A
LETTER
UNWRITTEN

*Two Women, One Man
and the Words That
Changed Everything*

RANDY RAUH

www.aletterunwritten.com

ISBN: 979-8-218-55999-1 (Hardback)
ISBN: 979-8-218-56000-3 (Paperback)
ISBN: 979-8-218-55998-4 (eBook)

Editor: Darby O'Shaughnessy
Cover and Layout designer: Damonza, a division of Booknack Limited

Publishing Company: KDP

1st Edition 2024

*To Megan, Matt, Ella, Gemma and all who
knew and loved these women.*

Chapter One

The Early Years Up to 1970

O NLY A COUPLE of generations ago, handwritten letters sent through the mail were the preferred form of communication. Before the 1970s, schools taught composition and penmanship to help develop letter-writing skills. Letters took time to compose, write, send, and receive. The art of letter writing has almost disappeared from society, replaced by email, text messages, and social media. In many cases, writing an electronic message or online post is done with abbreviations and emojis to keep pace with the amount of information being exchanged. Speed and brevity are foreign when it comes to handwritten letters. Words are carefully chosen. Paragraphs are assembled to tell a story that reflects the mood and intent of the writer. Letters received are eagerly opened and read. Some letters become treasured family heirlooms.

This is the story of two women from different generations who both possess the skill of letter writing. Their letters and the letters of others help tell their stories. Their lives, while complicated, do not include any significant event or action worthy of being included in the newspaper or any other publication. They have not influenced any social media trend, nor have any streets or buildings been named after them. Their comings and goings can easily be forgotten, as are those of countless women across generations. Libraries are full of the accomplishments of men, but the chronicles of equally incredible women are harder to find.

On a warm, sunny September evening in 2005, I escorted these two women to a night on the town. We dined at an Italian restaurant followed by a concert in a converted basketball arena where we enjoyed arguably the most famous tenor in the world, the great Luciano Pavarotti.

Tulsa, Oklahoma was one of only three locations on this final United States tour. The great tenor sat in a chair on the stage for the entire performance as he battled mobility issues. One of my dates for the evening also had mobility issues, which is why I purchased tickets on the arena floor. To my left sat my wife, and next to her, my mother.

This event took place late in our relationship. My wife and I were forty-seven when we went to that concert, and my mother was sixty-six. We had attended many other events: concerts, plays, school programs, graduations, ball games, weddings, and funerals, and my wife and my mother almost always sat together. Laughter was something we did often, as both of these women have a keen sense of humor. That night, we laughed about the spectacle around us as people made their way to their seats carrying popcorn, Milk Duds, and ICEE cups. We wondered what the great tenor must have thought of the sight. The three of us share a common love for music—but I am getting ahead of the story. Both my mother and my wife also share a love for reading and would never approve of their story starting in the middle…

My mother, Betty JoAnn, was born in the small town of Poteau, Oklahoma on the Choctaw Reservation on the southeastern side of the state in the rolling Ouachita Mountains. She was born at home on Ground Hog's Day, 1939. While her official name is Betty JoAnn, her close friends called her Jo, and most people I knew called her JoAnn. I just called her Mom.

One challenge Mom faced her entire life was being judged by her first appearance. She always struggled with her weight, which was compounded by a large port wine birthmark that covered much of the right side of her face and down her shoulder. While blonde as a child, as an adult, Mom was 5' 4" tall with short dark hair and a light complexion that made the ruby red birthmark even more visible. My mother always carried herself confidently, looked people in the eye, and greeted anyone who exchanged glances with her. However, out in public, strangers tended to avoid or ignore her.

When Mom was a child, her family moved around a lot. She did not share many childhood stories when I was young. She talked about a few cities she lived in but not much else. Mom graduated from Central High School in Tulsa in 1956. In 1957, she met Lee at a church function. She was eighteen, and he was thirty-six. Mom shared nothing about their relationship except that they met at a picnic. On July 14, 1957, JoAnn and Lee were married in Turley, Oklahoma, just outside Tulsa.

JoAnn's parents, Everett and Romagene, live in the small northern California town of Arbuckle. They had migrated to California from Poteau. Everett shares the same port-wine birthmark with Mom. Mom has one brother, Billy Joe—or BJ, as everyone calls him—who lives in California in the same town as Mom's parents. They made an annual trip by car from Arbuckle along Route 66 to Oklahoma every Christmas, with a side trip to visit us in Tulsa before staying with family in Poteau.

Lee's parents, Henry and Hannah, were first generation German or, more specifically, white Russian immigrants. They lived in western Oklahoma where we visited more often. Dad has a sister who lives near his parents and a brother in Texas. Dad dropped out of school after the eighth grade to work full-time on the family farm. He served in the Navy as a signalman during WWII—the person you see in movies flipping the spotlight, sending coded messages between ships. Like many veterans of every war, Dad did not talk much about his service. I recall him telling us only once about his time in the Pacific during WWII.

Dad worked in Tulsa near the airport as a machinist at the McDonnell Douglas plant where they made aerospace parts. Lee and JoAnn were living near 11th Street under some radio towers when, in 1958, their first child, Randy Lee, your narrator, was born on the afternoon of either May 30 or 31.

To this day we are not sure which date is correct! Mom said, "I was there, and you were born on May 30 at 5:00 in the afternoon," but my birth certificate says May 31. This eventually led to my driver's license, passport, and all legal documents listing May 31 as my birthdate. I recently turned sixty-five and applied for Medicare and discovered that, as far as the Social Security Administration is concerned, my birthday is May 30th. It seems Mom was right all along.

Shortly after my birth, we moved to Mingo, a small community north of Tulsa, and less than a year later—364 days to be exact—a second son, Ricky Lynn, was born. Mom confirmed his birthday is May 29, 1959, despite her best efforts to have him on May 30. For kids not to like their first or middle names is common, but my brother was different. He disliked the name Ricky and thought even less of the name Lynn. When he could communicate as much, he went by the name Rick.

In 1964, Lee and JoAnn welcomed daughter Leslee into the family. Given our five and six year age difference, Leslee was not much more than a nuisance to Rick and me. Mom often suggested we go outside and play to keep us from running around the house disturbing the baby, which we always obliged.

Mingo was a bedroom community located a stone's throw from the northeast end of the Tulsa International Airport and next to the American Airlines Maintenance Base. Mingo was not a town but consisted of three square blocks of houses with a smattering of residents living within half a mile of the mostly-rented houses that made up Mingo.

Our community's namesake, Mingo Elementary School, included first through eighth grades and was one of the first schools in Oklahoma to offer kindergarten in the early 1960s. Upon graduation from the eighth grade, most students transferred to Tulsa Public Schools. By the late 1960s and early 1970s, nearby Owasso Public Schools was also a destination for Mingo graduates.

Our rent-house was like all the others in Mingo: three small bedrooms, one bathroom, a living room, a small kitchen, a one-car garage, and a crawl space underneath the wood plank floors. On more than one occasion, we had to go under the house to retrieve puppies or kittens when our dark crawl space became their birthing center.

As was true everywhere in the 1960s, the only social media in Mingo took place in living rooms or across chain-link fences in backyards. These interactions were common as everyone knew everyone in this close-knit community.

The early community of Mingo had no restaurants except for Roy's Diner, specializing in hamburgers and serving the lunch crowd from American Airlines. You pumped gas, ethyl or regular at one of two places, and shopped at the one grocery store, Mitchell's.

Mitchell's Grocery was a converted house like the rest of the homes in Mingo, except it had a mobile home behind the store where the Mitchells lived. Behind the counter was a rack with rows of small notebooks or "tab" books. In the early 1960s, rarely did anyone exchange money at Mitchell's.

At an early age, Rick and I sometimes made multiple trips daily to Mitchell's. Dad worked nights and slept during the day. Most likely, we made many of these trips for as few as one item to allow Dad to sleep in peace. Dad had a quick temper and little patience when Rick and I made noise playing inside or outside. Knowing this, Mom spent a good part of her day keeping Rick and me as quiet or as distant as possible.

In our preschool days before Leslee was born, Mom would give us a grocery list, and we would walk the two blocks to Mitchell's. After examining the candy display, we would hand Mr. Mitchell the list. We were too young to read, so the Mitchells would gather and bag the items, select our tab book from the rack, and fill in the amount.

The Mitchells were particularly good at placing items correctly in paper bags. They always put the bread on top, which was too great a temptation. On our way home, we would tear into the top of the bread bag and destroy the first few pieces as we nibbled. We would try to conceal our destruction of the bread, but Mom never said a word and always managed to salvage the remainder of the loaf without drawing Dad's attention.

Mom was never overbearing or demanding in her role as our mother. She was firm when she needed to be and always loving. She was wise and dispensed good advice, usually with religious overtones that Rick and I sometimes took. If either of us came into the house upset with a scowl, Mom would say, "Go ahead, make that face. If you hold it that way too long, it will stay permanently." I remember thinking *how long is too long* and would forget what I was upset about.

Mom always told us to live by the Golden Rule. "It takes fewer muscles to smile than frown, so why not smile all the time?" She also had other sayings: "Make sure you always have clean underwear on. You never know when you may be in an accident and have to go to the hospital. You wouldn't want them to see your dirty underwear!" When we were young, she would inspect us after a bath, saying: "Show me your ears. I want to check for potatoes."

One time, I was upset about something and declared I was going to run away. Mom helped me pack a bag and asked me lots of questions about my plans without trying to change my mind. It was already dark, so I knew I had to get going. I said my goodbyes and, as I walked out the front door, Mom said, "Oh, one thing. Wasps are especially dangerous at night. Their sting is much more painful after dark." As she closed the door in my face, she added, "Don't forget to write." I stood on the front porch for a couple of minutes thinking about my fear of wasps and from which direction they would be coming. I went back inside and unpacked my bags.

Another time, Rick decided he, too, had had enough and wanted to run away, so Mom helped him pack his bags. When Rick started packing his favorite toys, Mom said, "Oh, no, you can't take any toys with you. Santa gave you those toys, so they have to stay here." That was the end of Rick's equally ill-conceived escape plan.

Mom did not have a driver's license, so Dad did all the driving. If the grocery list was too large for Mitchell's, Dad would go to Tulsa by himself to shop. Occasionally, Dad would drop us off at the library in Owasso or at a The Wagon Wheel shopping center in Tulsa.

On one of the first Saturdays during summer break, Mom would say, "Boys, we're going to get some clothes for school." This meant buying new jeans for the next school year. We were rough on the knees, but Mom always managed to patch any of our jeans or, in some cases, place patches on patches until the knees were too worn out, which made them candidates for summer cut-offs.

Our next stop after buying jeans was the adjacent fabric store. Mom would say, "You boys go pick out some material to make three shirts each." She then spent part of her summer making our new shirts for the next school year. We never saw her sewing these shirts because our entire summer was spent outside. We eventually noticed our new shirts hanging in the closet and were excited to wear our new clothes for the first time. I remember barely getting any sleep the night before the first day of school—not because I missed my classmates since we all spent the summer together, but because I was excited to wear my new shirt and jeans.

Dad was different from Mom in lots of ways. Because he worked nights, we rarely saw him during the week. When Rick and I were home, Mom spent a lot of time talking to us, asking how our day was, or telling us about what she had done. Dad's conversations were to the point and usually included tasks he wanted us to do. We would ask him what he did at work, and he would say, "My work is top secret, so I can't talk about it." This was probably true as McDonnell Douglas was a defense and NASA contractor. Since we did not see him much and could not talk about work, he spent little time getting to know us.

Dad was particular about many things. He only drove a Rambler, just like his dad. As soon as one Rambler was paid off, Dad would immediately trade it in for a new one. He washed his car almost every weekend and never allowed Rick and me to help, fearing we might scratch it. He mowed the grass regularly but never allowed Rick or me to use the mower. The little time we spent with him was usually doing some high-energy sports activity outside. He never played board games or put puzzles together. I never saw him read a book. Dad kept a razor strap and was not afraid to use it. He had a short fuse, and Rick and I were always a little worried when we were around him, as we never knew what would upset him next.

Dad had specific dietary demands. Friday night was payday and steak night. Mom would cook steak in the skillet; Dad rarely grilled outside. Other nights of the week were designated for his favorite dishes. Once a month, on Sunday night, breakfast was served, as Mom cooked pancakes with all the trimmings.

Only once did Dad take the two-week annual vacation offered him from his years of work at McDonell Douglass and later, at Rockwell International. Instead, he took the money and worked year-round except in 1965 when the family took a trip to Arbuckle to visit our grandparents. We kids were seven, six, and ten-months-old. The trip included stops at the Grand Canyon and several other points of interest along the way to California.

While in Arbuckle, the highlight for Rick and me was a trip to the grain elevator or what the locals called The Warehouse where our grandfather Everett worked. The Warehouse was used to store rice while it dried after the harvest. We had never been inside such a large building. The memory of the trip, or at least of The Warehouse, remained with us forever.

When Rick and I were young, we looked alike—so much so that many thought we were twins. Mom's disappointment over Rick being born one day shy of my birthday was quickly remedied as she routinely dressed us in the same outfits, most of which she made, especially when it came time for pictures. We also shared the same birthday party as if we were twins.

I do not recall seeing any kind of affection between my mom and dad. Mom was loving to us, while Dad remained distant. Mom was a different person when she was around Dad. She was not the funny, game-playing, adventure-seeking Mom we enjoyed when Dad was at work. Instead, she waited on Dad hand and foot as he usually complained about one thing or another. Mom could usually detect when Dad would be in one of his moods as she would send us on some errand or ask us to go to the store for something.

Even though Lee and JoAnn met at a church function, when Rick and I were young, they did not regularly attend church. When we were a little older, Mom took us to the Free Will Baptist Church in Mingo and to their Summer Bible School. Services at the church were full of fire and brimstone, and it was a very scary place for me. None of the rituals, such as the altar call or the passing of saltine crackers and grape juice, seemed sincere. I knew how some in attendance behaved when not at church, which caused me to see what was going on in church as an act. While I had my reservations about religion, Mom was a woman of faith. Although we rarely attended church, Mom told us many Bible stories and referred to prayer as something she often did. Many times, Mom would make her point about something by referring to a Bible passage.

Mom shared many of the same physical characteristics as Everett's siblings in Poteau who were all large people. Dad had an athletic build and enjoyed sports. When Rick and I were between ages four and six, Rick started to resemble Mom physically (less the birthmark), and I began to resemble Dad. Rick was not overweight or as skinny as I was. He struggled with early sports skills like playing catch. Dad got frustrated quickly and became impatient with Rick. He didn't seem to care that I was a year older and had further developed my hand-eye coordination. He would say, "Rick, just go inside and do something with your mother."

This early frustration with Rick's coordination started to form a wedge between Rick and Dad. At times Dad would come up to both of us and say, "Randy, come outside and play catch. Rick, you can just watch." Other times Dad would take me fishing and leave Rick at home, or he would only choose me to do other activities with him.

I don't know what Mom said to Rick when we were gone. I know that when we returned, Rick was never sad or upset, and he never resented me for spending time with Dad. Mom must have known what to say to Rick to help him get over what had to be painful as he watched Dad ignore him. Rick never shared what Mom said, and I never shared with Rick what Dad and I did together, as I was ashamed that he favored me over Rick.

When Dad was at work, Rick and I spent a lot of time in the yard playing catch. I wanted Rick to improve enough to catch Dad's attention. All my efforts failed as Rick and Dad became more distant while Rick and I became closer. We shared the same bedroom and were each other's constant companions on so many adventures. I was always upset and saddened when Dad excluded Rick because we shared everything except our father.

When family or friends visited, they always commented, "Randy looks just like his dad," which was often repeated. This observation may seem innocent enough, but words do matter. Rick was often dismissed by family or sometimes ignored. I did not want to be like my father. I wanted to be like my mom, but people could only see my physical resemblance to my father.

In 1963, I was enrolled in Mingo Elementary School in the

new kindergarten. The entire K-8 enrollment at Mingo was less than 150 students. Mingo School was unique because it was an Independent School District located inside the Tulsa City and Tulsa County Limits. In the 1960s, each school received the bulk of the tax revenue earmarked for the schools from the local businesses within their geographic school district. Mingo was the nearest school to two of the largest employers in Tulsa, American Airlines and McDonell Douglass, meaning Mingo School was by all accounts the richest school district in the state.

Mingo School was a great place to learn due to its small class size and highly qualified teachers attracted by Mingo's ability to pay more. Mingo's wealth also made the district a target of hostile annexation plans by both Tulsa and Owasso who knew what a cash cow Mingo's location could provide for their schools if they could get their hands on Mingo School and, more importantly, their money.

During the Mingo years, Dad would take the family to Poteau, sometimes on his way to visit his brother in Texas. The trips to Poteau were special. Never had Rick and I been around a family as close and loving as the relatives in Poteau, unlike our visits to our paternal grandfather who was cold and distant compared to our paternal grandmother who died when we were young.

Poteau visits centered around Grandpa Everett's siblings, many of whom lived in three houses within steps of each other. Everyone in Poteau was so kind, warm, and loving. We were always received as if we were special visitors. Everyone would make a big deal about seeing Mom as if she held some important role in the family that we did not understand.

One trait all the Poteau relatives shared was that, when they had a conversation with you, it was as if you were the only person who mattered in the whole world. This was especially true for Nanny, the family's matriarch. Visits to Poteau were always too short.

Everett's sister Bessie, a hugger with an infectious laugh, made a big impact on Rick and me. I think she would have hugged the mailman every day if she could have caught him. Everett's brother Earl always had a story to tell. We would watch in amazement as he rolled his own cigarettes, something we had only seen in Westerns on TV. A visit to Poteau was not complete without a family meal, which included too much of everything.

Mom shared the same talent for cooking as those in Poteau. Like other schools in the 1960s and 70s, Mingo School would ask moms to provide home-baked goods for special occasions. We're talking about real homemade food, not the prepackaged food kids today are required to bring.

Kids quickly learned whose moms were good cooks and whose were not. Rick and I were among the elite; Mom was a superstar when it came to cooking anything for school. There was nothing she could not cook. Many times, first thing in the morning on days when there was an event, students would stop Rick and me in the hall and quiz us on what our mom baked that day. Rick and I welcomed the notoriety, which to us was not unlike being the children of a rock star or famous entertainer.

Mom rarely wore shoes at home. She only wore shoes when she went out in public. Mom also liked having her hair done. She usually wore her thin shoulder-length hair straight, but she got a beehive bouffant for special occasions. She got her hair done at a house with a salon on the other side of the airport, but later, her neighbor got her own portable hair dryer that mom sat under when she got a permanent.

There were two times Rick and I refused to go into our house: when Mom was getting a permanent, and when she made tamales. We could not stand the smell of either and only came home under protest. Otherwise, Rick and I were on the receiving end of some amazing meals growing up—nothing fancy, but food prepared with an artist's skill and out of pure love.

Mom's sewing and craft work also made her popular in Mingo. She either repaired or created many of the costumes and uniforms used throughout the school. I would walk down the hall at school and be shocked to see Mom working in someone else's classroom. "You never know when you might see me helping any of the teachers," she explained to Rick and me. Realizing that we might run into Mom had a positive impact on our behavior at school.

Probably Mom's most sought after skill was her kind ear. She often left the house saying, "You boys fix your own lunch. I need to be with a friend." On other occasions, Rick and I would come home to see one of our friends' moms in our living room, deep in conversation, as Mom quickly would send us outside. Mom shared that same compassionate ear we had seen in Poteau during our visits.

Mom always kept a tidy house. Often Rick and I came home from school to find our bedroom transformed into something unrecognizable. I was always amazed at how many ways Mom could arrange two twin beds, a dresser, and a chest of drawers. Just when we thought it could not be done any other way, she would Rubik Cube our room yet again.

Mom made most of the curtains in the house, but the living room curtains were store-bought. During her annual spring-cleaning ritual, Mom took the curtains down to be washed. She knew Rick and I enjoyed playing with the curtain hooks that fit into the pleats—the kind of hooks with two feet and a curved top. If you lay on the ground and looked at them with one eye from the side, they looked like a fighter jet and canopy. Rick and I assembled our squadrons for battle. Mom watched as we scattered the hooks all over the living room, then said, "Let's gather all of those hooks and count them," which was another fun game she played with us as we guessed how many hooks there were. The truth is she only wanted to make sure we didn't lose any of them.

Mom always encouraged our imagination, whether we were pretending curtain hooks were airplanes taking off from an aircraft carrier or we were emptying her bottom kitchen cabinets so we could explore a cave. When the kitchen cabinets were not big enough, Mom helped us move chairs all over the house and place blankets on top of them to make our own Carlsbad Caverns. Mom never stopped us from going anywhere our imaginations led us. We frequently traveled to the Owasso Public Library where Mom encouraged us to read, further spurring our imaginations.

Mom also proved herself to be a fierce defender of her children. She once got into a disagreement (of which we were unaware) with a disgruntled mother. After school, Rick and I came home excited. "Mom," I said, "the principal called us out of the classroom to go to his office!" Mom was excited in a different way when she learned they were running their fingers over our heads.

The disgruntled woman apparently decided to get even by contacting the school office and reporting that Rick and I had lice. No parent wants to be told their children are carrying lice. In those days, lice carried the stigma that the child lived in a dirty house and had poor hygiene.

Disgruntled Mom's plan might have worked except for one essential requirement for lice to thrive: the host must have hair. Rick and I wore a shaved burr until we were in the sixth grade, so the claim had no merit. This logic did not matter to Mom as she literally ran out the door—too fast for us to tell if she put her shoes on or not—and hot-footed it toward school with a pace and determination Rick and I had never seen before (and hoped to never see heading in our direction). Nothing was ever said about lice again. I would not have wanted to be that other mother when Mom caught up with her.

Mom continued to encourage Rick and me to spend time outside the house, especially during the summer when we only saw Dad on the weekends since he worked the night shift and slept during the day. Our summers outside led to many adventures, most of which, fortunately, were never discovered by our parents. Occasionally, our best efforts at concealment would fail, and we got caught, like the time we decided to try cigarettes.

Dad smoked two packs of Raleigh's a day, most of which Rick and I bought at Mitchell's, so what could the harm be? The harm was Mom's finding out. "You boys sit right here on the couch," she said and went into the kitchen. She returned to the living room and handed Rick and me each a pack of Dad's cigarettes. "Let's see how much you really like cigarettes." She then forced us to eat one pack of cigarettes each. That neither of us ever smoked again should come as no surprise.

Some friends and I were hanging around a construction site. I noticed the keys still inside one of the bulldozers. No, I did not go on a joy ride, but instead, for some odd reason, I put the keys in my pocket. Later that afternoon, while Rick and I were home playing, someone knocked on the door. Mom called me, and as I came to the door, one of the guys said, "Yeah, that's the kid."

Mom asked if I knew anything about some keys, and I denied it. The guys told Mom about witnesses and explained it was a serious matter. I went to my bedroom and produced the keys.

Mom was stern in telling me how wrong what I did was, but she never raised her hand. My fear the whole time was what would happen when my dad found out. Mom knew Dad would have handled it very differently. Instead, she let the thought rattle around in my head. The next day, I knew Dad would get me after school. Eventually, however, it became clear that Mom chose not to tell Dad. Instead, she let me spend the next few days waiting for the hammer to drop, which was enough punishment for Mom.

Growing up in the 1960s meant corporal punishment in public school. Rick and I were on the receiving end of plenty of spankings in the hall by one teacher or another. With Dad working nights, Mom was the disciplinarian at home. Her weapon of choice was either a limb of the neighbor's willow tree or a flyswatter.

Even though many of our exploits remained concealed, we regularly got into enough trouble for Mom to require routine maintenance or replacement of her disciplinary tools. Rick and I, without doubt, earned and deserved every form of punishment our mother administered. She never was mean or angry or even yelled at us. She would explain why we were being punished, and everything went back to normal when it was over.

Dad's punishment was more severe and sometimes less deserving. One time, I went fishing after school with a friend. We found a recently drained pond with all kinds of fish flopping around in the mud. We gathered as many fish as we could carry. When Dad found out I did not catch the fish with a pole, he became furious and gave his razor strap a workout. He was convinced we used a net or snag line and did not believe my story about the empty pond. Rick and I always feared our father.

Mingo School, the hub of activity for the community, offered stability, making it a great place to grow up. We had some disadvantages, such as limited choices for sports and girls. Basketball was the only organized sport, and both Rick and I played on the school team. The band in which we both played was small—but we thought life in Mingo could not get much better.

In the late '60s, however, Dad started to change. First, he decided he wanted to be an artist. He bought a large box of fancy painting supplies, a canvas, and an easel. He made it clear that Rick and I were never to touch his paint equipment. Next, he tried his hand at photography. He bought a fancy camera and converted a closet into a dark room. Later, Dad told us he was going to start a second job selling products through a marketing company in Oklahoma City. We had no idea what any of this meant. Some might have called it a mid-life crisis since he was in his late 40s.

Just a few short years from retirement, Dad announced he was going to become a millionaire and quit his job at McDonnell Douglass to pursue this new venture full-time. He attached some magnetic signs to his car and ramped up his efforts, making frequent trips to the head office in Oklahoma City.

All this change confused Rick and me. Mom had to have been

more confused than we were, but she tried to reassure us. She would say, "I don't know why your dad is doing this, but he just wants the best for us." Mom had a way of explaining things to us that always made sense out of what, at the time, made no sense even to her.

Having worked his entire life either as a farmer or a machinist, Dad had no sales experience. His new job consisted of selling memberships to a club that provided some sort of merchandise. Only later did we discover he was really selling shares in an illegal Pyramid Scheme. Kids at school were asking why our dad was bothering their parents. We noticed some kids no longer wanted to hang out with us. Teachers treated us differently, too. After Dad had been turned away from all the homes in Mingo with no success, he started canvassing Owasso and other nearby towns. Sometimes on these sales trips, he would take the family with him when visiting relatives. Dad was not good at sales. While he spent more and more of the family money on sample kits and other schemes from the parent company, whether he ever talked anyone into joining is unclear.

For more than a year, as doors were being closed in his face, Dad's behavior became more erratic. Multiple times Dad would travel on sales trips with all of us. While in the car, he would start yelling at the smallest comment and force Mom and all of us kids to get out of the car in the middle of nowhere as he sped off. After we walked a long time on the side of the road, Dad would show up, and we would be on our way again.

Mom was so brave when this happened. "It's okay; he'll be back after he calms down." I knew she was trying to keep us from panicking, but each time he did this, I thought we would never see him again.

The evenings were worse as Dad took out his daily sales failures on Mom and Rick, sparing Leslee and me most of the physical harm. We all shared in the constant verbal abuse as the situation worsened. Sometimes, when Mom could tell Dad's abuse was going to be more severe, she would take Leslee back to our room and say,

"You boys protect your sister. Don't worry about what you hear from the other room." We would place ourselves between the closed door and Leslee, waiting for Dad to break into our room when he'd had enough with Mom.

Once, on a trip to Oklahoma City, Dad told Rick and me, "I'm not going to get passed by anyone today." He maintained a speed of over 100 miles per hour as we bounced around in the back seat in a time without seatbelts.

When Dad was away, Mom would say, "Let's pray for Dad. Everything is going to be okay. I'm going to protect you." This didn't change our always being on pins and needles when Dad was home. Rick or Mom's smallest random word or action would set him off again. The only positive occurrence happened when Dad insisted Mom get a driver's license, and he bought a second car. His reasons were unclear. He may have been too busy to deal with home duties like shopping, or maybe he wanted her to get a job. No one knows because events quickly spiraled out of control.

On May 13, 1970, Rick, Leslee, and I came home from school as usual, but Mom was not there. A couple of hours later, she arrived with a look on her face Rick and I had never seen. "Your dad has been arrested." She did not disclose any details then, but later that evening, after Leslee went to sleep, she explained to Rick and me that Dad had been arrested for public nudity in nearby Mohawk Park.

We were confused. This behavior made no sense and must have been a mistake. Rick and I hadn't had any indication of his nudist tendencies, which never took place at home. Mom explained that he belonged to a Nudist Colony in the area, which was another shocker to us. During our trips to the library or Wagon Wheel, he would visit the place.

Mom told us doctors had evaluated him. She was going to court the next day to sign papers to have him committed to Eastern State Hospital in Vinita. The facility, originally named Oklahoma Hospital for the Insane, was located about ninety minutes northeast of Tulsa.

Without warning, Mom, age thirty-one, faced no job, a stack of unpaid bills, and little or no money—with kids ages eleven, ten, and five to feed. Our world changed overnight. Mom was shaken but remained calm, saying, "We're a family, and we are going to get through this." I did not know what to say or think, but I always believed in Mom. Little did we know life was about to get worse, much worse.

While we were relieved that the daily physical and verbal abuse was over, we all knew Dad hadn't worked for over a year. We were barely scraping by before his arrest as Dad had managed to overextend our family's debt. The tab at Mitchell's was suspended, and only a few dollars were left in the bank. We emptied our piggy banks as Mom tried to figure out how to put food on the table.

Mom started the slow process of applying for Social Security benefits for us kids, which took time since Dad's legal issues were still unfolding. The local Free Will Baptist Church brought a box of food. However, there was no outpouring of support since Dad had burned most of the bridges in Mingo with his aggressive sales efforts to our neighbors.

Mom learned about government cheese and other handouts and left Rick and me at home to watch Leslee while she stood in lines for what she could bring home to feed us. These contacts led to even more handout lines that she stood in routinely until she finally got approved for food stamps, which only slightly improved our situation.

We almost always went to bed hungry during this period when ketchup sandwiches or gravy made from water and flour would be our only meal. While Rick, Leslee, and I ate whatever Mom put in front of us, we rarely saw Mom eat. We were either too young to understand what she was doing or just too hungry to make a fuss about what she was giving up for us.

Aside from the stack of bills was the issue of rent. The landlord was understanding and allowed us to remain in the house during those tough times. Kindness was shown to us in other ways, such as vendors Spiegel and Fingerhut, who sent compassionate letters erasing our debt. Mom did her best with the rest of the bills and managed to keep the water and electricity on most of the time.

Mom's car was repossessed, but she still had Dad's car, which was paid off. The phone was disconnected, so she had to use the payphone at Mitchell's to communicate with Social Security or make other important calls. She spent a lot of time at the payphone while Rick and I watched Leslee.

Mom's prospects for work were slim. She had no work history or skills other than housekeeping. Mom never seemed to be discouraged, but times were dark that summer as she tried and failed to get work. She repeated, "I am going to do everything I can to keep us together." Rick and I did not understand what she meant; Mom was barely hanging on by a thread.

If the landlord had not been so kind, we would have been homeless. The worst part for us kids was the pain of going to bed hungry and waking up with little prospects for food. On the other hand, Mom also privately worried about where we might sleep at night.

Mom sat us down at one of her lowest moments. "We're going to go meet some new relatives." Curious about who these distant cousins might be, she said, "You are going to meet your grandparents." Grandparents! This came as a complete shock. As if this were not enough, we were told that these new grandparents lived with an aunt just on the other side of Tulsa and we had another uncle and his family who also lived in Tulsa.

Growing up, we knew Everett and Romagene as our grandparents. Rick and I could not believe what we were hearing. Despite our shock, we never said or thought *what else is she hiding from us?* Instead, we knew Mom had to have had a good reason for having kept this knowledge from us. All Mom offered as an explanation was, "A falling out happened a long time ago."

After Leslee went to sleep, Mom sat Rick and me down and

began to tell us her story. Grandma Romagene was Grandpa Everett's second wife. Mom's birth mother's name was Opal. Opal divorced Grandpa when she was young and married Dan. Opal and Dan raised Mom along with her sister Carolyn Sue and brothers Dannie and Walter Richard. Mom explained that during her childhood, Grandpa Everett and Grandma Romagene lived in California, and that it was Opal and Dan who moved Mom and her siblings around the country when she was young.

Our mouths hung open as our world changed with every new revelation. "My parent's divorce was very bitter," Mom said.

"That doesn't explain why we never heard of them before," I said.

"The story is more complicated than that." She sighed. "When you were two years old, my mother, Opal, and Dan visited me while your Dad was at work. We were having a tough time, and my mother noticed our empty refrigerator and kitchen cupboards. Dan went out and bought us some groceries. When your dad came home, he asked where the food came from. Your dad raced over to Mom's house and got into an argument. He told them not to come over anymore, and that is why you don't know anything about your other grandparents."

When Rick and I went to bed, we talked for a long time about the bombshell Mom dropped on us. Our life had been on a roller coaster, going from one crisis to another ever since Dad quit his job, followed by his arrest and diagnosis of schizophrenia. Then we find out that Mom has been keeping secrets about her past.

One thing Rick and I agreed on: things must be really bad if Mom is reaching out to her mother whom she hadn't spoken to for ten years.

Chapter Two

1970 - Mid-1979

WE WERE ALL anxious and nervous on the ride to the countryside where Opal, Dan, and Mom's sister Carolyn Sue lived. "Boys, be on your best behavior," was not advice Mom gave us very often, as if we would have followed it, anyway. Her tone was different. A sense of dread filled the car. Mom did not say much more. All we knew was that this visit was serious if Mom was asking us to behave.

We arrived at a converted double-wide trailer with a barn on what looked like the largest yard we had ever seen. We lived a somewhat sheltered life in Mingo and assumed everyone lived in the same cookie-cutter houses and yards we knew. The place was probably only a two-acre lot, but from our perspective, it was more land than we had ever seen anyone own.

The atmosphere inside the trailer was cold, with Opal and Dan sitting in chairs as we walked in. "Well, here you are," Opal said, followed by a sarcastic, "What do you want?"

Dan did not say much.

Aunt Sue quickly took us kids outside to see her dog and horse. She was friendly enough, but clearly she was tough as nails and not someone whose wrong side you wanted to get on.

Uncle Walter, his wife Debra, and their toddler boys arrived. Walter and Debra were much warmer to us.

On the ride home, Rick and I asked Mom lots of questions, but Mom only said, "It all happened a long time ago. I'm sorry I didn't tell you about them sooner." She didn't want to talk about it. Clearly this visit was much harder on her than on us. When Carolyn Sue took us outside, I pictured Mom begging for money or food, but Rick and I were convinced that Opal and Dan were the last people on earth Mom could turn to for help.

Although my head was spinning, I was never prouder of Mom than I was that day and for all she did during those dark times to provide for us. She went through so much pain and fear worrying about our future, but never once did we see her scared. We always knew Mom would find a way to solve the next hurdle placed in front of her, including this visit, which could only have been made out of desperation.

Other visits to Opal and Dan's followed. Carolyn Sue and Opal warmed up to us as we played cards, a board game, or Opal's favorite— Yahtzee. Dan remained distant and usually left when we visited.

Mom managed to get a job cleaning newly constructed houses and apartment buildings. Carrying all the supplies up and down stairs was hard work as she scraped stickers off new windows and appliances then washed windows and bathrooms in every home or apartment until it was spotless. She would take us with her, and we would either wait in the car or sometimes come inside to watch or help her work. Most of Mom's house cleaning at home took place either while we were at school or running wild in the neighborhood. I remember marveling at how hard Mom worked and how amazed I was watching her.

Later that fall, we made our first trip to Eastern State Hospital in Vinita to visit Dad. He was quiet, calm, and happy to see us. I noticed his eyes blinking a lot and that he could not sit still. There were no incidents, and he hugged all of us before we left—not something he commonly did. I wondered if all the relatives who told me I would be just like my Dad might someday be right.

Eastern State was an awful place for kids, but Mom would say, "I know this is painful, but we are still a family, and family look after each other." This statement seemed ironic after meeting Opal and Dan's family, whom we had not known existed and who treated us as a nuisance on our first visit. Where did Mom learn her sense of family?

From what I saw thus far, Mom could not have formed her sense of family from Opal and Dan. In our lives, the only people I knew who exhibited the kind of love Mom gave us were Grandpa Everett's family in Poteau, where Mom's moral compass always seemed to point.

As we continued to complain about visiting Vinita, Mom would say, "He can't hurt us anymore. He's getting treatment to make him better." Her words, however true, did not change that the sights and sounds of that awful place still haunt me to this day.

When school was back in session, rumors about what happened had spread, so we were treated differently. The principal, Mr. Snodgrass, was a wonder man. He gave Rick and me jobs in the cafeteria after school, washing dishes and cleaning toilets. We were so happy to give Mom the extra money to help the family.

Later, Mom got a job as a hotel maid in Tulsa. When I say hotel, I mean she cleaned all the rooms in three different single-story hotels that were owned by the same person and located along a two-mile stretch of 11th Street or Route 66 in Tulsa. After Mom finished the first hotel, she drove to the next one and then the third. The work was hard, but Mom had an incredible work ethic—so much so that when she started, she was one of two maids but was such a hard worker, the owner realized Mom could do the work by herself and let the other housekeeper go cutting the owner's labor cost by fifty-percent.

Our band teacher offered me private lessons after school. I was transitioning from trumpet to baritone, so our bachelor teacher felt private lessons would help. Of course, we could not afford such a luxury, but Mom was shrewd. She offered the bachelor ironing services in exchange for private lessons. Mom would iron his shirts in the back bedroom while I got a lesson in our living room. She later branched out, providing the same laundry services for another teacher at Mingo.

The following summer, I worked as a laborer with a local brick mason. Mixing and hauling mortar was hard work, but it paid well, and I was so proud when I would give Mom my paycheck every week. She, in turn, always left the room—no doubt to cry over her son's doing a man's job at thirteen.

We took occasional trips to Poteau, which comforted Mom and us although the Poteau family did not have the resources to offer much assistance. Everett and his family, on their annual Poteau and Tulsa visits, helped as much as possible. The family finances remained tight, but Mom managed to keep the family together, fed, and with a roof over our heads. She changed jobs and started working for a pavement company as their secretary.

In early 1972, Dad was released from Eastern State, and Mom, without hesitation, took him back into our home. He had changed and was no longer a threat to the family. Instead, due to his heavy reliance on medication, all he did was pace the floor. He could only carry on a conversation for a few minutes. He never said a coarse word or made the smallest threatening move or gesture.

We later found out that shock treatments were routine while he was in Vinita. After a while at home, he would get more agitated—not with the family but with himself. He would eventually ask to be readmitted to Eastern State. This cycle of release, moving back in with us, and then returning to Eastern State was repeated for several years.

Also, in 1972, Dan, Opal's second husband, died. Mom said,

"We're not going to the funeral." We did not know Dan very well. He always kept his distance when we visited, so it was not a big deal to Rick or me. Mom did not elaborate on why we would not be going.

In May of 1972, I was set to graduate from Mingo. The family had a difficult decision to make. We had to choose whether I would go to Tulsa or Owasso for ninth grade and high school. Both schools were roughly the same distance from Mingo. The advantages of going to Tulsa included being where most of our shopping and other needs were. We weighed this benefit against Owasso, where our family doctor and the library we loved were.

Mom did not need my input in making this decision, but she left it up to me, for which I never thanked her or gave her credit. We had been through a great deal, and Rick, Leslee, and I were forced to grow up quickly due to our life struggles. Mom valued my opinion on where I wanted to go to school, even if my motives were questionable.

As mentioned, Mingo only had a school basketball team, but I wanted to play football. All I knew of the sport was what I saw on TV or while listening to OU or Notre Dame games on the radio with Dad when I was young. I pleaded with Mom to play football, so her first thought was costs. Mom called Tulsa Public Schools about enrollment and asked about football. She was told there was a sixty dollar equipment fee, and they would be glad to have me try out for the team. She called Owasso Public Schools, who informed her they did not charge an equipment fee. The sixty dollar fee sealed the deal, and Owasso now had a new transfer student into the ninth grade. Little did the family know this decision to go to Owasso over sixty dollars would change the family's future.

My relationship with Mom started to change. I felt like I was more grown up than my years indicated. I considered myself the man of the house, which Mom supported. I did not boss anyone around, but I felt like I did not need to confide in or consult Mom like I should have.

The fall of 1972 was exciting for me as I started ninth grade at Owasso. I had never been around so many people. Mom drove me to Owasso every morning, or I carpooled with others from Mingo. I enrolled in band and, more importantly, football. Football practice had already started earlier in the summer. When I got to the first practice, I was asked about my football experience, of which I had none. I was given equipment and a schedule of practices. At the first practice, I learned how hard football practice was in the summer. I struggled with too much running and other complicated drills while wearing heavy pads and a helmet that I could hardly see out of. My lack of skills landed me a last-string offensive guard position.

My football career consisted of making it into one or two games for only a few plays. At the end of the season, I gave up my football ambitions. I had about the same success with basketball. By Christmas, my sports dreams were over.

During this same time, I was also part of the Pride of Owasso band, learning how to march and perform at high school football games. I was a little better at band than sports but didn't show any special talent there, either. Still, I was settling in and began making friends with the band kids. My friends were not just other freshmen but older students who were accepting of this new kid from Mingo. Band trips to football games, parades, and contests helped us bond.

Many friends like Kenny, Doug, Tim, Johnny, Robert, and Thomas sat near the baritone section. Thomas was cool because he had a girlfriend who was the Freshman Band Attendant in the Band Royalty, which meant she was honored at the Band Homecoming football game. In addition, she was quite a looker.

Mom came to every game and quickly became popular as she was able to connect with my friends in the band who called her "Mom" as a sign of affection. Mom became as much a valued member in Owasso as she was in Mingo. My friends would tell me how much they liked hanging out with my mom, which was a little unsettling.

One thing lacking in Mingo was an assortment of girls. It was simply a numbers game. Besides, I was always too busy having fun at Mingo to think about girls. My only exposure to girls in Mingo was in the Playboy magazines that my friends kept stashed in our many forts.

Although Mom played the role of both mother and father throughout my teenage years, we never had any discussions about sex, so I learned what I could from the aforementioned publications, idle gossip, and the occasional health department movie shown to eighth-graders at Mingo.

I was enjoying my time in the band more and more and became closer to the band members. A group of us would hang out at lunch, and the topic of girls would always come up. Thomas, being the one with a girlfriend, didn't have any time to share tips as he was too busy hanging all over his girlfriend.

Around Christmas, Thomas and his girlfriend broke up. It was an ugly split from what I could tell, not having experience in such matters or knowing the girl very well. There was lots of finger-pointing as girls huddled around Thomas's ex, but it was great for me as Thomas could now hang out with us more. Later that spring, Thomas's old girlfriend moved on and started hanging all over an eighth-grader who lived down the street from her.

The atmosphere in the band room was loose. The band director was not much on discipline. From what I could tell, his philosophy was to allow the upper-level students to be in charge. This may be why the older students were so engaging to young members like me who had never been in an organized band before. All we did at Mingo was play a concert or two. I knew little about how a real band was supposed to work, but I quickly realized band was a lot of fun.

I enjoyed bus rides to football games. All the parents were nice, and Mom quickly made friends with them. One dad stood out. He drove his pickup truck to games, hauling large instruments like my baritone. Kind of a loud character, he picked on everyone and was a bit annoying. I couldn't imagine what it would be like to be his kid.

Towards the end of the ninth grade, I arrived at school to find the band room was buzzing. The band director had been fired. There was talk of a meeting at someone's house that night where a group planned to attend the school board meeting to fight this injustice. I had known the band director for less than a year. While he was a nice guy, I did not have an opinion either way. I was certainly not as passionate about his firing as almost everyone else. The local paper, the Owasso Reporter, was full of letters to the editor, including:

Firing of Director Resented by Student

I am writing in reference to the firing of one of the best band directors Owasso has ever had. The school must not have much pride in the "Pride of Owasso" when every time we get a great Band Director, they fire him. This year, the high school band brought first-place trophies and a "Big 1" in contests.

We are going to State for the first time in five years—requiring band members' effort and an Outstanding Band Director's help and guidance.

Doesn't the school want to be known for having a great band? Or does the school just want to be known because of the football team? You've never fired a coach when the football team was having a winning season, so why do it to the band when they finally have a winning season?

As a student in band for five years, I've had at least six different directors, and each had a different teaching style. Every year, it got a little bit harder to get used to the different teacher and his teaching style.

If this keeps happening, instead of the "Pride of Owasso," it will be "The Shame of Owasso." I hope the school administration and everyone involved are proud of themselves because they are losing the respect of all the students in the school. The new band director will have trouble working the band up again to where it is now. They'll probably never get the pride back that our Band Director achieved.

A concerned student,
Bonnie Helm

Bonnie Helm was our Freshman Band Attendant and my friend Thomas's ex-girlfriend. The band room was in turmoil. None of the students' efforts to change the decision had any effect. There was talk of a mass walkout, but cooler heads prevailed. When the band kids realized the decision was final, we got on with our end-of-year concerts. Soon we learned that our band director's replacement would be a husband-and-wife team from Texas.

Early May meant the arrival of our yearbooks. Our Mingo yearbooks were only about twenty pages. The Owasso yearbook was huge. We were allowed to take our yearbooks to class to have them signed. In band, all we did was sit around and sign yearbooks since the band director was marking time. By the end of my first year, I'd made a lot of friends in the band, so I had fun that day.

My hormones were causing me to think about girls more and more, and Owasso had so many pretty girls. I was awkward around girls and didn't make much headway. I had never so much as held a girl's hand, much less kissed or anything else. I wondered if I would ever have a girlfriend. I noticed several couples among older band members but saw no path forward toward getting my own girlfriend.

I never shared any of my love life concerns with Mom. She would have been a sympathetic ear, but I saw myself more as an equal with her instead of a kid with lots to learn. My mother was so wise at dispensing wisdom to others, but I pushed her away. When I acted like a big shot, all Mom would say was, "I think someone is getting too big for his britches."

A couple of older girls who were good friends signed my yearbook, so I had no fear of approaching other girls. My friends wrote all kinds of silly things. For some reason, I asked the activist, Thomas's ex-girlfriend Bonnie, to sign my yearbook. She handed me hers as she started writing:

Randy,
I've really enjoyed knowing you this year. I hope that we're friends again next year.
God Bless.
Love,
Bonnie Helm

After I read what she wrote, I quickly wrote in her yearbook:

Bonny,

I have enjoyed knowing you. I wish you would stay like you are.

Love,

Randy

Yes, I misspelled Bonnie—but it was because I was still in shock over one word in Bonnie's message: Love. No girl had ever written Love as a closing which prompted my Love in reply. The thought that she had probably written Love in everyone's yearbook never occurred to me. For all I knew, Love was a personal message to me and only me. In my hormone-ravaged mind, a girl just used the word Love to me! This was all I needed to gain the courage to approach her, but I was still incredibly awkward around girls. Nonetheless, I now had Bonnie on my brain.

Did I go home and share this with Mom? Of course not. Mom would have been able to put in its proper place what I clearly took out of context. Instead, all kinds of thoughts were going through my head as I tried to come up with a way to approach her—with stalking not off the table.

School was almost out, so I didn't have much time to act. However, there was the issue of her new boyfriend. John was a younger eighth-grader, but his arms were larger than my thighs, and he lived a convenient two doors from Bonnie. I was not about to go near Bonnie for fear of John's snapping me like a pretzel. Besides, they were always locked arm-in-arm at school, so I had no opportunity. I figured all was lost.

As the school year ended, I was ready for a fun summer back in Mingo with my friends riding around on our bikes like we had done all the summers before. One of my older band friends with a car came over and told me about a gathering they were going to have on Memorial Day weekend. Mom knew most of the kids, so she approved.

On May 28, 1973, several cars full of band kids went to a small campground on Spring River, about ninety minutes from Owasso. We were having fun running around a sand bar when I noticed Bonnie was there and John was not. We started up a conversation— the closest I had ever been to her. I noticed behind her glasses were the prettiest eyes I had ever seen. Probably my hormones were just taking over, but my heart was pounding. This conversation was the first one-on-one with this girl since the Love entry in my yearbook.

I can still picture Bonnie that day. She stood 5' 8" tall with shoulder length, strawberry-blonde hair that was always well-kept. She was not overly thin; rather, her medium build was well put together with broad shoulders and long legs—longer than mine. She was always smiling. She carried herself like a ballerina or a delicate porcelain doll, always making dainty moves with little or no wasted motion. To simply watch her move any part of her body was to behold a thing a beauty.

"Do you want to go for a walk?"

Did I ever! I could not believe we were walking off from the group. While she continued talking to me, I glanced back. No one was following us. My heart pounded as Bonnie, an experienced woman with at least two boyfriends, was taking me on a walk into the woods. Stepping out from the trees into a small meadow, we stopped and looked at the water while continuing to talk. Bonnie sat on the thick green grass, and I sat beside her. I clearly needed to follow her lead as I had no idea what would happen next or what would be expected of me.

She lay down on her back, looking at the clear blue sky dotted with small clouds. I lay on my back beside her. She pointed at different clouds, describing each one. "Doesn't that one look like a rabbit? I think that one looks like a train." I'd never had a conversation like this before and enjoyed every moment as we made each other laugh at the silly images we tried to point out in the sky.

I rolled onto my side resting my head in my left hand. I slowly put my hand on her stomach expecting some form of resistance. Bonnie turned her head slowly towards me as she looked into my eyes. I had seen this in the movies, so I leaned over to kiss—

My elbow slipped from under me, and I completely missed her face! My lips ended up somewhere near her ear. I mumbled something like, "I've never done this before."

"That's okay," she said. "Let's get back to the others."

As we walked back, she took my hand, and I almost passed out.

We returned to the group to the sound of giggles. I seized the moment and confidently put my arm around her. We may have arrived in different cars, but we left in the back seat together, arm in arm. In her driveway when we dropped her off at home, I got a second chance at a kiss. It wasn't much better than my first attempt, but at least I hit the mark. While getting out of the car another couple invited us to join them for dinner that evening at Arthur Treacher's Fish & Chips in Tulsa. It was the best day of my life.

I went home and announced to the family, "I met a girl." I neglected to mention the yearbook comment or that I'd been plotting to stalk her. Mom was excited and sincerely happy for me. Rick was not nearly as excited. He preferred to talk about what our next adventure might be and only saw Bonnie as a distraction.

From that day on, my life was never the same. Nothing would ever be the same. My interest in having a good time with Rick or my friends was all but over. All I could think about was Bonnie. I hardly slept as I could not get her out of my mind.

By then, we had a phone again, and Mom started a new job at a Tag Agency in Tulsa. Her job was to type license plate renewals and registrations. In Oklahoma during the '70s, all car tags were renewed at the same time of year. This meant long lines at tag offices as everyone had to endure this inconvenience together. The time spent in line was directly proportional to how fast the clerk could type registrations.

Mom quickly became something of a freak of nature in the tag office world. She could carry on a conversation while typing registrations three to five times faster than anyone else. In time, people would come to the tag office just to watch Mom type. To make extra money, Mom brought a typewriter home with a large stack of registrations and knocked them out while refereeing disputes among us kids.

Mom became a favorite of car dealers who brought their registrations to her because they knew she would get them done faster than anyone else. Watching her type was like watching a great athlete or dancer. Her fingers never stopped as she finished one registration after another seconds after feeding the form into her typewriter.

Bonnie and I started our summer of 1973 by spending a lot of time on the phone. While her parents were at work, Bonnie was left in charge of the home and her two brothers who were three and four years younger than we were. Mom never tried to limit our time on the phone. We would talk for what seemed like hours.

During our many phone conversations, Bonnie asked lots of questions and patiently waited for me to answer because she wanted to learn about me and my family. I told her as much as she wanted to hear, but what I enjoyed most on the phone was listening to her sweet voice. Bonnie suggested I come over the following weekend to meet her parents.

I was nervous as Mom drove me over. I wore my best clothes, including some new purple and gold tennis shoes we'd gotten at a thrift store. I slowly walked to the door and knocked. To my shock, the Equipment Truck Driver answered the door! He looked me in the eye, looked down at my shoes, looked me in the eye again, and slammed the door in my face. I stood for what seemed like the longest time before Bonnie came to the door while her dad, Richard, sat in his recliner laughing.

Richard was the same as when he was hauling our band instruments. He gave everyone crap. If you didn't like it—too bad. *What had I gotten myself into?*

Bonnie's mother Virginia was much quieter. We eventually had a good initial visit. When I got home, I told Mom about Richard's greeting to warn her, but she just shrugged. "Oh, I can handle him. Don't worry about how they treat you." She paused. "So you really like Bonnie?" I told her how much, and she said, "That's all that matters. Don't let her parents scare you."

Mom was so patient with me as I acted all grown up. After my dad's mental breakdown, I saw myself as Mom's peer and not as a son who still needed her guidance. She no doubt wanted to talk to me about what I was feeling and experiencing, but I kept my feelings inside and didn't give her a chance.

During the summer, with her parents' permission, I rode my bicycle as often as I could from Mingo to Bonnie's house in Owasso. We lived about seven miles apart, which took a while on my Stingray bicycle, but I never tired of each trip as I felt like I was riding on air.

On one of my first visits to Bonnie's house, we were sitting on the couch when we heard a knock at the door. It was John, the muscle-bound boyfriend who lived two doors down. He saw me and turned to Bonnie. "What's he doing here?"

Bonnie told me, "I'll be right back."

Five minutes later, she returned and sat on the couch as I stared at her. She watched TV for a few moments, then slowly turned. "That's taken care of."

I never asked what she said to John, but I always had a healthy fear of him after that—and maybe even more of a fear of ever getting crossways with Bonnie.

Early on, I told Bonnie about my dad and his time in Vinita. Bonnie listened quietly, never passed judgment, and expressed compassion for my situation. When Bonnie met my mother, they immediately hit it off without any of her father's drama.

Richard's over-the-top demeanor never changed; he insulted me with one derogatory comment after another each time I came over. "You're shorter than the guy who was here yesterday" or "Hey, Bonnie, your other boyfriend's here" or "Are you lost? Do you want me to call your mommy?" He continued with other such comments, always trying to get a rise out of me.

Virginia was nothing like my mom—or my family in Poteau. Virginia was clearly in charge but kept everyone at arm's length. As I learned later, this included Bonnie.

Summer also meant vacations. Bonnie's family planned a trip in Richard's camper shell that was mounted on his equipment truck—or should I say, Chevy pickup. They were headed to Wyoming. On one of my visits before her vacation, I learned firsthand how tough Bonnie really is. She stood up and started to walk. Her body faced west, but her knee faced due south. We both just stood there staring at her kneecap when she reached down and popped it back in place, saying in her sweet, soft voice, "Ow, that hurt."

Her injury was more serious than her reaction, and she was rushed to the ER. The incident only put a minor cramp in her vacation as she managed to travel in the camper shell while wearing a bulky knee brace. She mailed me a couple of postcards that I read over and over and over until I almost wore off the ink. Her postcards were just like talking to her on the phone. I was amazed at how much she could say on something as small as a postcard.

Mom also planned a vacation. She surprised us kids with a ten-hour road trip to the beach in Galveston, Texas. To save money, we stayed in the cheapest hotel near the beach and ate bologna sandwiches and other food brought from home. The trip was special for all of us.

As the summer progressed, Mom found a rent-house in Owasso. Rick would be attending Owasso in the fall, so it was time to turn the page on our life in Mingo. Leslee would continue to attend Mingo School so we still had a connection, but it would never be the same. To this day, I am convinced that in the 1960s, Mingo was the best place for a kid to grow up.

I was excited about moving to Owasso; Bonnie was now less than a mile away. We took bike rides together and played tennis or walked in the park. Summer band was fast approaching, and we were all concerned about the new band directors—especially Bonnie, given of her vocal support for the previous director. The new band directors were secondary for me as I was having the best summer of my life spending every moment I could with Bonnie.

Although our family still had money problems, we were in a much better place than we were two years earlier. While I was in high school, Dad was released from Vinita a couple of times. Mom and Dad eventually got a quiet divorce about which I knew nothing until months later. We weren't surprised about the divorce. Mom never said much about it, and we didn't press her. After that, Dad was no longer a part of our lives when he was released. He never reached out to us, and we drifted apart.

The time arrived for summer band to start. I rode my bike to Bonnie's, and we rode to the band room. We walked in the door, and a large man looked us in the eye. "Hi, Bonnie and Randy. My name is Harlon Lamkin." He continued to greet everyone who walked in the door *by name.* Our faces all wore the same bewildered expression. Obviously, Mr. Lamkin's preparation for coming to Owasso included memorizing every band student's name and face. Clearly a new sheriff was in town. One kid showed up a few minutes late. "You're late, "Mr. Lamkin said. "Take your stuff and go home. You're out."

Someone said, "You've got to be kidding." Mr. Lamkin gave that student his walking papers, too. Several others were kicked out or quit during those first few days of summer band. Under the previous band director, the kids were in charge. Mr. Lamkin knew this and was not having any part of it.

If we thought the uproar over firing the previous band director was a big deal, the entire city erupted as parents wanted to run Lamkin and his wife out on a rail. Meetings were held almost daily at different parents' homes to discuss strategies for getting rid of the Lamkins. No matter how many letters were written to the editor or how many protests were held at school board meetings, the school board and administration stood firmly behind the Lamkins and would hear no other point of view.

Summer band practice progressed. We all soon learned that Harlon and Wileeta Lamkin were more than tough taskmasters. They knew what they were doing. Eventually we realized the Lamkins knew how to build a winning band program.

During our first summer together, Bonnie asked me to meet her one Sunday at Lake Oolagah where Rick, my friends, and I often rode our bicycles looking for summer excitement. Bonnie explained they were having a gathering. Mom dropped me off at the lake, which was twenty minutes from Owasso, and I recognized several of my classmates. I soon discovered this gathering was a church outing. The subject of Bonnie's religion or church had never come up, so I was surprised to see a Catholic priest there. Granted, my feet barely touched the ground when I was around Bonnie, so she may have mentioned it, but my heart always pounded too loudly in my chest to have heard her if she did.

Bonnie told me the priest was going to say Mass, which was the most unusual church services I had ever seen. Aside from the unique setting beside the lake, no one yelled, pounded their fists on tables, or waved their hands. Instead, the service was quiet and respectful despite everyone's wearing swimming trunks and flip-flops. Several had draped towels around their necks for a quick dip in the lake as soon as Mass was over.

Later, Bonnie asked me to come to a regular Mass at church with her. I could not pass up an extra hour to spend with Bonnie, so I started attending Mass at St. Henry's Catholic Church in Owasso. I did not understand anything that was going on in the small church. Bonnie was so patient as she guided me through the missalette, which I thought was a clever playbook that Protestant churches should copy.

The best part of Mass came afterward when we all went to Grandma Helm's, Richard's mother's house. Grandma Helm was not Catholic, but she hosted a regular post-Mass gathering every Sunday with cookies or some other treat. She was kind and warm, and we hit it off immediately.

Grandma Helm's husband passed away shortly before I knew Bonnie. Later, after Bonnie and I got our driver's licenses, we continued the Sunday morning tradition of visiting Grandma Helm after church. Sometimes I would visit Grandma Helm by myself. She reminded me so much of my Poteau family: she had the same gift for making me feel like I was the center of her universe.

Bonnie's maternal grandparents, Troy and Anna Tilman, lived on two city lots only half a mile away. They had turned the second lot into a huge garden. The garden was an extended family project, with Bonnie's family spending lots of time preparing the soil, planting, weeding, harvesting and canning. Troy and Anna Tilman had five children including a son, Donald, who lived with them. They were not as easy to connect with as Grandma Helm but easier to get close to than Bonnie's mother.

As summer band wound down and school was about to start, I knew tenth grade with Bonnie would be my best year ever. Since Bonnie and I became a couple at the start of summer, we had no chance to schedule classes together. Instead, Bonnie memorized my schedule and passed notes to well-placed girlfriends in my classes who discreetly delivered the notes.

I tried to keep up with writing love notes back to her, but because I took so long to compose them and lacked her letter-writing skills, my notes couldn't compare with what Bonnie could crank out. She used every inch of a piece of paper, stringing sentences into circles or other geometric patterns, then folded the note so that, if intercepted, the contents would only be visible after considerable effort.

Although Bonnie was the center of my universe, I didn't spend time responding to her notes. When I wasn't with her, I hung out with my band friends or with Rick. I don't know how Bonnie found time to write so many notes. I think she wrote a lot of notes after our phone calls each night. She didn't have someone close in her family like Rick to spend time with her.

The first band marching season under the Lamkins got into full swing. Bonnie and I had some of our best times on band trips to football games or contests. We would sit together on the bus and talk while holding hands. We were just fifteen, so on the bus was the only time we could be alone. Although thirty other kids and adults were on the bus with us, we felt like we were the only people on the planet. Bonnie's dad went to every event, but he drove his equipment truck trailing behind, making the bus our private domain.

Near the end of the season, Owasso designated one of the home football games as Band Homecoming. Bonnie was the Freshman Attendant the previous year, and my girlfriend was named the Sophomore Attendant that year. She wore a sash and sat in a convertible, and I got to walk her out onto the field for the ceremony. I was having the time of my life.

Bonnie's parents would invite me to dinner at their house, or, sometimes, we would all drive to Tulsa for dinner. Her dad was relentless, continually picking on me or calling me by some new taunting name. Her mom was more reserved and didn't talk much. When Mom met Bonnie's parents, she quickly put Richard in his place. Richard had more than he could handle with Mom and never gave her any trouble. I never felt Mom and Virginia hit it off, but Mom kept her opinion of Virginia to herself.

Nothing Bonnie's parents could say or do would have kept me from her. I was completely under her spell and found it difficult to breathe when I was not with her. I found myself head over heels in love with Bonnie.

I quickly learned that words mattered to Bonnie, and it didn't take much to upset her. Because I hadn't chosen my words carefully, I would unintentionally say something insensitive, and Bonnie would get mad. I'd try to figure out what I'd said that upset her or how I could fix whatever dumb thing I'd said that time.

Bonnie never mixed words or got off-topic. On the other hand, a friend or any shiny object would easily distract me, which sometimes happened when Bonnie was serious about something.

As our first year in the Lamkin band program continued, we began succeeding at contests, so the Lamkins planned trips out of Oklahoma, which was a first. The uproar died down about removing them, and the following year, the band's size increased due to our success and the promise of some fun out-of-state trips.

As school finished at the end of May, I turned sixteen and got my driver's license.

Immediately I asked if I could go for a drive by myself, and Mom agreed. (Family finances were tight, so we shared the car.) I drove over the old Bird Creek bridge onto a gravel road and couldn't resist trying to fishtail on the gravel—and landed the family car into the middle of a large oak tree. I walked to a phone and called Mom who had a friend tow the car home.

I'd totaled the Ambassador, so Mom now had to scramble to

find another car. One of her car dealer friends from the tag office found her a 1964 Ford Galaxie—a long, two-door boat in faded Phoenician yellow. As long as we had that car, its tires were always different brands or sizes. We would go to the local tire barn where Mom would pay from five to ten dollars for the best worn-out tires we could buy to keep the Galaxie on the road. Rick and I added the car's most redeeming feature when Mom allowed us to put bright red cherry bomb exhausts tips on the back.

I mentioned instances when Mom allowed Rick and me liberties other parents might not have, such as putting cherry bombs on the family car. Maybe Mom was liberal because of what we all went through during Dad's illness, or perhaps she just wanted us to enjoy our childhood in a way she had not experienced herself. Either way we only loved and respected Mom more for how she treated us.

Now that I had a car (granted, it was Mom's), I drove to Bonnie's almost every night. Bonnie's parents allowed us to drive, at first for ice cream or pizza, and later, to the movies. We could only go to a drive-in with another couple, which we did occasionally, but mostly we went to an indoor movie theater. We also spent a lot of time sitting on the couch at either house watching TV. Mom was so sweet as she would leave us alone. She would read in her bedroom while keeping Rick and Leslee out of our hair.

Bonnie and Mom quickly became close. They shared a love for cooking, sewing, and crafts. I never saw genuine affection between Bonnie and her immediate family, especially her mother. During our phone calls, we talked about the tension between Bonnie and her brothers. Bonnie would change the subject telling me how much she liked my mom and how lucky I was to have her.

That summer, Bonnie had to wait for her driver's license because her birthday wasn't until September. After failing her first diving test, she passed, and her dad took her shopping. They came home with Bonnie's first car: a green 1971 Camaro. She got a job at K-Mart's counting money in the cash cage, and I worked in Tulsa dipping ice cream at Braum's Ice Cream and Dairy Store. Bonnie needed her job to make her car payments and insurance, while my earnings were for gas money and helping around the house. The Camaro became our date night car as Bonnie would come over and pick me up.

Our junior and senior years, 1974 through 1976, included great date night movies: *Young Frankenstein, Airport 75, Earthquake,* and *Towering Inferno.* Other memorable date night movies were *The Four Musketeers, Rocky, Carrie, Logan's Run, The Other Side of the Mountain, Jaws, Superman,* and *Carrie,* along with an Elvis concert.

Junior year at school was going to be different. Bonnie and I coordinated our schedules to take classes together, which seemed to make sense at the time. I soon learned taking the same classes with Bonnie was not a good idea. Bonnie loved school. She always sat in the front row and never missed an assignment. She got straight A's and took homework seriously. I struggled with most subjects, preferred to sit in the back, and hated homework.

Bonnie liked to come over to do homework together. I enjoyed the together part but not the homework. Bonnie was not about to let me fail. She was so patient as she helped me get through classes I struggled with. During our nightly phone conversations, she'd say, "Are you done with your homework? I finished mine after dinner." She liked talking about school and enjoyed every class she took.

As Band Homecoming approached, Bonnie was named junior attendant, so Mom thought she would do something special. She contacted one of her car dealer friends and asked if they would donate convertibles to drive the girls around the football field. She got the green light, and I had to narrow my list of friends to three to go with me to pick up the cars.

Friday after school, we went to the dealership (which will remain anonymous) and picked up four new two-seater convertibles. (I'm not going to give away the make or model, either.) The dealer told us he was leaving town for the weekend and asked us to bring the cars back on Monday.

What was he thinking?

After school on game day, we did our duty by first driving the girls to the parade and later around the field during the game. Once our official duties were over, the fun began. Between the end of the game and Monday morning, we put nearly 1,000 miles on each car. We spent all day and night driving all over the place, usually in an unsafe manner. None of us got a ticket, nor did we do any damage to the cars other than the ridiculous mileage. Needless to say, Mom was blacklisted among the car dealer community and was never again offered any dealer cars for kids to drive.

By this time, Bonnie and I were excelling in band. Bonnie was first chair flute and piccolo, and I was first chair euphonium—a baby tuba if you've never heard of it. The band was doing better than ever, winning every competition we entered. Bonnie and I won ribbons at solo and ensemble contests. I was encouraged to try out for the all-state band and made the first alternate which was as far as anyone from Owasso band made it under the Lamkins.

Because of my improvement, Mr. Lamkin spent extra time challenging me with more complex music and finding band pieces with euphonium solos. As much as I enjoyed band and spending all the time I could with Bonnie, I had no illusions about my music career extending beyond high school. Mom was barely making ends meet, so college wasn't a dream let alone something we discussed at home.

Our junior year also meant the junior prom. Bonnie made her own pretty red velvet dress, and I rented a tuxedo. Bonnie enjoyed bringing her dress over to show Mom who helped her. They spent a lot of their time laughing and would sometimes stop their conversation when I entered the room making me think *my ears are burning*.

I was a social wallflower with dancing one of my worst nightmares. I wasn't much fun at the prom and spent most of my time visiting with friends. Bonnie just wanted to dance, but I wouldn't even try. Despite her disappointment, Bonnie never remarked or commented.

Bonnie and I frequently talked about the future. From my

perspective, the future was next summer or the next band trip, but this was not what Bonnie had in mind. Like many other high school couples, one of our routines was to go "parking" after a movie or outing. I knew lots of good places where we could have privacy with the only interruption being another couple stumbling onto our spot.

Aside from the usual necking and consensual exploring of each other's bodies during these high school rituals, Bonnie would share her plans. I remember the first time she said, "When we get married, we're going to…" A shiver went down my spine. Marriage! I hadn't thought about it; marriage scared me. I had no clue what I would do after high school, much less how I would support a family. I was having too much fun being a teenager.

Bonnie would then talk about children as she shared her wish for at least three kids but reminded me that some Catholic families have many more. While I acted all grown up around my mom, I was just an immature boy. Bonnie was the mature one, always thinking and planning. She was never pushy when sharing her dreams and plans and would back off at the slightest resistance on my part.

Here I was with the girl of my dreams, who I loved more than air itself, yet I could not think or talk seriously about the rest of our lives together. I know this had to frustrate her, but she just loved me more. Thoughts about my dad still kept me from sharing Bonnie's excitement about the future.

Part of me saw my future as the man of the family with Mom, not moving on as an adult with Bonnie. In the furthest reaches of my mind, I still feared turning out like my father who did so much harm to our family. I cannot explain the feeling other than an inner voice that kept reminding me of my resemblance to Dad.

As if Bonnie and Mom were working together behind the scenes, Mom also talked to me about Bonnie and my future plans. I worked at night, so Bonnie often came over to visit with Mom instead of sitting at home. I did not fully understand the dynamics at her home, but Bonnie often said, "I can't wait to get out of that house."

When I started getting what at first appeared to be random letters from colleges asking me to visit, my college prospects changed. I had no idea how colleges even knew I existed until I learned Mr. Lamkin was sending letters to various colleges on my behalf. These letters encouraged me to try harder in the band. During my senior year, I was fortunate to make second chair at All-State, which was a big deal for the Lamkins as they continued to grow the Pride of Owasso.

My band success meant that letters from schools now included scholarship offers. I do not know who was more excited about each letter, Bonnie or Mom. At times I caught Mom crying while holding one of my letters. Only a handful of years earlier, Mom was on the verge of homelessness and uncertain if she could keep her three kids together. Now, her son was being offered full-ride scholarships to the college of his choice.

While Mom and Bonnie were always my biggest fans, I never acknowledged Mom for all she did to get me to this place. My pride and ego made me think my success was solely due to my talent when it was Mom's grit, wisdom, and sacrifices that led me to this pivotal point in my life.

Bonnie and I were now starting to see a path forward, as it seemed certain I would be going to college. My resistance in discussing Bonnie's future plans changed. I was now saying yes and nodding when she told me details of her vision.

Bonnie's dad made microscopes for a small local business while her mother worked in a bank. Her parents did not have the resources to send Bonnie to college, but she was not discouraged. She took two years of Technical School in high school and planned to enroll herself in a local community college while working to pay her own tuition. While my path to college was falling in my lap easily, Bonnie had to make her own way by herself.

My first college visits were to University of Tulsa, Oklahoma State, Oklahoma University, and Oral Roberts. I liked each school, and they all offered full-ride scholarships. Choosing Tulsa or Oral

Roberts meant I would stay close to Bonnie. We both knew I would not focus on school if I were to stay at home. D-1 Schools in Kansas, Texas, Missouri, and Indiana made offers. Over a dozen different colleges offered full scholarships.

Next, I visited the University of Arkansas, unaware that Mr. Lamkin wanted to develop a relationship with the University of Arkansas as a resource for future Owasso students. Mr. Lamkin drove me for my meeting with Director of Bands Eldon Janzen. I was nervous as I met Mr. Janzen in the band room. We talked for a few minutes, then Mr. Janzen stood. I asked if he wanted to hear me play. He said it was not necessary, which surprised me. For the other schools, I'd done a full try-out including sight reading. Mr. Janzen must have noticed my disappointment because he sat and asked me to play something. I played for less than a minute when he said, "That's enough." I went on a campus tour and fell in love with Fayetteville.

This day was special for me but more special for Mom. Mom was a woman of faith who experienced difficulties from childhood through adulthood. Like Bonnie, Mom never complained or got discouraged. During even the most challenging times she would say, "I put my faith in God, and He will protect us." No doubt Mom prayed for much throughout her life. Today's miracle in Fayetteville meant her children might enjoy a future when just a few years earlier, all she worried about were the basic necessities of life.

Bonnie and I got serious about our plans since I was off to Fayetteville in the fall. Bonnie's plans included, in a manner-of-fact fashion, our marriage. The truth is, I never proposed to Bonnie. She referred to "after the wedding" so often I felt no need to propose. We both knew we were too young to get married now, so we kept our plans a secret, which included waiting until I graduated. Bonnie's plans included getting her associate's degree and transferring to Arkansas while working to support herself.

Our senior year also included some complications. Bonnie's

mother thought we were getting too serious, which, of course, we were. Virginia told Bonnie she needed to see other people, and I was not to come over anymore. We would meet in secret, usually at my house where Mom had no problem with our hanging out. Mom was upset over the forced breakup. In fact, she always wanted Bonnie to come over—so much so that Bonnie once told me she was closer to my mom than she ever was with hers. That Bonnie's mother would decide during our senior year, with my college plans in full bloom, to pull a stunt like that seemed strange. The more I knew Virginia, the more I realized she was a control freak. Bonnie and I were making plans without her approval, and she wanted to take control.

To appease Bonnie's mother, we devised a plan that included Doug, one of our good friends from band. We convinced Doug to ask Bonnie out. I helped him with where to go and how to handle Bonnie's dad. The "date" went off without a hitch, which caused her mom to stop trying to separate us.

When it came time for Band Homecoming, the committee asked Mom about cars. After last year's sports car disaster, Mom knew borrowing cars was out of the question. Instead, she used her considerable connections to find some guys with roadsters who volunteered to drive Bonnie and the other attendants into the stadium.

For our senior prom, Bonnie made a pretty off-white dress. We met several other couples at a fancy restaurant for dinner where a waiter dumped a tray of iced tea down Bonnie's back, ruining her dress. I drove her home so she could change into her last year's prom dress. We returned to the prom, making the most of the evening except for my continued lack of interest in dancing. Bonnie still wanted to dance, but I made one excuse or another.

Time arrived for the 1976 Owasso High School graduation, which was exciting for both Bonnie and me. We had planned our future and were ready to move forward. Our summer following graduation was busy with Bonnie and her cousin Jeannie planning a trip to Florida to visit Jeannie's sisters. At the same time, I attended an exclusive band camp in a secluded part of southeast Colorado. I was to report to Arkansas in late July for summer band, so the remainder of our summer went too fast.

I had one small problem as I got ready for college. I needed a car. The husband of one of mom's co-workers gave me a 1967 Ford Galaxie. It was in rough shape and needed a paint job, but it was perfect.

When I arrived on campus, I was busy with summer band and trying to fit in. In no time I regretted attending a school so far from Bonnie. Every chance I got, I drove the two hours to Owasso and stayed as long as possible before returning to Fayetteville.

Bonnie was settling in at nearby Rogers State College, making her usual straight A's and taking every class seriously. The notes she passed in high school were replaced with letters she wrote and mailed to Fayetteville. To say she wrote lots of letters is an understatement. Sometimes I got a letter every day. She also spent a lot of time visiting Mom. Bonnie said she could talk to my mom in a way she couldn't with her mother.

Many of Bonnie's letters were about the trouble she had getting along with her younger brothers. She also wrote in detail about work, how her classes were going, and the dreams we shared for our future. I, on the other hand, was awful at letter writing. She begged me to write, but when I was not busy with band, I was hanging out with my new friends. I think she spent a lot of time in her room writing to escape her home situation. Bonnie felt unappreciated by everyone at home as she balanced work, school, and constant home duties.

When I first met Bonnie, I noticed she always worked around the house after school. Her brothers would just sit on the couch watching cartoons while Bonnie cleaned, did laundry, ironed, and started dinner. I called her Cinderella a couple of times as a joke, but not for long as the term was too close to the truth.

When I read Bonnie's letters, I felt like she was sitting next to me, holding my hand, and talking to me. She could write anything and make it sound like a conversation. She would answer her own questions, share new ideas or plans, or just vent about someone or something. She was always looking forward to the next time we would be together. Her letters were full of life as I read them over and over.

When she could, Bonnie included a few dollars in the envelope, which always helped. My full scholarship did not include spending money. The money I'd saved from working at Braum's quickly disappeared, so letters with money from Bonnie and my mom helped me socialize with friends off campus.

Bonnie soon traded in her green Camaro for a 1974 red Camaro with white stripes over the hood and trunk and a white vinyl roof. The Camaro was a great muscle car and a major upgrade. I acted foolishly when she told me on the phone about her purchase. Being too big for my britches (as usual), I was upset at not having been there to help her pick it out. Of course, Bonnie always knew what to say to calm me down. Her dad tried getting her to buy a Corvette as if she could afford it, but Bonnie wanted no part of her dad's idea. Turns out Bonnie did not need my help anyway; she always knew what she wanted.

Time came for the band's first home game, which meant a three-hour bus trip to Little Rock. Arkansas plays half their home games in Little Rock and the other half in Fayetteville, which seemed odd to me. Lots of donors and politicians in Little Rock and politicians get what they want. The first two home games were in Little Rock, with the Hogs beating Utah State and Oklahoma State.

The next home game was in Fayetteville against the University of Tulsa. I got tickets for Mom, Bonnie, and Leslee. In preparation for her first drive to Fayetteville, I mailed Bonnie a map—not your typical Rand McNally, mind you, but a hand drawn map on yellow notebook paper taped end to end to form an approximately ten-foot scroll. My map showed every turn, bridge, store, stop sign, and rough patch from Fayetteville to Owasso.

The girls made it to Fayetteville safe and sound despite my map. Sharing my campus life and showing them the sights was exciting. They commented on an odd smell in my room. I explained that marijuana was common in the dorm. One of my biggest fears when I went to school was dealing with marijuana, but the guys in my dorm were so good about it. They asked once, and when I said no, they closed their door and proceeded.

Bonnie and Leslee had other surprises. Our dorm was male-only but had a women's bathroom downstairs next to the game room. On at least one trip to the bathroom, they were greeted in the hall by more than one naked guy heading to the common shower located on each floor. The Hogs lost the game 9-3.

In early 1977, Bonnie's life changed.

Bonnie had a grand mal seizure and was diagnosed with epilepsy. She also experienced smaller petit mal seizures where she would be looking at you, then her eyes would appear blank as she zoned out. The grand mal diagnosis meant getting used to new drugs, and, more importantly, her driver's license was revoked. The loss of her driver's license was a major blow as she now had to rely on others to get to school, work or doctor's appointments. It wasn't easy, but she used her significant planning skills to make it work.

Bonnie was afraid I would think less of her or find that her epilepsy made her undesirable. On more than one occasion, she said that maybe I should find someone else—not because she wanted out but because of how much she loved me and wanted me to be happy, even if it that meant my being with someone else.

Nothing could ever change my belief that Bonnie and I were placed on this earth for each other. Neither her epilepsy nor anything else could keep me from wanting Bonnie at my side for the rest of my life. Bonnie's sweet nature always made her concerned about others even as her own health complications came her way one by one. She, too, knew our connection was so strong that asking me to move on would never work.

Despite simple daily tasks becoming more difficult without a car, Bonnie continued writing letters that remained, for the most part, positive. Knowing what a hard time she was having only made me want to be with her more, so I came home every chance I could.

My first year at college ended. I returned home and worked at Braum's because I needed money to get a different car so Rick could use the Ford. Rick graduated from Owasso and was coming to Arkansas on a half-scholarship to play in the Razorback Band as he pursued a degree in history.

When my second year at Fayetteville started, I was even more determined to spend my free time with Bonnie, which meant I chose to skip the college social experience. In contrast, Rick embraced the social side of college with both arms and quickly became popular in the dorm and band. Sometimes I returned from Owasso to hear how much of a party animal Rick had been that weekend. Friends repeatedly told me how Rick was the life of the party. Amazed, I just shook my head. Rick was a party animal to the extent that some probably doubted we were related, especially since I was becoming more and more of a recluse as I struggled with depression because of my poor grades and lack of focus. In fact, I habitually dropped any core class that was problematic, including English. Fortunately for you, my editor was able to make grammatical sense of these words I put on paper. My grade point average continued to drop, putting me further behind on my graduation path.

Another casualty of my constant trips to Owasso was my relationship with Mom. Although I was back in Owasso every weekend, I never stopped to realize that I hardly spent any time at home. Bonnie was not the only one sending me letters. While Mom's letters were nowhere near the volume Bonnie cranked out, she sent letters including this one in September 1977 at the start of my second year at Fayetteville:

Hi,

How are you doing? We are OK. How are classes going? Have you heard anything about private lessons? [A group of us were going to travel to high schools to teach lessons to make a few dollars.] I talked to Bonnie a couple of times this week. She seems to be enjoying school. It gives her something to do.

Did you get moved or have a different roommate?

Randy, I wish you wouldn't leave mad every time. I don't know what I do to make you mad, but if we could just talk it over, maybe we could get back on at least talking terms. I guess I'm a motor mouth to you. Randy, I'm so nervous around you anymore. I talk too much. I'm human, too, and I don't want you to hate me, which is what you seem to be on the way to doing. But I said I'm human, and I love you very much. I know you think I'm partial to Rick, but I'm not. It is easier to talk to Rick because he at least listens, even though he may not want to. Randy, I don't have anyone but you all, and I don't have anyone to talk to. I guess that is unfair to you because you have to listen to all my day-to-day ramblings. But honey, I don't want us to grow apart. We used to be close, and I don't even want us to be like me and my mother. I know you think I'm too nosy and possessive, but I'm really trying, Randy.

I'm just interested in everything you do and maybe you find that too confusing. I realize you aren't interested in our lives anymore. Babe, I'll try to keep my mouth shut more often. If you try, maybe we'll make it.

I love you,

Mom

I had been such a fool. I was so wrapped up in myself that I ignored the one person who gave me so much. She thought I was mad at her; I *was* upset at many things, but never her. First, my heart broke every time I pointed my car east toward Fayetteville after leaving Bonnie. Second, I knew I was squandering my opportunity to earn a college degree, which would eventually upset Mom and make her disappointed in me. Immediately I called Mom and explained I was never upset with her, but I did not share any of my other fears, which I regret.

When I accepted the scholarship, I was to be a music major and become a band director. Bonnie looked forward to being a band director's wife so we could continue the fun we had together in high school. I was coming to terms with my increasing disillusionment with the prospect of teaching beginner band students as a career. As I became fixated on major symphony orchestras, my musical tastes turned me into a musical snob. However, none of this mattered because the reality was that the scholarship and college were my only way out of poverty, and while I was enjoying all my music classes, I was failing everything else.

After Rick came to Fayetteville, Mom and Leslee moved into a small apartment in Owasso. The rent-house she had been living in was falling down around her, so she had to make a move. Finances were tight. Mom was still working at the tag office, but that didn't stop her from shopping for her boys in college or sending what money she could spare.

In the fall of 1977, Bonnie got a job at Saint Francis Hospital in Tulsa as a nurse assistant and was eventually assigned to the pediatrics unit. She enjoyed her job but was still reliant on others for transportation. Her life at home was not getting any easier as she struggled with her brothers and lack of support. Her letters to me were sometimes hard to read as she was ready to move out, offering one plan after another that would get her out of her house and closer to me.

Struggling with the epilepsy diagnosis and a separate illness, Bonnie was at a low point. She kept mailing me letters, but I was not sending responses. I could say I was busy, but just like in high school when I was not in class, I was either having fun with my new band friends or my other friends in the dorm. Bonnie mailed me this letter:

Nov. 7, 1977 Monday

Hello,

You know, I don't even know why I'm writing this letter. I told myself I wouldn't write another letter until I heard from you first.

But I guess it's always the girlfriend who gives in. I'm sorry I didn't get to come this weekend. I was really looking forward to it. I was hoping you would call me last night, but I guess you didn't have time for that either. I'm not all that sick, I've got strep throat, so it'll be Wednesday or Thursday before I can return to work, I sure hope I don't lose that job. I had those months when I wasn't working to get sick, but I had to wait until I got a new job.

I've lost 2 lbs. in 4 days. I guess I'm on what you call a liquid diet. I can hardly swallow those capsules for my seizures! Donald [her uncle] went and got my prescription for my throat, and those dang things are horse pills.

Randy, please write some letters. I can hardly stand it. It makes me feel like you don't even think about me anymore, which I know isn't true. Even a postcard with something that's going on would make me happy. It's just not getting a letter, card, or call which makes me upset. I like to know what you're doing so I can at least be with you spiritually. You wrote to me quite a few times last year.

Randy, even though you have nothing to say, an "I love you" would make me very happy. I want you to know that I've written you 2 or 3 letters I threw away because I wanted you to feel it too. What if you didn't get one letter from me in a week, wouldn't you get worried? Please don't use the usual excuse: "I don't have the time." I don't want to keep writing letters you don't have time to read.

Please. Randy, I love you, and I need to know whether or not you tell me in letters if you still love me. Please take 5 minutes to write even an "I love you" on a postcard and send it to me. I'd know it would be from you, so you wouldn't even have to sign it.

I love you!

This letter, the only unsigned one I ever received, got my attention. I immediately went down the hall, called Bonnie, and apologized. We talked for a while, which helped us both. She wrote this letter right after my phone call:

Nov. 8, 1977 Tuesday

Hi Randy,

Thanks so much for calling me last night. I felt a lot better afterward. It looks like I won't make it to work tomorrow (Wednesday) either. My throat is so sore that I can feel it clear down in my chest when I swallow. I sure hope those pills are helping.

Sometimes, I think they're part of my sore throat problem—they're as big as horse pills! No, I'm not a horse, either!

You know I really hate days like this. It's been rainy all day long. I'm sleepy, too, but I can't go to sleep. I'd much rather be at work. Besides, I wouldn't have all this time to think about you. It only makes me depressed.

I sure hope you're not so busy next semester. It seems like it has been a whole year again, but you know it's only been 4 months.

Well, we're almost halfway through. In five months, you'll be home for a while. I'm glad you'll have a chance to go to a bowl game. It would be a grand (sorry) great experience! These next few years will be your only chance to go unless your high school band is the greatest. Have you really thought about what it will be like to be a teacher and have your own band? I bet you're really excited.

Whenever I think of the future, I get so excited I can hardly wait. But then, later on, I'll probably wish time had gone slower. I just wish these next couple of months will go by fast. It looks like it'll be around Jan. or Feb. before I can move out. I've thought of some things I'll need to get or save for before then. By then I hope you can take me looking. There are quite a few apartments around St. Francis.

Anything close around there would be closer than Owasso. Which do you think would be best or cheaper, furnished or unfurnished? I know the furniture would cost more, but if I got it unfurnished, the money saved would be used to buy furniture. What do you think?

Randy, Christmas is coming soon, and I need an answer from YOU. What do you need or want? I was thinking about a digital watch, clock radio, tools, or clothes. Which do you want me to get you? I WANT you to give me an answer too. I don't want to get you anything you really don't want or need. Don't say you want it to be a surprise. It's OK if you have an idea of what it is, or even if you have a special item picked out, you could tell me.

Besides, you're getting two gifts this year. All I have to find is a bigger box or lose some more weight!!

I really ought to be signing off. Please tell Kathy [my friend David's girlfriend, whom Bonnie stayed with on one of her visits to Fayetteville] not to water her plants. One of my plants spoiled and stinks awfully bad. They're all in the garage now, but my poor room still stinks! Sunday, I smelled something in the hall, and later on, I walked into my room, and I almost got sick! I took out my jade because I thought it was that, but then I could still smell it, so I took out the other by the door. Yesterday was just as bad, so I took the rest out of my room. So please give Kathy a warning for me!

Dad's plane looks pretty good. He has the big one hanging up at the sports shop now for looks. I think this one's prettier. I'll tell him not to go fly it and wreck it until you get to see it!

I really ought to be going. The mailman is across the street.

Write to me on Friday about your trip and ANSWER the Christmas questions!

Love Ya,

Bonnie

P.S. I love you, Randy

Whenever Bonnie and I disagreed or misunderstood each other, we quickly resolved the matter. This letter is a testament to how quickly Bonnie could regroup after a setback and how much in love we were and are.

The reference to her dad's plane introduces his fascination with models. When Richard and Virginia got married, it was model trains. When I came along, he was into remote control model airplanes. Richard was a master R/C plane builder who built hundreds of planes for himself and others over the years. Many of his planes hang in the Tulsa Air and Space Museum & Planetarium. Richard's planes were up to one-third scale with a chainsaw engine and twenty-inch propellers. Bonnie told me when she was young, her Barbie dolls routinely went missing. She would discover her doll as the new pilot in one of her dad's big planes. Many of her Barbies were destroyed in various aviation disasters.

Richard tried to interest me in model airplanes, but I never had the time. I was always afraid of crashing. Many a time I watched him spend six months building a beautiful plane only to see it nose-dive into the flying field. He would always say, "If you're afraid of crashing the damned thing, you should never take up the hobby." He would shake off a crash as fast as Bonnie bounced back from a setback.

Bonnie was trying to solve how we could get married. Her plan included getting married and working in Fayetteville while I finished school:

Nov. 12, 1977

Hi Sweetheart,

All I do anymore is think about this, so if I went ahead and wrote and got it off my chest, I'd feel better. I'm not sure I should because I don't know how you feel about it. I only wish you were here or I were there so we could talk together.

I am willing to work while you're at school. You told me

that I could go back to school after you got your job if I wanted. If we both worked hard this summer, we could get my car paid off, so we won't have to worry about it. I can make two or almost three car payments monthly, and we can fix your car, too. I'm putting a little bit of money in the bank every payday and leaving it there so it'll grow for emergencies. If we can't get married before you start back to school, we could still find an apartment, and you could live in it while going to school. I could still stay here and work, and we could slowly get everything together and then, around Christmas, get married. If you're worried about never going out with the guys, we could set up evenings where you could go with them without me tagging along.

We don't even need to worry about a honeymoon right now. Just being together would be great right then. We could save then and go on a honeymoon the next summer. That way, we would be spreading things out.

Randy, we could make it. I shouldn't say this, but Mark and Carla [friends who married in high school] have made it. Look how happy they are. I truly believe they aren't using Marcia [their daughter] as an excuse to stay together, either. We won't have a little one to worry about either.

Every time I think of you, I hear, "Are you truly ready?" I've been thinking about this a lot this past week, Randy. I am very much ready to cook your meals and wash your dirty clothes. I know that we wouldn't have many dates then, but we would have every night together. We wouldn't have to worry about those expensive long-distance calls, or you wouldn't have to worry about writing a "dumb" letter.

Please think about it seriously, Randy. If you don't want to yet, please tell me. Yes, it'll probably hurt right at first, but it's better than letting me "dream" to come to a crash. If you want to try, I'll stay home and pray things work out, knowing I'll be with you soon. But if not, I'll go ahead and move out on my own now. I know you probably think I'm using my home problems as an excuse to marry. No, Randy, that is not true. I'd move out right now even if I knew you wanted to get married, but this way, it would save money.

If you wanted, and if Kathy sold my flute, we could get the rings this Christmas and make the engagement announcement. I just want the whole world to know we want to get married. I guess that's just every girl's dream.

Please think about what I've said here, and please write back.

I want and need to know your feelings. I cannot know unless you write and tell me. Please, I need to know before I get my hopes up too high. I just don't want my "bubble" to burst if it is left to grow for too long.

Randy – I love you !!

Love,

Bonnie

Bonnie & Randy
P.S. This way, you wouldn't have to worry about Tony locking you out of your room. I would never lock you out of our room! Never.

Bonnie was always thinking of a way for us to be together. Of course, I followed up this emotional letter with… a phone call. The reference to Tony, my roommate, is about the time he had a girl in our room and locked me out for good reason.

Even when we were younger and getting around on bicycles, Bonnie was always open and honest about everything. She even shared her menstrual problems and her visits to her gynecologist. She suffered from severe cramps and difficult periods. All I could do was hug her and just tell her how much I loved her. On the other hand, I was never as honest with her about my feelings in the same way I kept them from my mom.

Bonnie would even include in a letter before I came home for a weekend if she was "feeling good or not," her code for whether or not she'd be having her period when I came home, as if it mattered to me. In this letter, she tells me about getting birth control pills at the advice of her gynecologist—not for our personal use but to help with cramps:

Nov. 28, 1977 Tues.

Hi Randy,

I thought I would write a short note before I go to bed. I'm really tired today. I worked back in the back today in infants, and they wore me out. All four were under a year old, so it took a little more time. Later, I could go to a special school for a year and become an LPN (licensed practical nurse). She's the one who prepared medications and shots. It doesn't bother me so much now that I've been around that stuff. But then, someone else is doing it. I don't know yet. Time will tell.

Well, I got that medicine today (for my cramps). I'm still a little scared about taking them. Mom still doesn't know yet, and I won't tell her for a while. Since it's supposedly against our religion.

But I'm not using it for that reason. I don't ever want Grandma Tilman to find out—NEVER! I got a month's supply, and it was only $3.50, I was afraid it would cost a fortune. Time will tell.

Well, I better be going. I think a nice, warm bed sounds great right now. I believe Mother Nature still hates me! I'm off on Thursday, so that'll help. Then Monday will be my next day off. Good luck with your test, and tell everyone "Hi" to me. By the time you get this letter, it will be 9 days before I see you again. I promise I'll be in a happier mood! Well, God Bless!

I love ya!

Love,

Bonnie

Bonnie & Randy

(just 26 days til Christmas!) OH NO

Bonnie and I talked about the pill. We knew exactly why she was taking them, and I completely agreed. Taking advantage of the pill to have sex was not something we would ever consider. That is not to say we did not fool around. We just did not have intercourse for fear of Bonnie's becoming pregnant, which would change our plans.

In the previous letter, Bonnie referenced Tony locking me out of our room. I was better at planning than Tony. While some weekends Bonnie spent the nights in Kathy's dorm room, other weekends, when we told our parents she was staying with Kathy, she stayed with me. The difference was that I chose weekends when Tony was home with his parents.

When I came home for Christmas, the break was shorter than usual as Arkansas was heading to the Orange Bowl to play Oklahoma, and I would be taking my first airplane ride. While I was home, Bonnie and I went shopping—not for presents, but for rings. We decided to buy wedding rings on layaway and make payments. When the rings were paid for, we would announce our engagement.

The jeweler we selected for such an important purchase was... Sears & Roebuck, of course. They offered layaway, so we planned to pay them off with our tax refunds. We waited to make the final decision after we did our taxes to be sure we could afford the rings. Of course, news of our engagement would surprise no one as all our family and friends had long assumed we'd get married.

Bonnie and I never discussed how I would ask her dad for her hand in marriage. Aware that Richard picked on me all the time, Bonnie knew how badly that conversation would have gone. The truth is, I never asked Bonnie or her dad for her hand. When the time came, Bonnie simply told her parents in much the same way she informed me. Here is Bonnie's letter shortly after I went back to school after Christmas break:

Jan. 10, 1978

Hi Randy,

I hope you made it back to school ok. Are your new classes working out for you? I sure hope so. Work has really been busy these last two days. My feet are really hurting.

Next payday I'm going to get a second pair of shoes so that I can trade off and on. I can't wait til Thursday gets here.

I'm already ready for a day off.

Well – I talked to Mom. I told her of our future plans.

She said she knew something was probably being planned but she didn't want to ask questions. She said she thought if she asked, we would think we were trying to rush things.

She said she thought it was great but she wanted us to be sure we could afford it before we did get married. I showed her the rings we were thinking about and she said we should check at Oertles too because they're supposed to have good jewelry. So maybe the next time you come home.

I talked to Mrs. Heath, my head nurse, about next month. I'm supposed to be off the 4th (Sat.) and the 5th (Sun.) then I'll work Thursday and take that day off Tuesday the 7th and I'll work Sunday and be off Monday the 6th. In other words, I'll work Sunday and be off Saturday and Monday and Tuesday.

So, you check to see what the bus fare would be or you could drive home Sunday night and get me then I could ride a bus home Tuesday afternoon. Please check into it ok?

I really ought to be signing off for now. I need to dish up some ice cream for Dad then go wash my hair. I really am getting tired of washing it every night so on my day off I'm going to put a conditioner on it. I hope that will help.

I hope I'll get to see you this weekend but it might be harder since we can't see each other very much.

Remember that I love you very much and I miss you.

Be good but have some fun too.

Love you!

Bonnie

Bonnie & Randy

P.S. I love you !!

Not long after this letter, Bonnie finally got her driver's license back and was already storing furniture and buying blankets and all sorts of home goods. Her spirits improved daily, and complaints about her home life almost disappeared.

I gave a joint recital in February with Kathy's boyfriend David. David played the trumpet. It was on a Monday night and a big deal to a music major. We had programs printed, and Bonnie and Mom came. A nice crowd filled the performance hall. Both Mom and Bonnie sent me letters after the concert. Mom wrote:

2-12-78

Dear Randy,

Here is one of those letters that you'll say, "Oh no" or "Brother, she's at it again." But I'm writing it anyway. I want to tell you how proud of you I was on Monday. You always stop me if I start to tell you how I feel. I guess you think I'm a little silly. But someday, when you have children, you will only know how I feel. My heart was so full of pride I thought it would bust.

I know you are working very hard at school, and it really showed Monday night. Sometimes, it gets rough going, but honey, it is worth it. I know you've had such a rough time of it so far, no money as it would be easier. And I know I haven't been a perfect Mother. I try, and sometimes I try too hard and end up looking stupid.

I know you are the worst critic of yourself. But don't be too tough on yourself. You remember you are in the process of learning. Sometimes, it can be pretty tough sledding. But you've set your goal and are within sight of it. I know you had it rough growing up, having to become the man of the family when you were barely a teenager. I know sometimes it seems like you have been grown up all your life, and you feel you've had to take care of me. All of this will probably make you chuckle, but honey, how proud and pleased I am with how you have become a man. I love you very much.

Mom

No matter how thoughtless I had been all those times I came home and spent less and less time with Mom, she was still my biggest fan.

During spring break, Bonnie and I decided to get married after school ended in May of 1979. That would give us enough time to prepare and get one year closer to graduation, which I blindly thought would happen even though I remained behind in my studies. Bonnie sent me this letter with more of her plans:

March 29, 1978

Hi Randy,

There's not too much going on, so I am writing you a letter. Everything here is fine. I called and told your Mom [I left some keys at home], *and she said she had your keys and an extra key for her car, so do not worry.*

I took my ring in after work to get it sized. They are cutting it down to a size 5! It's a little hard to get it over my knuckle, but this way, I won't lose it down the laundry chute. It will take a week from Friday before I can get it back. I already miss it!

I went to see Grandma and Grandpa [Tilman] last night. They both seemed happy. They said I could have an old chest of Grandpa's grandmothers and use it as a hope chest. It's up in their attic, so Donald said he'd look for it sometime. They said it was an old round-topped one, and the inside would probably need to be redone. Maybe we could revarnish the outside.

I know this is or seems to be soon, but people are already asking about ideas. I thought we should at least decide what colors we would like for rooms. I think I want avocado green in the kitchen.

Beige or light brown would be nice in the bathroom, or any color would go well there. I was thinking of blue for the bedroom since we both like blue, but I was hoping you could decide on that color.

That's probably where I'll see you the most, if not in the kitchen!!!!

I also talked to Patty [lifelong friend] the other night, and Dan [her fiancé] was up there. They plan on next summer and maybe June 15th. I wish we could have an April wedding, but that's when all your finals are, and most of your studying will be. Maybe the middle of May would work or May 28th. That way, we could keep our tradition!! Everybody was teasing me all day Tuesday at work.

Then today (Wed), they all came by to see if my arm was still working or if my finger had broken yet! They are all *taking bets on how long we'll make it. They said one year is impossible!*

It's getting late, so I had better sign off. I'll write again as soon as I can. Remember, I love you very much. Donald was very happy when I told him. Mom's happy—she's already helping me fix a recipe box! Write if you ever have time. Dad's leaving Friday for Houston and won't be back until next Thursday. That's the day I have to go see Dr. Duffy. Hopefully, he'll let me cut down on the Dilantin.

Love Forever,

The future Mrs. Randy L. Rauh

Bonnie's Uncle Donald was a favorite of ours. He was a bachelor who lived with Bonnie's grandparents and helped them a lot. Mom and Donald were good friends. Donald came to my house once to show me his new motorcycle. Mom came out, one thing led to another, and off they went down the street and out of sight. Their return seemed to take a long time; when they did come back, they were both laughing. Mom told us they were pulled over for speeding and got off with a warning.

While I was home for the summer, Mom found me a job in a small machine shop in downtown Tulsa. I shoveled chips all day and wheeled them to a dumpster. Later, they allowed me to run a couple of basic machines, which I enjoyed.

That fall, Bonnie and I made one of many important decisions. We got a dog. Bonnie's cousin Terry and her husband Carl's Samoyed had puppies. Bonnie could not resist, so she took one of the puppies. She had grown up with a Jack Russell terrier, Daisy, whom she missed very much. We named our new dog Jasper.

Bonnie's wedding plans were in full swing. We would have the wedding at St. Henry's, which made sense except I was not Catholic. Bonnie told me we would have to attend classes with the priest, Father Fulton. One subject that came up was my intention to join the church. I told Bonnie I would be joining, which seemed to satisfy everyone. Father Fulton would officiate at our simple non-Catholic service.

As the time grew nearer, we both became more and more excited. Bonnie was busy with all the things she had to get done. She was making her own wedding dress and the bridesmaids' dresses, too, with the help of her neighbor, Jessie. We never asked Bonnie's parents or my mom to pay for anything related to the wedding. Ours would be a low-budget affair with Bonnie and me—Bonnie mostly—paying the expenses.

My cause for excitement was different from Bonnie's. Mine was more of a carnal nature from the sex education I learned from *Playboy* and similar publications. I knew we would be having lots of sex after we got married, even though Bonnie had made no such overtures or promises. I just figured it was a switch that got turned when you say, "I do."

While we wanted our wedding on May 28th to honor our first encounter on Spring River in 1973, we realized it was Memorial Day weekend. So, instead, we chose May 12th and decided on a 10:30 a.m. Saturday wedding. Bonnie had received a solicitation from Hot Springs Village Resort for a 3-night stay if we attended a real estate seminar. So, the honeymoon arrangements were made. With the wedding in the morning, we would have time to drive to Hot Springs before dark.

As our wedding drew near, Bonnie discovered we had scheduled our wedding on the day before Mother's Day, which meant a shortage of flowers. She called all over, looking for flowers, and finally found just enough for the ceremony.

We were to have three attendants each. Bonnie chose her friend Patty, with whom she grew up, her cousin Jeannie, and my sister

Leslee. I chose college friends David and Jim and my brother Rick. Friday night before the wedding was the rehearsal, followed by supper at Roy's Diner in Mingo. They decorated the place for the special occasion. Being back in Mingo for such a special day was like old times. Instead of the usual burgers, Roy went all out and cooked steaks.

That night the guys took me out for a typical bachelor's party: we went bowling. While Rick knew how to live it up, David and Jim were more like me in that we did not do the bar scene, and anything more risqué would have been out of character.

Our families attended our wedding, as did Opal, Carolyn Sue, Walter, and Debra. While we continued to visit Opal's family, we were never close. Mom was in rare form as she was so excited about this day and welcoming Bonnie into our family.

Carolyn Sue and one of Bonnie's uncles spiked the punch twice. When the short ceremony ended, Bonnie and I left in my car, but not before Carolyn Sue dumped some rice down my pants. They decorated my car as expected, but Bonnie's Grandpa Tilman allowed us to hide her Camaro in his garage, which was the real getaway car.

After we changed cars, we were on our way to Hot Springs. Back at the church, lunch plans were not in our budget, so Bonnie's dad went to the local KFC and picked up some buckets, and those who were left enjoyed a post-wedding lunch.

The drive to Hot Springs was long, and it was almost dark when we checked in. As we took our luggage to our room, I did what I thought all new husbands were supposed to do: I picked up Bonnie and carried her over the threshold, smashing her bad knee on the door frame, causing us both to fall to the ground.

We laughed about it, but Bonnie was really hurting. She took a warm bath to help her knee. I pretty much knew what was about to happen next without any consideration for Bonnie's pain. She got out of the tub, dressed, and limped to bed, saying, 'Randy, I'm too tired to do anything but sleep." We kissed and went to sleep. I realized *Playboy* had it all wrong, but it didn't matter. We were now married and looking forward to the rest of our lives together.

While we enjoyed a healthy sex life, one where we were always more interested in pleasing each other, the truth is many of our most intimate moments were not during sex. We enjoyed intimate moments just embracing or simply holding hands and looking into each other's eyes. Bonnie and I were connected by much more than what sexual pleasures in themselves could have ever brought either of us.

The next day, we went on our required tour and seminar, where they tried to talk us into buying a timeshare. Once we explained we had no money, they stopped talking and took us back to our room. When we got in the car, the Camaro would not start. Someone helped jump our battery, and we returned to the resort. We noticed a puddle of liquid under the car and realized our battery had a hole in it, so we decided to come home early. We packed our bags, got another battery jump, and headed back to Owasso.

Chapter Three

Late 1979-1992

OUR IMMEDIATE PLANS included finding a place to live in Fayetteville and finding Bonnie a job. We didn't have a place to live in Owasso, so we moved into Bonnie's dad's camper shell that sat on cement blocks in the backyard.

Fortunately, we didn't have to live in the camper shell for long. Our prayers were answered when Roy from the band in Fayetteville told me about an available house his grandmother owned that was within walking distance of the campus. We made an appointment to meet with Roy's grandmother. Her only requirement was that we bring our marriage license. "I'm not going to allow anyone to live in my house in sin," she said. Our documentation satisfied her, and she agreed to let us rent her house for ninety dollars a month.

The next good news happened when McElroy Bank in Fayetteville hired Bonnie. She earned three hundred dollars a month, which, given our rent, allowed us to make ends meet. Along with a night job I got at Shipley Bakery loading delivery trucks, we were able to move out of the camper sooner than expected. We borrowed Terry and Carl's truck and, with all our furniture and Jasper, moved to Fayetteville to start our new life together.

McElroy Bank was downtown a short drive from our house.

Bonnie settled into her new job working in the loan department. From our house, I walked to class. Across the street was a Catholic church; down the street was King Pizza take-out, Dillon's Grocery, and the laundromat. We could not have started out in a better location.

My work at the bakery ended with summer band starting, so we relied one hundred percent on Bonnie's three hundred dollar monthly salary. Bonnie was cost-conscious, so Hamburger Helper was our mainstay. 1979 was the year of the oil crisis and gas shortages, which meant Bonnie's Camaro with its ten miles per gallon was costing us too much in gas. We decided to sell it for a more practical car, an Oldsmobile Cutlass—but I always regretted selling Bonnie's Camaro.

As school and football season started, Bonnie attended all the home games and went on the bus with me to a few Little Rock games. I quickly got back into the grind of school, and while Bonnie and I enjoyed what time we had together, Bonnie was alone a lot.

Having spent the last three years skipping almost all social interaction at college, I had no college life to share with Bonnie. As odd as it seems, she became homesick—not for her home life, but for her familiar surroundings and her church community at St. Henry's. We took frequent trips back to Owasso, but Bonnie's boredom in Fayetteville remained the same. We did go to drive-in movies with other band couples who started as freshmen with me: David and Kathy and David and Jana (who played French horn in the band and whose father, Mr. Janzen was the Director of Bands).

Everyone who met Bonnie always enjoyed her company. I, on the other hand, was a social wallflower. I didn't help Bonnie meet many people because I didn't make the effort to attend gatherings. I'd said no so many times in the past that people assumed I would say no if invited. Rick, on the other hand, continued to blossom. He met a girl, Kim, from Charleston, Arkansas who played clarinet. Rick was a favorite among band members who included him in every social gathering.

One of the highlights of Bonnie's and my first year together in Fayetteville was Everett and Romagene's visit. Everett's health was failing, but they made the extra effort to make a side trip from Poteau that we've always treasured.

Mom was now working as a counter agent at Thrifty Car Rental where her people skills allowed her to advance into management. She'd come a long way from trying to find her first job and dealing with a major family crisis to becoming a successful manager. No surprise. We knew her crisis management skills would make her a great boss. We would visit Mom at her apartment but stayed with Richard and Virginia because they had a guest room. Leslee was in high school now and also in the Owasso Band where the Lamkin's were still in charge of the Pride of Owasso.

Our Christmas holiday was cut short because I was off for New Orleans and the Sugar Bowl to play Alabama while Bonnie stayed in Owasso. While in Owasso, Bonnie visited her neurologist as she was still having petit mal seizures. The seizure would last only a few seconds to a minute; then she would snap out of it and complain of déjà vu, the feeling that she was experiencing something she had experienced before. These seizures were usually followed by a severe migraine.

Bonnie also had her first grand mal seizure, which was completely different, when I was with her at home. Thankfully, her grand mal seizures only happened at night while we were asleep. I knew to keep her on her side to prevent her from biting her tongue.

As I lay across her to keep her on her side, she would beat the fire out of me as all she wanted to do was get out of bed. She would slur, "I want to get up, let me up." She sounded like her tongue was swollen and could barely fit in her mouth. These events could best be described as twenty minutes of terror as I did my best not to hurt her, and—more importantly—I didn't want her to hurt herself. When the seizure was over, she would usually go back to sleep, and both of us would be sore for the next day or two.

As school started to wind down, I needed a summer job. Uncle Walter, a machine tool salesman selling CNC machines, made frequent visits to Fayetteville on business trips. He found me a night-shift job in a small machine shop in Rogers, Arkansas, a thirty-minute drive from home. During the week, Bonnie and I did not see each other as Bonnie was still at the bank when I left for work, and I didn't get home until 2 a.m., but we needed the money.

My car was showing its age, so I sold it and talked Bonnie into my buying a motorcycle to save gas. Bonnie had serious reservations but reluctantly agreed.

During the fall, Bonnie's gynecologist told her the menstrual pain she had always complained about was finally diagnosed as endometriosis. She explained her wish to have children, and he told her we had better get it in gear. I liked the getting it in gear part, which seemed simple enough, but Bonnie was much more scientific about it. She would calculate the days of the month, consult the phases of the moon, and who knows what else to decide when was a good time to try—none of which was very romantic, but I did what I could.

Our house on Leverett Street was on the side of a steep hill. Across the street was a small bluff with some houses above it. At some point, a guy from one of the houses on the hill across the street came over to talk to Bonnie. I don't know how it progressed, but Bonnie, as you know, has a history of taking care of herself. She told me about it and assured me she would take care of it. At some point, she rebuffed his advances and told him to take a hike. In retribution, he allegedly would sit on top of the bluff across the street and take potshots with a pellet gun at our Cutlass, which had over two dozen dings along the side. I spent many nights sitting under a tree in the front yard trying to catch him, but never had any luck.

Not long after the pellet incident, someone broke into our house. Only our high school class rings and some very personal items of Bonnie's were stolen. The police were of no help, but we, of course, had our suspicions. Now Bonnie was not only lonely, she was scared.

At that time, Mom changed jobs. She went to work for rival Avis Car Rental, which has a large reservation center in Tulsa. Mom's work ethic was paying off, but it was still a struggle. She suffered discrimination due to her weight by people who did not take the time to get to know her.

One of Mom's great strengths was her ability to make and keep friends. People were quick to judge her at first glance, but once they spent just a few minutes talking to her, they found her to be a kind person with a sympathetic ear. She quickly became popular among her peers with many of the younger workers regarding her as a mother figure, just like she was the mom to all of Rick and my friends at Mingo and later Owasso.

Mom started volunteering as a counselor for the Tulsa Chapter of Domestic Violence Intervention Services (DVIS). This organization was new and something for which she showed a passion. She was also involved in Avis's United Way and Corporate Challenge efforts and enjoyed being a team captain on the Corporate Challenge.

1980 was an important year. I remained worried about Bonnie's safety, and I was scheduled to start student teaching. As part of the process, I was to meet with my counselor. I dreaded the meeting because I was behind in my studies. When the meeting started, my counselor asked why we had not met before. "Someone as far behind as you should have asked for help." I was hit with the cold hard fact that graduating in my fifth year of college was impossible, and my scholarship would expire. I could enroll in the fall, but I would have to get a student loan to continue.

I went home and gave Bonnie the sanitized version, which consisted of my scholarship running out and the need to get a student loan. The crazy part is that I lived with a woman who loved school and would have helped me with any of my classes had I asked. This would not be the first time I kept something inside that could have been easily fixed had I only asked for help.

I told Bonnie my heart just wasn't in being a band director. As I met other band directors, I saw adults in their thirties and forties still teaching beginner bands. I was such a snob I could not see myself teaching band for a living. I suggested we move near Owasso where my uncle could get me a full-time job in a machine shop. I enjoyed my work in the Rogers machine shop and felt something was calling me to this profession.

Bonnie agreed, and we made plans to move home. I think Bonnie was more relieved to leave Fayetteville than upset over my failure. Bonnie and I visited Fayetteville many times in the future. We never talked about the guy across the street or any other fears she had in those last few months in Fayetteville.

We found a rent-house in Collinsville just north of Owasso. We borrowed Terry and Carl's pickup truck again, loaded all our belongings along with Jasper, and left Fayetteville.

I could never explain why Bonnie never hinted at disappointment or made any offhand comments about my obvious failure. Her dream was to be a band director's wife, and I'd ruined those plans with my lazy attitude toward my studies. Clearly, I still had a lot of growing up to do.

My uncle got me a job at a small machine shop in Oolagah, a ten-minute drive from Collinsville. The pay was good, and I worked the day shift. Bonnie got a job as a bank teller in Tulsa.

In 1981, Grandpa Everett, age sixty-four, died in California. Afterward, Romagene made several trips to Oklahoma as the two always went on a road trip together when she came to visit. Since Mom worked for Car Rental companies, she used her discount to rent a car for their trips. Mom's rental of choice was always a convertible. Mom's brother BJ and his wife Carla became close as they continued their visits to Poteau.

Bonnie and I were settling into our new routine, but despite our best efforts, Bonnie was unable to get pregnant. In March of 1982, she had an episode that doubled her over in pain. We rushed to the

ER to learn that one of her ovaries had burst. The doctors said she could still get pregnant with one ovary, but the clock was ticking.

Sadly, two months later, she had the same abdominal pain. Her second ovary had exploded, the doctor told me, and she had to undergo a hysterectomy. It was up to me to break the news to Bonnie after she came out of recovery. It was the hardest thing I ever did. I looked her in the eyes and told her what happened as I broke down sobbing on her shoulder.

My emotional breakdown was about more than her dream of having children being over. I was riddled with guilt because, deep down, I did not want children. I still carried around the notion I would be "just like my dad" and didn't want to pass on his gene for fear of my or their becoming psychotic or worse.

Bonnie, however, took the news of having a hysterectomy at age twenty-four as just another setback. She contacted Catholic Charities to start the adoption process. I gave only tacit approval and support because I didn't want children, adopted or otherwise, to experience what we went through as kids. Looking back, I clearly was struggling with an undiagnosed and untreated mental illness.

When driving home from work, Bonnie had another setback. Heading north on Highway 169 at an estimated speed of sixty miles an hour, she had a petit mal seizure and drove the Cutlass off the 76th Street overpass. The car landed on its side on 76th Street, and Bonnie was rushed to the hospital. The only major damage was a broken nose requiring reconstructive surgery and twenty-four stitches inside her mouth. Bonnie was not out of work for long.

The day they removed the plastic splint inside her nose, I was sitting perpendicular to Bonnie, looking at the side of her face. Holding the splint in place, the doctor took his long scissors and clipped the stitches inside her nose. He then took tweezers and started pulling the splint out of her nose. My vantage point was the best and worst view of the procedure. As the splint emerged from her nostril, I kept waiting for it to be over, but the white plastic kept coming and coming as I clutched the sides of my chair with both hands. Bonnie never made a sound as I said, "How in the world did they get that big thing in there?"

Not long after, a friend invited us to go to a meeting about a new housing addition being built outside of Collinsville. One thing led to another, and, after looking at our finances, we decided we could make it work within our budget. So, we signed a contract to build a small, two-bedroom house and were involved in all the joys and heartaches of building our first home.

Mom was also making changes. After Leslee graduated high school, she and Mom moved to Tulsa to be closer to work. Mom found an apartment much nicer than the old one in Owasso. She also started spending time with Opal and Sue.

After construction on our house began, we frequently visited the site, which was located on a hill with a view of downtown Tulsa. We were so proud to show our parents the construction site! We spent time adding extras, like insulating all the interior walls, and we made other minor additions ourselves.

At some point in 1983, we were having a family gathering at our new house when someone knocked on the door. It was Dad and his new wife. He had managed to track down my new address. Leslee was nervous about seeing him, but the visit went without incident. I was glad to see him. I felt for him as I could tell he was nervous. He gave me his contact information and left.

Not much later, I needed to visit him. I do not recall the reason, but when I arrived at his apartment, he said, "Give us a minute." Unfortunately, the window in the door did not leave much to the imagination as they both had to dress. Clearly, Dad was still living the nudist lifestyle, but at least this time behind closed doors.

In 1984, the hospital contacted me. Dad had died of a heart attack. He was sixty-two years old. We buried him with military honors in a Tulsa cemetery.

Many changes took place in 1985. The first happened after a

former coworker suggested I work with him in Tulsa at a mold shop. The job meant a raise, but it was on the night shift. I would go to work at 3 p.m. and get off at 3 a.m. Bonnie supported the decision. We made the most of it, enjoying each other's company on the weekends and hoping for better days ahead.

The only time we had together during the week was when Bonnie started working the early shift. This meant we drove to and from work at the same time. Our daily routine was that we would meet at 2 p.m. at a Tastee Freeze in Owasso. Our private joke was that we came from different directions in different vehicles, held hands in the booth, and hugged and kissed before leaving in opposite directions. The workers had to think we were having an affair, which we always got a kick out of.

Back in Owasso, Bonnie was near our house driving home from work when she had another petit mal seizure. She drove the car off the road into a concrete culvert, which totaled it. Fortunately, no other cars were involved, but the accident resulted in a major back injury that required surgery. She would not get a paycheck during her extended recuperation period.

We soon got behind on our mortgage payments, so Bonnie called the mortgage company. We agreed to move out of the house and turn it over to the lender. The decision was painful, but one we could not avoid. We found a rental house near where I was working in Tulsa and made plans to move. None of this affected our relationship. We remained as close as we had ever been.

Bonnie was upbeat despite her long rehabilitation and our having lost the home we built. She focused on working with Catholic Charities for an adoption. I was busy with my 3 p.m. to 3 a.m. shift and was still not as supportive of Bonnie's adoption efforts as I should have been. She knew I was working long hours with lots of overtime, so I had little time for much else.

About this time, Leslee got married and moved to California. Not long after, Mom moved to California to help Leslee who had two kids. The bond between Mom and Leslee is so strong. During our family crisis, Rick and I leaned on each other, while Mom and Leslee did the same, making their bond much closer than that of most mother-daughter relationships. Mom found a job in California in a construction company office where she quickly became a valuable asset and close friends with her coworkers.

Back in Owasso, the coworker who convinced me to come to the mold shop started talking about us starting our own company. His dad owned a molding company in Tulsa and did not have his own mold shop, so we thought we could eventually get some of his business. We were both naïve. Like me, he had a young wife, so we figured if twelve hours a day we were not working, we could start by 8 a.m. and work until 2 p.m. at our new business before going to our real jobs.

One thing led to another: we quit our jobs, started our own mold shop, and eventually got into the CAM software business. CAM software is used to write programs for CNC machines such as mills and lathes. We were burning the candle at both ends, working 120 hours a week or more. Bonnie would visit me at night and brought dinner when she could. She was so supportive of what I was trying to do. I knew I could not keep this pace up for much longer as I started making some dangerous mistakes like driving away from a gas pump with the hose attached—twice. The worst incident was when Bonnie came to meet me for dinner. Afterward, I returned to work for another all-nighter. The next morning, someone came in and asked, "Why is your car running?"

My partner and I eventually split. I took over the software side of the business, and he took over the mold shop. I opened an office in Owasso to focus on selling software and services, and we moved to a rent-house in the older part of Owasso. I remained busy with my new business, which now included lots of road trips.

During all my time burning the candle at both ends, Bonnie was quietly and patiently working on the adoption with Catholic

Charities. Bonnie spent almost five years getting approved for adoption. Then she started meeting potential birth mothers—alone—since I was always working. Bonnie would try to talk to me about baby names, but I showed little interest. She never pressed me, but I knew how disappointed she was. Bonnie chalked it up to my working too many hours. The truth is, I was still battling demons in my head.

In early 1988, Bonnie informed me about a home study, a final step toward adoption. We learned the cost that, while modest, was more than we could afford, so we borrowed money against our life insurance policies. We were a little short, so Bonnie's Grandma and Grandpa Tilman helped us meet our goal. Grandpa Tilman was quite ill at this time, having been in and out of the hospital. He was at home on what we would now call hospice care.

In July 1988, Bonnie got the call. A baby girl was available. Did Bonnie want to meet her? Bonnie was so excited, I doubt the social worker could finish her sentence before Bonnie asked when and where. In this case, Bonnie did not meet the birth mother of the two-month-old baby girl who was in foster care on the other side of Tulsa.

When we arrived at foster parents Don and Sheila's house and met the baby (whom they called Toya), as all my concerns about being like my father and not wanting children disappeared. Bonnie and I sat on the floor and just looked at each other as we beheld the most beautiful baby we had ever seen. Her piercing blue eyes—a shade of blue I'd never seen—were the size of silver dollars. Bonnie's dream was coming true as we both fell in love with this baby at first sight.

We explained Grandpa Tilman's grave situation and our hope that the adoption process was finished so we could take her to see him. Don and Sheila were amazing. They suggested we take the baby to see him saying simply, "We won't say anything if you don't."

The drive across town usually takes fifteen minutes, but this trip took at least thirty since I drove as if I had the Queen of England in the back seat. I stayed well under the posted speed limit and braked so softly a bowl of goldfish on the front seat wouldn't have sloshed a drop.

On the way, we talked about the baby's name, a topic Bonnie had often wanted to discuss but we hadn't due to my prior lack of interest. Bonnie said she liked the name Megan, to which I responded with multiple spellings—

"No, it should be M-E-G-A-N." So, Megan it was.

In case the plan fell through, no one in the family knew about our visit to Don and Sheila's to meet the baby, so no one knew we were bringing her to see Grandpa Tilman. We arrived at the Tilman house and found it filled with family standing vigil. They were all amazed as we walked in with a baby, brightening everyone's spirits. Bonnie took Megan, went into Grandpa Tilman's bed, and laid her beside him. He had the biggest smile as she introduced him to his new great-granddaughter. In the other room, I was being congratulated with everything short of cigars.

As we headed back to Don and Sheila's, I could see Bonnie in my rear-view mirror, the most excited I had ever seen her. She was leaning over beside Megan talking to her, making the most of every second with her. We arrived safely and gave Megan back to the protection of Don and Sheila with our profound thanks for the great gift they had given us.

Two days later, Grandpa Tilman died.

During her six-year journey, Bonnie had fully stocked the baby-room with little participation from me. I could blame my busy work schedule, but it would not be completely true. Even though Bonnie had to have sensed my reluctance to adopt, she never confronted me or berated me for my lack of interest. None of this mattered after my first sight of Megan.

Bonnie had already decorated the baby's room with drapes she'd made and other personal touches. Bonnie's many sewing skills included cross-stitching. She placed a note on the back of one of her projects. Her cross-stitched baby picture had this note on the back:

"Started stitching [this] *in 1987 after approval for adoption process.*

Stopped counting after talking and meeting 8 birth mothers.

Found out much later if they didn't look you in the eye [they were] *not serious.*

We got the call in July of 88."

Although Bonnie was clearly in pain as she felt she'd been rejected by eight different birth mothers, did she complain or badger me to get more involved? No. That was not Bonnie's style. Was I there for her when she was in so much emotional pain? No. I was too busy traveling for work, and my mental issues kept me from engaging with her about her adoption journey. Did this affect how close we were during that period in our life? Not at all. We remained as much in love with each other as ever as we enjoyed each minute together.

A couple of weeks later, with the adoption finalized, we went back to Don and Sheila's this time to get Megan forever. We could not have been happier as we reflected on the six years Bonnie worked through the adoption process. Bonnie was so patient when I had not shown the same enthusiasm. None of this mattered now as we drove to our little rent-house with our new baby on the happiest day of our lives.

We quickly wrapped our world around Megan. My business was doing well enough that we could afford for Bonnie to stop working and become a full-time mom, a dream she'd always had, and I was happy to let Bonnie do what she had always wanted: be a mother. Foregoing the career she could have chosen over becoming a stay-at-home mom was easy. She never gave up on adoption and made raising children her goal. She's always been the smarter of the two of us and could have had a career doing almost anything, but instead, she put raising a family before herself.

Bonnie bought a "First Year's Calendar" and meticulously entered all of Megan's *firsts*, including the day she got the call from the social worker about Megan and the three baby showers. She also placed stickers on milestones like Finds Hands, Eye Focus, Begins to Creep, Shakes Rattle, Rolls from Back to Tummy, Finds Feet, First Solid Food, and Drinks from Cup—with the list of special days covering an entire calendar year. Bonnie also marked a car accident, the result of a petit mal seizure. The car wreck would be her last and one of her last seizures.

When I was home, everything I did centered around Megan. If I had a project or honey-do job, I placed Megan right in the middle of whatever I was doing. She was swinging a hammer when she was two, and we quickly realized Megan was fearless and tough as nails.

When Megan would fall or, in some cases, literally jump off things, she would just dust herself off as if nothing had happened. I do not understand how it happened, but Megan seemed to be biologically as tough as her mother. The problem is, while she was as tough as Bonnie, she was also as reckless as I was at her age.

When Megan was four, I put together a tall UBuildIt cabinet for Bonnie's sewing room—you know, the kind of cabinet with the heavy white laminated MDF plywood. With Megan's help, I was almost done but needed a tool from the garage. When I returned, I could not find Megan. I called for her and heard her muffled voice. I saw the cabinet on its side with one of Megan's arms sticking out from underneath. As I quickly lifted the cabinet off her, she never made a sound. The incident scared her more than it hurt her. She must have decided to climb up the shelves when it fell over.

Bonnie likes family pictures on the walls. We used several professional photographers and took Megan for a photo shoot at least once a month. Bonnie made most of her outfits that always looked better than anything from a store. On several occasions on the day before a picture appointment, Megan would run into or fall off something that would leave a bruise, scrape, or black eye. Bonnie would do her best to hide the incident with makeup before the picture.

By 1990, Megan was turning two, and the business was doing well, so I started looking for a larger house. We had no idea where our credit stood. We were able to buy a car without issues. Still, we were concerned about what the house we had abandoned would do to our chances for a mortgage.

Driving the neighborhoods of Owasso alone, I pulled into a cul-de-sac and noticed a large, two-story house with a handmade sign: "For Sale by Owner. Assumable Loan." I pulled into the driveway and met the owners who showed me around. They had built the house two years earlier and needed to move out-of-state to be with family. They wanted someone to assume their mortgage, and, after two years, we would need to refinance and change the mortgage into our names.

"I think I found a house!" I told Bonnie. I was excited as I drove her to the cul-de-sac and pointed out the house.

The outside's light gray with peach trim immediately appealed to Bonnie's sense of color, but she shook her head. "We could never afford this house."

"Let's go in and take a look."

The bottom floor had a living room on one end, a game room on the other, and two fireplaces, one on either end of the house, as well as a formal dining room and a large kitchen. The carpet throughout was—as Bonnie called it—mauve, but it just looked pink to me.

All three bedrooms were upstairs. The first two were average size, but then we entered the master bedroom. Dramatically, I flung open the two doors to the oversized master bathroom. Bonnie gasped. The bathroom, with its large shower and two-plus person whirlpool tub, was larger than the living room in our rent-house. Mirrors, positioned all around the room, made it look even larger.

Bonnie leaned over and whispered, "We can't afford this."

"Come downstairs with me so we can talk about it." We discussed with the owners who explained their need to trust whomever they turned the house over to. We must have made a good impression because later that same night, they called to tell us the house was ours if we wanted it. I still had to convince Bonnie we could afford the payments, which was one of my most successful sales pitches ever.

Chapter Four

1992-1997

During this time, Bonnie was experiencing back, hip, and shoulder pain, the lingering results of numerous car accidents. The back pain was ongoing because of her surgery years earlier. Still, the other pain was not diagnosed until much later when it was found to be early onset fibromyalgia. Bonnie also suffered severe migraines, which would leave her in bed all day in complete darkness as her only relief. In addition, she was having some wrist pain, which was diagnosed as carpal tunnel syndrome and resulted in yet another operation.

Bonnie took any surgery in stride, but what she struggled with was anesthesia. She experienced severe nausea and vomiting after every surgery: the first burst ovary, the second burst ovary and hysterectomy, her nose surgery, her back surgery, and now after carpal tunnel surgery.

In 1992, we planned a summer trip to California. At the last minute, Bonnie had a minor fall at home and hurt her back, which required yet another back surgery. Bonnie insisted Megan and I go to California without her. Mom, Leslee's family, and Rick's family were all living in California, so it was a big deal for us to visit. Leaving Bonnie behind was so hard, but all she could do was lie in bed. We made home movies to bring back to her. Every time I called home, she remained upbeat and was excited to hear about our daily adventures.

Bonnie continued having various medical issues over the next couple of years, including two knee surgeries and removal of her gallbladder. Pain management was quickly becoming a serious issue. We eventually had to find a pain management clinic where she was subjected to routine injections in her neck, shoulders, and back. She even resorted to acupuncture to relieve the pain.

Our visits to the pain clinic were sad as we observed people in tremendous pain with mobility issues. Bonnie would say, "I don't know why I'm here. These people need help so much more than I do." Had there been a shortage of medication, Bonnie would have been the first to volunteer her shot for someone else.

In 1993, Mom decided she had had enough of Los Angeles and moved back to Tulsa. I think Mom was running out of ways to avoid traffic, but in truth, she missed home. Mom found an apartment in Tulsa and a new job at another utility service company where, as at every other job, she became indispensable.

A few months after Mom moved back to Tulsa, her mother Opal died. Their relationship was complicated, and they were never close. With her other grandchildren living elsewhere, Mom took advantage of the move back to Tulsa to be close to Megan. As with all her grandkids, Mom quickly developed a special bond that was no truer than it was with Megan. Mom loved Bonnie so much that she shared every moment she could helping her as much as possible.

Mom had another unique skill: She was an expert at baby talk. Her voice dramatically changed at the sight of a child or even when talking about a child to another adult. Bonnie did not mind, but I became annoyed and even a little embarrassed. The truth is that Mom's baby talk, in ways I will never understand, made her closer to her grandchildren and any child she encountered under the age of ten.

That Christmas, we made a home movie to send Leslee and Rick. This movie served two purposes: first, to show them around our cul-de-sac house because they hadn't been back to Owasso since we moved in. I played tour guide, following Megan age two as I filmed a house walkthrough. The second reason for the movie took place downstairs.

After a little staging, I announced from behind the camera, "Where are the girls?" while walking into the living room where Mom, Bonnie, and Megan were sitting on the floor having a tea party. Mom was hamming it up like she always did when playing with her grandkids, and Megan was serving tea. All three were modeling the dress-up accessories including the fancy hats and frilly boas that Bonnie had made for Leslee's three girls for Christmas. We shipped the gifts to California along with the home movie.

Our house was full of joy and laughter. Bonnie and Megan were always going somewhere on an adventure or daily outing. They rarely sat at home. Megan was so funny and not afraid to try anything. Sometimes, she caught us off guard when she would attempt some new daring act—or should I say, dangerous feat?

Bonnie enrolled Megan in Wee Angels Pre-School at St. Henry's, the church where we were married. Bonnie enjoyed helping at preschool every chance she could. About that time, the popular TV show *Full House* appeared featuring the Olsen twins who were about the same age as Megan. In her pre-school years, Megan was the spitting image of the twins, so much so that people would routinely stop us in stores and restaurants asking if she was the girl on *Full House*.

After preschool, Megan attended the public grade school just up the hill from our house. Bonnie was no stranger there, either, as she involved herself in every activity she could. While I attended Mass with Bonnie and Megan, I had not yet joined the church as promised.

Things going on in my head prevented me from getting close to God. Back in 1987, when I started my software business, tax time came around. I asked my former partner who he used for taxes and took my business to the same accounting firm. When my taxes were done, I was presented with my $1500 tax bill and $1200 accountant fee. I could not pay both, so I paid the accountant and figured I would pay the tax bill later with interest.

I either never saw, or I misplaced a follow-up letter, got busy with work, and forgot about my tax bill. The next year came and went as I waited for something from the IRS. I now needed help, so I hired an employee. I knew I would have employee withholdings, so I paid a tax service for payroll. At the same time, I continued to neglect filing my personal or business returns for another year. Bonnie knew nothing about this.

I kept my head down, working hard to provide for my family as the business grew, putting any tax concerns out of my mind. My reputation for customer service and doing whatever it took to satisfy my customers led to even more business. Sometimes, this meant spending half the night downstairs working or making some crazy road trips that, just like the years apart in college, meant coming back home to Bonnie and Megan as quickly as I could.

I always felt a euphoric excitement when I packed my bags on the last day of a trip, and, like college, I felt the same way each time I headed home to see Bonnie and Megan. When I got into the car after class, I would immediately call or text Bonnie to tell her I was on my way. I never lost that tingle of anticipation when coming home after a long road trip.

Bonnie and I played a little game where I would predict my arrival time when I departed. I got surprisingly good at this even when I had only paper maps and no car navigation or cell phone maps.

My routine was to drive until I needed gas: I would start pumping, lock the doors, use the bathroom, and get something to eat. The goal was to make it back to the car before the gas pump clicked off. On many occasions, I would get home on the dot as predicted, with Bonnie always accusing me of parking at the end of the street to make sure I arrived on time.

I do not know how it is with other couples, but I think what we have is special. Bonnie and I often came up with the same thought or idea at the same time. Often we finish each other's sentences. We never argue and rarely disagree. We are both particular about a lot of things—rarely about the same things, though. My fascination with precision is a byproduct of my work in CNC programming where every letter and number must be exact. Bonnie's focus on detail is different.

Bonnie is highly organized. I recall not long after we moved into the big house (only 2,400 square feet, which is small by today's standards, but in 1990 was a large home for common people like us), I changed the toilet paper roll in the downstairs bathroom. Not long afterward, Bonnie walked into the living room in a huff saying, "Come with me." She led me into the bathroom. "This isn't how you load toilet paper." She removed the roll, turned it around, and replaced it, explaining the physics of the proper way to dispense toilet paper. I never made that mistake again.

Bonnie is a wonderful cook, as my waistline can attest. She kept everything in the kitchen in a specific order that I've done my best to learn in an attempt not to interfere with her delicate balance.

As her passion for crafts and sewing expanded, we turned the game room into her sewing room, which was just as organized and neat as her kitchen. Bonnie had a place for everything, and everything was always in its place.

While I am particular in other areas of my life, I am not nearly as organized as Bonnie. She always gave hints and suggestions or bought me organizers for my garage or the backyard shed.

Work colleagues shared with me how much they enjoyed working from home. I always told them I could never work from home because Bonnie would constantly be reorganizing my workspace, and I would never find anything.

Although my office was only half a mile from home, I enjoyed having a separate place to go to work every morning. Undeterred, Bonnie would do her best to organize or decorate my office, too. I tried to keep it tidy, and I instructed everyone who worked with me on how to properly replace a toilet paper roll.

One thing we agreed on was that we did not want Megan to be an only child. Bonnie checked with Catholic Charities, but the waiting list for a first child was so long she was told getting a second child would be almost impossible. We started talking to private adoption agencies and attended a couple of seminars focused on adopting foreign children, which was fine with us.

With Megan's approval, I am sharing a family crisis that occurred when Megan was seven. We were on our way to visit Bonnie's brother's family in Arkansas when, out of the blue, Megan said something about someone touching her. We were driving, but we asked questions and she gave us names. We stopped at a park where Megan told us the details and added in a soft voice, "I don't mind, Daddy," as if that would keep the matter from escalating.

When we got home, I demanded a meeting with the two boys' father and grandparents. I told them the boys needed counseling at the very least and made it clear they were to stay away from Megan. Their grandmother wanted to brush the incident aside and defended them, saying it had happened to her when she was young. She said such incidents were common, even within churches—which I took out of context and in anger stopped going to Mass.

Bonnie and Megan continued to go to church, but I refused. I blamed God for having allowed this to happen. I never shared these thoughts with Bonnie. I just told her I didn't want to go. I should have turned *to* God, but, like I treated my mother as a teenager, I thought I was all grown up and did not need to consult God or my mother. While I had made peace with my mother, God was a stranger to me.

Despite Megan's being as tough a little girl as I have ever known, after the incident, she became quieter and more withdrawn. The situation was complicated because severing ties with the other family was impossible since we were related and attended many family functions together. Megan never got the space she needed to heal, as the grandmother believed putting Megan and the boys who did this together at gatherings would fix things. None of us ever healed from this incident.

Bonnie turned to God; I blamed Him.

Chapter Five

1998-2003

As TIME PASSED, we became even more convinced we wanted Megan to have a sibling, and, if possible, a sister. Bonnie's cousins at the time were nannies to Garth Brooks who was raising his children in Owasso. They asked Garth and his wife Sandy, whose family also went to St. Henry's, for advice. They recommended an attorney in Beverly Hills who helped with private adoptions.

We made an appointment with the attorney and made our initial visit to his office off Rodeo Drive. He explained the process: he would find a pregnant girl without resources, pay to house her until the birth, and provide her with expenses to get back on her feet after the adoption. The process started with a retainer and the promise that he would find us a baby. We were told upfront that we would have to act quickly and understand how expensive his services could get.

The business was doing well, so we paid the retainer and went to LAX to head home. We stood at the gate all set to board, watching the passengers deplane. Bonnie gasped, "Look! There's Tom Selleck!" Sure enough—Tom Sellick walked right past us as Bonnie stood, her mouth wide open.

Everyone has a heartthrob. In her teen years, Bonnie adored many musicians, but among actors, Tom Selleck was her favorite. She never missed an episode of *Magnum P.I.* and made sure we went to all his movies. I had my heartthrobs, too. Rachel Welsh was a favorite. In fact, when I was in college before we got married, for Christmas Bonnie gave me a pillowcase with Rachel Welch's face on the front, as she said, "Think about me every time you put your head on this."

Seated on the plane and still excited, Bonnie said, "I wonder what seat he was in."

I rolled my eyes as the plane took off and started climbing out over the ocean—when the cabin filled with mist or a faint smoke. The captain announced we were returning to the gate. We boarded a different plane and Bonnie missed out on three hours of breathing the same air as Tom Selleck.

Our next step, scheduling a home visit, took place about two months after our initial trip to LA. We were to provide our biographies to our attorney who created a brochure he would show prospective birth mothers.

Once we made the initial steps, we wanted to announce to our family that we planned to adopt another child. We chose to be a little sneaky when we told my side of the family. We had a gathering and brought takeout Chinese food over for dinner. The day before, Bonnie and I bought a fortune cookie. Using some of Bonnie's fancy sewing tweezers, we surgically removed the fortune from the cookie and replaced it with our typed fake fortune that read: *You're going to be a grandmother.* When dinner was done, Mom opened her fortune cookie and screamed—it was such a thrill for everyone!

Aside from adoption plans, we were busy with another project. Across the street from Bonnie's parents was a house that had been empty for ten years. One of the boys who grew up there was in the same grade as Bonnie and I. Not so secretly, he'd had a big-time crush on Bonnie.

Rick was now married to Kim from the Arkansas Band, and they had a son named Sam. They moved around with Rick's previous job as a Regional Manager, but they now lived in Owasso where Rick worked with me. Rick and Kim secured the mortgage, and I paid for the significant renovations. We eventually moved Mom into the house, which was convenient and much better than her apartment. She was so happy with her new house that she decorated it with every knickknack under the sun. She made her own drapes and turned the place into a home only Mom could create. Roosters and miniatures were a common theme, along with stencil art on the kitchen cabinets.

Bonnie and Mom's love for decorating and crafts was only eclipsed by their love for cooking. We enjoyed many meals at Mom's house as she always enjoyed entertaining. This meant that Mom now lived across the street from my in-laws. When Mom moved in, the fun began, as Richard and Mom would yell at each other across the street any time they were outside. Later, when Leslee's kids would visit, they called Richard "the grumpy old man across the street."

The house was but a small gesture from Rick and me and nothing compared to what our mother had done for us. If we could have bought her a castle, we would have. She always cared for others, and attended every softball, baseball, basketball game, concert, and awards program. Mom was now fifty-nine, and her health was becoming problematic as she developed painful thrombosis in her legs and had constant UTI issues. None of this mattered to her. If there was a game or event involving her grandchildren, she would park as close as she could and carry her folding chair as she limped to the stands. Her attempts to get proper medical care were many times met with prejudice by nurses and doctors alike who appeared to have disdain for treating a morbidly obese woman. None of that mattered to Mom who never made an issue of the lack of medical care she was receiving.

Over the next few months, the attorney in California contacted us each time a girl took one of our brochures only to be told she chose someone else. The attorney kept encouraging us and told us to remain patient. Still, Bonnie took each rejection personally, wondering what they did not like about our brochure or us. This was so like the rejections Bonnie experienced during her long adoption process with Megan.

During spring break 1998, we planned to visit Bonnie's cousin Maria and her husband Pat in Castle Rock, Colorado. Maria had transferred from Phoenix College to the University of Arkansas while we were there and was on the track team for two years where she met Pat from Tulsa. They married, and Bonnie was a bridesmaid at their wedding.

Bonnie and I visited them in Phoenix when their first son Justin was born. We also visited them in their beautiful old house in the heart of Castle Rock. They had recently moved to a larger home we were excited to see. Their new house was on the back side of a traditional housing addition. However, their lot was secluded and backed up to a natural canyon. They had a stable and a couple of horses.

Megan was having a blast playing with cousins Lia and Adele. The girls raised and showed rabbits—*lots* of rabbits—and Megan enjoyed the animals. We all enjoyed hiking the canyon behind their house. We found their place to be the most picturesque home we ever visited.

I have a habit of making impulsive decisions and purchases. In 1992, I surprised Bonnie at Christmas with our first cruise to the Bahamas. My first gift was a wrapped shoebox with a bottle of suntan lotion. The next box held the trip tickets, which prompted Bonnie to immediately ask, "Is she going?" while pointing at Megan opening gifts on the floor. I shook the camcorder sideways saying no as her dad chimed in explaining this was why Megan got so many gifts.

Back in Castle Rock, I had the bright idea of taking Megan on a day trip skiing. Megan had skied before, but I knew not to invite Bonnie because of her skiing history. After we got married, we reconnected with a group of high school friends and would go to each other's homes for dinner or to the movies. They had motorcycles, so we made some bike trips for breakfast and other short rides together. We also played board games and Atari, which was all the craze, and Bonnie loved Pac-Man and Frogger. We all laughed and had a great time together. None of us had kids yet, so we decided to go on a weekend skiing trip.

The nearest place was Taos, New Mexico. None of us had much money, so the trip was on a shoestring budget. We decided to squeeze into one car and share one hotel room for one night, go skiing the next day, and then drive straight home. None of us had ever been skiing before. We considered lessons but could barely afford the lift tickets. We talked about what we had heard from others who had been skiing and figured, how hard could it be?

We arrived at the ski resort, rented our equipment, and headed to the bunny slope. We made it up the chair lift with minimal falls at the top. We all stood together discussing the snowplow technique. As we started to discuss the method's finer points, Bonnie managed to shift her skis parallel to the slope, and—

Off she went! We did our best as first-time snow-plowers to follow her, but Bonnie was on a beeline downhill like she was on an Olympic course. She was screaming the whole way while we yelled, "FALL DOWN! FALL DOWN!" As she neared the end of the bunny slope, she lost control and tumbled head over heels in a cloud of snow. We finally managed our way down the hill to where she lay motionless on the ground and asked if she was all right.

"I'm fine," she said, clearly irritated, "but I can't find my glasses." We looked around and found her glasses in a small debris field. Bonnie was nearsighted and had worn glasses since the third grade. Without them, she couldn't see objects more than three feet from her. We guided her to the snack bar where she sat while we skied the rest of the day, checking in on her after each run.

So, NO—Bonnie would not be going skiing.

Continuing with my impulsive tendencies, I had no idea where Megan and I would ski. My plan consisted of driving until I saw a resort that was not busy and looked easy for beginners. We found a place and began our day on the slopes. Megan, a natural athlete, took to skiing with ease.

Back in Castle Rock, Bonnie was enjoying a quiet day with Maria.

Things in Owasso were not quite so peaceful. Rick and Kim were listed as contacts for our attorney in Beverly Hills. After being unable to reach us at home, the attorney called and talked to Kim. He informed her that she needed to contact Bonnie and me ASAP. Kim explained our whereabouts, and he told her a baby boy was available in California. He needed a commitment from us if we wanted to take this baby.

Rick and Kim knew Bonnie and I wanted a girl; they didn't know if we would take a boy. They contacted numerous family members until they finally found Maria's phone number and called Bonnie. Bonnie called the attorney and faced a life-changing decision for her family all by herself.

Bonnie did not hesitate. "I'm on my way to California," she told the attorney. Pat helped book her on the first flight from Denver to San Francisco. He drove her to the airport, and off she went by herself to meet the birth mother and our future son.

I, overthinking as usual, left my cell phone in the car for fear of falling on it, so Megan and I were completely out of the loop. While Bonnie was in the air, we finished our day on the slopes and returned to the car where I noticed a bunch of missed calls. Despite the poor cell reception, Pat briefed me on the situation as we drove back to Castle Rock. Pat and Maria played travel agent again as they figured out how to get Megan and me to San Francisco as fast as possible. I next talked to Rick, who was still in need of oxygen as he was recovering from the frantic events.

We found a flight that arrived at 10 p.m. We packed our bags, and Pat drove us to the airport. By this time, Bonnie had landed in San Francisco and had to find her way to Antioch, over fifty miles from SFO. She was advised to take the BART train and went to the station to get her ticket. It was dark as the train left the station. The BART from SFO through Oakland to Antioch is not something a woman traveling alone would be advised to do, especially at night, but Bonnie was determined. She arrived at the Antioch train station where she took a cab to the hospital.

Inside the hospital, she met the birth mother and beheld this beautiful baby boy with a head full of black hair who had been born just twelve hours earlier. Bonnie returned to the waiting cab and asked him to take her to a hotel where she booked a room and waited for the skiers to arrive.

We landed at SFO on time, rented a car, and at midnight, arrived at the hotel where we were reunited with Bonnie. We shared our joy and planned for the day ahead. We lay there in our beds, talking about the amazing day we'd all had and what tomorrow would bring. Exhausted but too excited to sleep, we laughed and talked for a while before finally drifting off.

The next morning, we drove to the hospital where we, especially Megan, could hardly control ourselves in anticipation as we met the birth mother and two of her daughters, and patiently waited for the baby to come into the room. The nurse finally brought in the baby. With Megan by her side, Bonnie held Matthew Richard. To honor Bonnie's dad, we used his name as Matt's middle name. My relationship with Richard—or Dick, as I called him—had come a long way since he slammed the door in my face when I was fourteen.

After all the excitement, we exchanged a couple of phone calls with the attorney and filled out some paperwork. We also faced some immediate logistical challenges: most pressing was that all our baby stuff was back in Owasso since we had been on vacation. Before leaving the hospital, we needed to make a quick run to Target for a car seat.

Next was where to go. Our car was back in Castle Rock, but instead of heading to the airport, we decided to drive to Leslee's house in Los Angeles to show off the baby. By 3 p.m., we were walking out of the hospital with Matt when we realized we needed more than a car seat. We spent the next hour at Babies"R"Us getting everything else we needed, which were mostly duplicates of what we already had back home.

The five-hour drive to Los Angeles was so much fun. Bonnie and Megan were in the back seat on either side of Matt getting excited at his every move and giving me a play-by-play as we all laughed, making it one of the best road trips ever—second only to the drive with Megan to visit Grandpa Tilman.

Leslee had three girls and a son and was pregnant yet again. She was notorious for going to bed early to have the bathroom to herself at 5 a.m. before it was overrun by her four kids and husband, so it was too late to visit. We decided to stop in Thousand Oaks for the night. Usually, I would go into the hotel and get the keys. However, we were still so excited we all went into the lobby, savoring every moment we had together. I stood at the counter with the clerk signing the registration form. Bonnie was behind me, holding Matt in his carrier on one arm and her overnight bag on the other. Megan was leaning over, looking at Matt.

We were all laughing when the clerk glanced at Matt. He looked back at his papers, saying, "That's a small baby. How old is it?"

I looked at my watch and toward the ceiling as I did the math. "Thirty-seven hours."

The clerk stopped what he was doing. He looked carefully at Bonnie, down at Matt in the carrier draped over her arm, and back at Bonnie, repeating *thirty-seven hours* a couple of times. During his obvious confusion, none of us said a word. He eventually looked at me and said, "Here are your keys."

Not until we got to the room did we realized the clerk must have thought Bonnie was Wonder Woman carrying a baby and suitcase with ease just thirty-seven hours after giving birth. Knowing how tough Bonnie is, the scene would probably have been the same had Bonnie actually given birth.

The following morning, we arrived at Leslee's where Matt was surrounded—or more accurately, smothered—by his new cousins. We all laughed when Matt took the opportunity during a diaper change to pee on Leslee's girls! Everything was going great until I got a phone call from the attorney who sounded anxious. He asked where we were and was pleased we were still in California. He told me there was a problem: our home study expired a couple of weeks ago, and we needed a new one from the Oklahoma Department of Human Services (DHS) before we could legally complete the adoption. He cut to the chase. "Until we get a new home study done, you can take Matt anywhere except Oklahoma. Doing so would put the adoption in jeopardy because the adoption has no legal standing in the state of Oklahoma." This blow was huge as Bonnie and I were now faced with living like nomads for however long it would take to solve this crisis.

We discussed our options, which included returning to Denver because our car was there. We decided we'd fly to Denver and figure out what to do when we got there. While at Pat and Maria's, we looked not only at locations near Oklahoma for us to take Matt but also for a flight path that would not cross Oklahoma air space. We took the attorney's words seriously.

Bonnie and I chose Springfield, Missouri, but only Bonnie and Matt would go there. Megan and I needed to drive the van home so Megan could go back to school, and I needed to get back to work. Kim volunteered to drive to Springfield to help Bonnie. Bonnie had done the same for Kim when their son Sam was born in Savannah.

The following day was difficult. Megan and I had to head back to Owasso, leaving Bonnie and Matt behind in Castle Rock waiting for their flight. Megan was upset as we left Matt and Bonnie.

The drive from Antioch to Los Angeles just days earlier had been the best road trip ever; this one was among the worst. Our parting reminded me of the countless times I'd left Bonnie's house to drive back to college, but now Megan shared my pain.

At home, Megan had quite a spring break story to share, and I went back to work. On Friday afternoon, we made the three-hour drive to Springfield to resupply Bonnie with some of the baby gear she had stockpiled at home. The drive to Springfield was the opposite of the drive from Denver; I had the same shortness of breath and adrenalin rush I had experienced so many times as I anticipated being with Bonnie and now Matt.

In what could only be described as a misunderstanding, I thought we had the green light to come home, so Kim loaded Bonnie and Matt in her car and drove home. They had barely arrived when the attorney called to clarify his instructions: Matt had to remain out of Oklahoma. In a panic, we decided to move Bonnie and Matt to Springdale, Arkansas, an hour closer to Owasso. The following weekend, we led a small caravan of cars, including my mother and Bonnie's parents, to Bonnie and Matt's temporary home at the Hampton Inn in Springdale.

Bonnie and I worked with DHS to schedule a home study, but there was a backlog. She was told it might take up to two months before they would send someone out! We continued our weekly routine of driving to Springdale after school on Friday, only to return home every Sunday night for another week of work and school. Bonnie and I talked on the phone every night like high school when we spent hours on the phone.

Nearly two months later, our home study was finally scheduled. Of course, it needed to happen at our home in Owasso. The plan included driving Mom to Springdale to stay with Matt while Bonnie and I returned to Owasso to conduct the home study for a baby with whom we'd been living for the past two months.

The visit went well. We showed them our house and baby room, which was sparsely supplied due to the relocation of many items to the Hampton Inn. Soon after the home study was completed, our attorney called to give us the green light to take Matt home. We arrived to a cul-de-sac full of cars and a Welcome Home banner in the yard. We enjoyed the party at our house where everyone who knew the story met Matt and heard about our ordeal.

Later, when all the legal work was completed, we met with the judge to finalize the adoption. We were blessed to have Matt's adoption handled by the same judge who performed Megan's adoption ten years earlier.

The following year, I decided to treat the family to our first trip to Hawaii. We took Mom and Leslee's youngest daughter, Kaci, who was close with Megan and nearly the same age. I made two classic travel mistakes Rick Steeves would have never made. First, I underestimated the sheer bulk of extra provisions required to travel with an eighteen-month-old baby. Second, I arranged a much too ambitious itinerary. Despite my poor planning, we had a great time, and the trip was a real treat for Mom.

When we got home, I faced some hard facts about my business. The software I originally sold had been acquired more than once and was slowly fading away. I needed to sell a different CAM Software, which meant starting over with the four families who relied on my business for their livelihood. My plan included keeping everyone on during this downtime while we learned new software and introduced that software to our territory.

I chose to maintain staff by financing the business on credit cards and lines of credit. Applications for both would appear in the mail daily, and approval was as easy as signing my name. As a result, I ran the business on credit cards for two years as we ramped up with the new software. This meant I was making huge monthly credit card payments, but we were blessed with enough business to remain in the black as I covered payroll and debt.

As Matt got older, we noticed he was not like other three and four-year-old boys. At family gatherings, he preferred to socialize with adults rather than peers. He attended the same preschool at St. Henry's and the same elementary school Megan attended, and none of the teachers voiced any concerns.

We worried about Megan, too, when she started her teen years. Bonnie grew up in a house where her mother controlled everything. While not as severe as her mother, Bonnie had expectations that Megan rebelled against. They drifted apart, which resulted in a few difficult years with me in the middle playing referee.

With Megan in high school and Matt in grade school, Bonnie got bored and decided to work as an assistant at St. Henry's Wee Angels Pre-School. Bonnie loved children and her work at the pre-school, but Matt was less pleased. He told his mother, "I don't like you playing with other kids while I'm at school." We thought his point of view was odd, but it told us Matt was not wired like other kids.

In 2003, Mom's sister Carolyn Sue died. Mom and Sue still saw each other after Opal died, but they were never close. Uncle Walter called and asked if we were coming. He wanted to make sure we attended the funeral, to which I agreed. After the funeral, Mom and the rest of us were asked to go into a side room where Walter, Debra, and their two sons had gathered with someone I didn't know seated behind a desk.

The man behind the desk told us he was going to read Sue's will. Sue did not have much, so I didn't know why we were there. Sue was fond of Walter and Debra's boys, so I assumed they would inherit her possessions.

The man started by saying the El Camino would go to one of the boys while the pickup with the Shark license plate on the front would go to the other boy. He listed other items that also went to the boys as expected. He then said, "To my sister JoAnn, I leave nothing because nothing is what she deserves." The attorney continued to rip into Mom, reading Sue's manifesto while we stood in shock. Mom stayed strong and never moved a muscle.

When we left, Mom held her head high as if nothing had happened. Later, I visited her to discuss the incident, but she refused. I offered her my theories as I recounted the first time we met Opal, Dan, and Sue and how uncomfortable that first meeting was. In passing, she said, "Dad was embarrassed about what he did to me when I was little." I stopped asking questions. I didn't want to know the details of what Mom was trying to tell me.

After some time passed, I sat with Mom, and she gave me more facts about her childhood, which I later supplemented on one of my visits to Arbuckle with information from Uncle BJ and Aunt Carla. The following is based on conversations with Mom and documents I found much later that I am including to provide as much of a picture of my mother's history as I can.

JoAnn's parents, Everett and Opal, were raised in and around Poteau. Everett was born in Poteau, and Opal was born in nearby Braden, Oklahoma. They were married in March 1938 and divorced by early 1940, only months after JoAnn's birth. The divorce papers listed Abandonment as the reason; there is no other explanation. Opal married Dan in March of the same year.

Shortly after their marriage, Opal and Dan began a series of moves across Oklahoma, then to San Diego and Phoenix. Around 1950, they moved to Fort Smith, Arkansas, and later to Tulsa. With all this moving from one city to another, JoAnn managed to skip a grade, so she was a year younger than her classmates.

When I was young, I remember Mom always encouraged me to make friends. "I never had any close friends growing up," she said. "I got tired of making friends only to move away in the middle of the school year." Mom never said much about her schooling—not because she wasn't smart or because of her grades, on the contrary. Instead, Mom told us stories about the blackouts and rationing in

San Diego during WWII and other storied about places they lived but nothing about any of her friends or childhood.

Mom mentioned an uncle who was a Pentecostal minister. At a young age, she was quite a hit entertaining crowds at his tent revivals and at other church services with her singing. I recall one picture of Mom, around five, standing on a table in front of a crowd in a revival tent. Her love for music and singing always remained with her. She had a beautiful voice and would break out in song at every chance, especially when a musical came on TV.

Everett remained in the Poteau area until 1942 when he enlisted in the Army and served in the Philippines. After the war, he moved to California to look for work and eventually settled in the small farming community of Arbuckle, about an hour northwest of Sacramento.

In 1946, Everett married Romagene who, ironically, grew up in Poteau and knew Everett's family. Romagene, her widowed mother, and her four siblings moved to California in 1943. In 1947, their son Billy Joe (BJ) was born, followed by Everett Eugene, who died at two in 1953.

These are the facts, but we already know there is more to this than a divorce between Everett and Opal.

As we dig deeper into JoAnn's story, this family tree may help you keep the two sides of JoAnn's family straight.

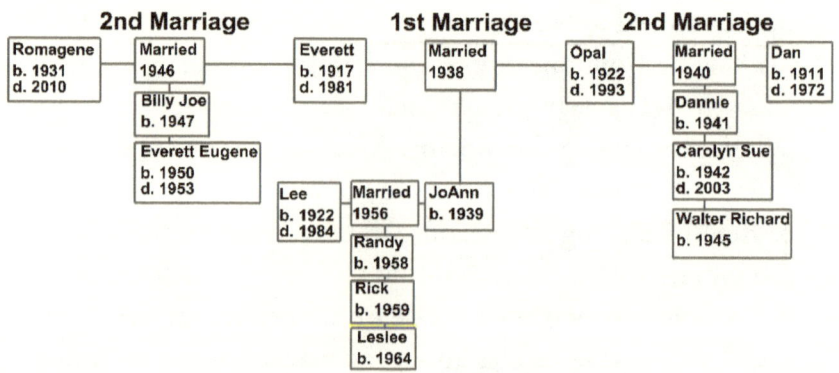

One of the first things to notice in this family tree is that Everett and Opal were married in 1938, and JoAnn was born in February 1939. In March 1940, when JoAnn was barely one year old, Opal married Dan. At the same time, the three started a series of moves from Oklahoma to California and back to Arkansas before settling in the Tulsa area.

The next curious fact is that JoAnn's last name was changed from Everett's to Dan's without formal adoption or legal documentation. This may have been a common practice at the time. We have no explanation for the hasty marriage to Dan, for JoAnn's name change or for the series of moves across the Southwest.

This story started in Poteau, where Everett was one of ten children. All of Everett's siblings lived most of their lives in Poteau; only Everett settled in northern California away from his family.

Having been separated from Everett when she was less than a year old, JoAnn could not have known that Everett desperately searched for her since Opal and Dan left town in 1940. When he was able in 1947, Everett and his family started their annual pilgrimages to Poteau. These trips occurred around Christmas when the rice and almond harvests were completed.

They made the long trip on Route 66 every year except 1952 due to Everett Eugene's health. These trips continued throughout the '50s, '60s and '70s. Oddly, they never stopped at the Grand Canyon or any natural wonders between California and Oklahoma. Instead, on these trips during the '40s and '50s, they spent most of their time in Poteau looking for JoAnn. While Everett was back in California, his siblings, led by his sister Maylene, continued the search.

Why would someone accused of Abandonment go to such great lengths to find the daughter he last saw when she was only months old? Why would his second wife and siblings in Poteau spend so much time and effort helping in his search?

In 1953, Everett finally tracked JoAnn down at school. Multiple sources confirmed that while he was waiting in the office, someone contacted Opal. She took JoAnn out the back door and disappeared. When Mom learned that Everett was her father is unknown. She never told me. Mom did say that when she found out the truth, Opal told her about a bitter divorce and nothing else reminiscent of how Mom told us about Opal and Dan's existence.

JoAnn said that her family would hear that Everett or one of his family members was in town, and the family would move in the middle of the night. She told me this story more than once.

What harm could there have been in allowing Everett to see JoAnn? Or—should we look at this from a different angle?

Is it possible JoAnn knew something Opal and Dan wanted to keep from Everett? Many of these questions remain unanswered, but some details help us draw some conclusions.

Remember that JoAnn's mother remarried when she was barely a year old and her mother and stepfather changed JoAnn's name while never telling her or her siblings she had a different father or name. There was never a formal adoption, so there was no termination of Everett's rights as father.

Given that there are always two sides to every story, perhaps Opal was protecting JoAnn from Everett. This hypothesis does not explain what would motivate a family with as many as four children to abruptly move when they learned Everett or one of his relatives was in town.

In 1955, when JoAnn was sixteen, Everett located her at Central High School in Tulsa where they reunited briefly. Sadly, a five-year gap intervened before they were together again. Nothing is known about why this gap took place.

In 1956, JoAnn graduated from Central High School at seventeen. She did not share many stories about her high school years other than a run-in among her half-sister Carolyn Sue, her, and the Catoosa police. Catoosa is located on just the other side of Tulsa. While she did not share details, she always avoided driving through the small town. If she was in my car when I drove through town, she would say, "Be careful. You can't trust the police in this town."

One unusual story concerned a boy who did or said something to one of her girlfriends. JoAnn and her friend got on top of his car and, well, urinated on his roof. Mom laughed when she told this surprising story which came out before the incident at Sue's funeral. I think a lot of Mom's teenage years were spent with Sue, and after the funeral incident, Mom did not want to share any more stories about her teenage years.

At some point before August 8, 1960, JoAnn called Everett's sisters in Poteau. More than one person talked to her. This conversation was jointly brokered by Everett's sister Maylene and Jessie Allen, JoAnn's aunt on Opal's side of the family. Remember, Everett and Opal had deep family ties in the Poteau area.

In a letter from Romagene to Everett's sister Bessie in Poteau dated Monday, August 8, 1960, she says:

> *Bessie, you can't imagine how surprised we were to hear that JoAnn had called.*
>
> *I never saw anybody as happy as Everett was and still is. He is so anxious to know more about her and the call. He gave me a list of questions to ask you about it. Who did she talk to, where did she call from, where does she live, and when is she coming to Poteau? In other words, if you would tell him every word, she said it might satisfy him. So, whoever talked to her, please write or dictate a letter and tell us all about it.*

This letter included the following unusual PS written upside down in different handwriting:

> *JoAnn, this is the letter we got from your daddy when we wrote him about you.*

Clearly Romagene's letter to Poteau was forwarded to JoAnn. This letter was followed by four letters in quick succession:

August 24th, 1960

Dear JoAnn,

This letter may come as a surprise to you, but I hope you will be a little glad to hear from me, just half as glad as I would be to get a letter from you. Your Aunt Maylene of Poteau sent me your address. She wrote to you and told you about talking to your Aunt Jessie. She told Maylene and your grandmother that you wanted to see me and get to know me and all of the family.

JoAnn, honey, I can't tell you how much I wish I could see you, and if you feel the way your Aunt Jessie says, maybe you know something about how I feel. I'm almost afraid to believe that we may get to know each other at last. I hope it's not just a dream. We plan to go to Poteau for Christmas and get there on December 19th. I am hoping with all my heart to see you while I am there. All the folks are anxious to meet you. Mom was out here this summer and said, "I'd give anything if I could see JoAnn just one more time."

They tell me that you have two boys, Randy & Ricky. I just today learned their names. My grandsons. I want to see them. I want to see you, JoAnn.

You are my daughter, and I love you. This is an awful short letter to cover so many years. There are so many things I'd like to say, but it is hard to know what to say without knowing how you really feel. Please write to me and let's make a start we should have made many years ago.

All My Love,

Daddy

PS Please write, JoAnn. It would make your dad and me so happy,

Romagene

It is hard to reconcile how someone who could write such a beautiful letter from the heart could have ever been accused of Abandonment This letter and the annual trips to Poteau searching for JoAnn bring into question the circumstances surrounding Everett and Opal's divorce, her whirlwind marriage to Dan when JoAnn was barely a year old, and JoAnn's name change. The following letter adds an even greater cloud of suspicion:

September 19th, 1960

Dear JoAnn,

I feel rather strange writing to you, though you have, in a sense, lived with me for 14 years, for Everett has talked of you a very great deal. I don't know you, and you know even less about me. But it is my duty and right to tell you of your father. You have heard many things about him from your mother and her people. Still, quite probably, you have never heard a good word spoken on his behalf, as you have never had any contact with any of his family or friends, a situation I hope will soon be amended.

20 years ago, I didn't know your father; therefore, I cannot state as a proven fact that he didn't treat you and your mother as you have described. I can only tell you of him as I have known him for 14 ½ years. I have lived with him in the closest of all relationships for 14 years, and I feel that I know him as completely as any human being can know another.

We have built a good, solid marriage on Love and trust in one another.

Though he is not rich, handsome, or suave, I would not exchange my husband for any man I have ever met. He has many other worthwhile qualities that are more important to me than those surface things. He is kind, warm-hearted, generous, hardworking, good-natured, and everything a woman wants in a husband and a father for her children. He has always been the best of Daddy[sic] *to Billy Joe and the beloved son who was so painfully taken from us. I feel sure he would have done as well by you had he been given the opportunity.*

Everyone around here likes him, and my family thinks he is a great guy. Sometimes, I almost believe they think more of him than they do of me. I'm not trying to give you the impression that he is perfect in every way. He is only human with human failings, but aren't we all? He gets impatient at times, not nearly as often as I, and can never wholly forgive a wrong done him. He swears, not at anyone, just pure habit; he smokes too much, indeed. I am not blind to his shortcomings, but they are no more than in any average person.

I know that it is true that people do sometimes change over the years. Still, I find it impossible to believe that the Everett I know could have ever been the awful person you have been made to believe.

Of course, all of these things coming from me may mean little or nothing to you, but I hope it may help you. Also, I hope I have said nothing to hurt or offend you. If so, I am truly sorry if I have in any way talked out of turn. I want very much for...

Sadly, what appears to be the last page is missing. Romagene clearly wrote this letter, which paints her as a strong woman who wanted to help her husband reconnect with the daughter he tried so long to find. She also knew from the beginning about Everett's previous marriage and daughter.

One can only imagine the conversation between Aunt Maylene

and Aunt Jessie, who were on opposite sides, as Maylene convinced Jessie to make the initial contact with JoAnn on Everett's behalf. Jessie was always close to JoAnn and her kids. She lived in the Tulsa area, so they saw each other regularly. The following letter was included with the previous letter from Romagene:

Dear JoAnn,

This is your brother Billy Joe (age 13). Just a few lines to say hi. I've always known I have a sister, and it looks like I'll finally get to see you.

Anyway, I'm hoping to see you at Christmas. Tell Randy and Ricky hello for me. I think I will like being an uncle to two boys. Write to us soon and tell us all about you and your family.

With Love,

Billy Joe

Between the two letters from Everett and Romagene, JoAnn sent her own letter to Arbuckle. We do not know the contents of this letter. It is safe to assume that JoAnn's letter and Romagene's may have passed each other on Route 66. In 1960, First Class Postage was $0.04. Still, I wonder how much longer it took a letter from Oklahoma then than it does today to reach California.

September 22nd, 1960

Dear JoAnn, Lee, Randy & Ricky

We received your letter yesterday, and I was so glad to hear from you again. I was worried since your last letter, afraid you might not believe me, and I am so happy to learn that you still feel the same way about wanting to see me.

I can hardly wait to see you and the family. The three months from now until Christmas will seem like a year. My busiest time at the warehouse will be starting in about a week. The rice harvest will begin then. They bring it in from the field, and we dry and store it. I'll be working 12 hours a day, 7 days a week, for quite a while. Then, this winter, we go back to 40 hours a week. I've worked there for almost 10 years now. We live just across the Street from the warehouse. Arbuckle is a small town with less than 1,000 people. We may get lost trying to find you in a city as big as Tulsa, but I'll see you if it takes my whole vacation.

By the way, which of the folks came up to see you? I haven't heard from them in a couple of weeks. I understand about you all not going to see them, and I'm sure they will too. I hope you, Lee, and the boys can come to Poteau for Christmas. I can tell you it would be the best Christmas present I ever had just to be with you on that day. I think you all would enjoy it too. Mom loves for people to come, and there is always a crowd at Christmas and other times. Lee might feel out of place for a few minutes if he's not much on big family get-togethers but they would soon make you both feel at home. They are all plain common people who don't know what the word stranger means, and Randy & Ricky would carry on as they spoil them for you. That's something I sure would like to get a chance to do, carry them around and play with them.

I guess they may be pretty shy with me, but I hope not for long. Sure hope they will like their grandpa and their new grandma, too. Romagene & I both love children, and yours will be special to us; if you and Lee don't have any more babies, we've got Randy and Ricky to love. I was so proud to see the pictures. They helped me get to know you a little more. I'd like photos of you all over again. I missed all of your growing-up life and the important times in your life. How I wish I had spent those times with you. But we have the future to look forward to, don't we? I'm sending you a few old pictures. We haven't taken many in the past few years, but we will try to get around to taking some soon and send them to you.

Billy Joe got your letter today. He seemed awfully pleased and is very interested in everything about you and your family. He's got lots of friends, but I think he's always felt lonely and left out that he doesn't have brothers or sisters in the house. He was crazy about Everett Eugene and missed him so when he was lost to us. I hope the two of you like each other so much, and I believe you will. I think you will like Romagene too and I know she will like you too. She's only 8 years older than you, so you two should get along pretty well. I hope you're not shocked at our ages, but I don't think age matters much. It's made no difference at all for us. We get along very well, though we've had hard times, too, like most people. It's made no difference at all for us. We get along together very good though we've had our hard times too, same as most people.

I can't understand your mother making more trouble for you two, but I'll say no more about that, just that I'm sorry that she feels the way she does about many things.

I'm glad you liked the almonds. They were very plentiful here, and they didn't cost me anything. I'll send you some more later. Also, I'll send you some dried apricots if you all like them. We have quite a few of them around here, too. Billy Joe worked in the field last year, the first job he ever had was he ever proud of himself.

I hope this letter will be of some help to you one way or the other. It's up to you if you believe one of us, both of us, or part of us. If we could only forget the past and start over new from here but I guess it isn't possible for you. I hope with all my heart that there will be happier times for you and me. I have never for one moment stopped loving you and wanting to be with you. I'll go on hoping. Please answer soon. I'll be anxiously waiting for your letter. I'll be anxiously waiting for your letters ahead for you and for me. I'll go on hoping. Please answer soon. I'll be anxiously waiting for your letter.

All My Love,

Dad

PS Hello to Lee & Randy & Ricky

Notice how the tone of this letter changes in the last paragraph. It is unclear if something in JoAnn's letter was troubling them or if they were just cautious and did not want to assume JoAnn was as excited about a reunion as they were. It may have been as simple as a phrase that JoAnn used in her letter that was not interpreted the way it was intended.

When this last letter was written, I was only two years old. This was at about the same time my dad had his falling out with Opal and Dan causing their family to be erased from my memory.

While the letters discussed JoAnn's possible trip to Poteau for Christmas, for some reason, she didn't go. Instead, in December of 1960, Everett, Romagene, and BJ drove from Poteau to Tulsa to meet the family, which must have been an exciting visit for everyone. I was too young to remember anything about the visit or to understand the history that led up to this event.

In 1960, the drive from Poteau to Tulsa took three hours, and the first visit only lasted a few hours. The lost time was too much to make up for in such a short visit, but JoAnn and her father were never separated again.

Everett and his family faithfully made their annual sixteen-day Christmas trip from Arbuckle to Poteau, with a detour to Tulsa. Of note is that Everett did not have a driver's license for most of those years. Yet, he made countless trips from California to Oklahoma, including his visit to Fayetteville in 1979.

One interesting fact is that the letter written by Everett was penned by Romagene because Everett could not read or write. Everett would have dictated what he wanted to say to Romagene who put his words on paper. One can only imagine the love between Everett and Romagene as shown in the tender words written, no doubt, through tears by Romagene: first, as she heard and dictated his spoken words, and then in her following heartfelt letter.

After feeling the love of the amazing family in Poteau, it seemed impossible for Everett to have abandoned an infant with his siblings never forgiving him. In fact, the motives for Everett and Opal's divorce and rapid marriage to Dan followed by their immediate departure from the Poteau area bring much into question.

Sadly, we never got the real story behind Everett and Opal's divorce. The stories had too many gaps, and all the participants passed away, so we couldn't accurately pinpoint a reason for the circumstances surrounding that bitter divorce. Then, after Carolyn Sue's funeral, there was Mom's comment about what Dan did to her as a child.

Mom's volunteer activity and passion for DVIS now made sense, as did other conclusions I am confident in making. Dan and Opal must have been in a relationship during her marriage to Everett. Why else remarry when her baby was barely a year old and the ink wasn't dry on the divorce? Why would they keep Mom from Everett all those years unless they were hiding something? What other explanation could there be for this behavior? I am convinced that Mom was abused as a child; hiding her from Everett was how they kept this abuse secret.

None of this explains Carolyn Sue's slap from the grave at Mom at the reading of her will—unless this was payback for all the moves she, too, made when she was young. Mom gave no indication of any falling out before Sue's death.

I later learned Carolyn Sue was cremated. She'd asked Walter and Debra to spread her ashes in the Gulf of Mexico. When Walter dumped the ashes, some stuck to the box, so he tossed the entire box into the water. He and Debra noticed a pair of fins swimming near the box, and wondered if those could be sharks as they remembered the shark license plate on the front of Sue's pickup. Read into that what you will.

Much about my mom's early years will remain shrouded in mystery. She suffered so much pain in both her childhood and marriage. Nothing ever came easy for Mom. Her children and grandchildren as well as the close friends she made at every place she worked were her only source of happiness. In spite of this, anyone who knows my mom always describes her as a warm, caring, and loving person who would do anything for anyone. Sounds a lot like the way people described Everett in the letters. How does someone who is the product of a difficult childhood and marriage become such a beloved person, amazing mother, and adored grandmother? None of us ever fully appreciated how strong my mother was and how she managed to find the courage to face all the challenges that plagued her entire life.

Chapter Six

2004-2008

Bonnie and I marked our twenty-fifth wedding anniversary in 2004. I wanted to do something special for Bonnie, so I arranged a trip to Maui to renew our wedding vows. I hired a wedding coordinator and planned an authentic wedding on the beach. Like so many other past trips or gifts, this one was meant to be a surprise, but AAA ruined it by calling the house and asking Bonnie what kind of room she wanted at the resort.

AAA's spoiling my surprise allowed Bonnie to plan what each of us was to wear, which was a good plan, after all. Megan (16), Matt (6), Bonnie, and I (46) traveled to Maui where we prepared for the ceremony along with the photographer and videographer (part of the package). We were given a place to meet and told to stand and wait on the beach. Megan wore a scowl most of the time, but we did the best we could.

At the other end of the beach, on a bluff between palm trees, a large man in Hawaiian attire appeared over the rise. Quite dramatically, he raised a conch shell and blew a signal, then sang a native welcome song. He made his way to the beach, and we met him in the middle. He sang another song as we put leis on each other and then on Megan and Matt. We recited vows and put our Sears

& Roebuck rings back on each other twenty-five years after that Saturday morning at St. Henry's.

Matt was squirming and moving around the whole time as Megan, knowing the camera was rolling, tried to keep him in one place while never smiling. The ceremony concluded with our celebrant singing a final love song as he suggested we dance on the beach.

One small problem: I still do not like to dance. Never have, which was something I know always bothered Bonnie. (When we were alone at home, she would take my hand in the living room, play soft music, and ask me to dance. I would go through the motions but never made much of an effort.) So, we stood and stared into each other's eyes during the song as I disappointed Bonnie once again by not taking the perfect opportunity in this perfect location to take her into my arms and dance with her without thinking how foolish I might look. It is one of the greatest regrets of my life.

Megan's scowl was something to which Bonnie and I had become accustomed. Megan and Bonnie's relationship at that time was tumultuous at best. Simply put, Bonnie and Megan were oil and water during Megan's teenage years.

In high school, Megan tried to balance being in band with playing volleyball, activities at which she excelled. Bonnie and I, because of our history, wanted her to be in band. We were also excited to have Megan in band because of the band directors who replaced the Lamkins. We were so proud that our dear college friends David and Jana Gorham, were now leading the Pride of Owasso. You may recall that Jana's father is Mr. Janzen, my band director at Arkansas. Under David and Jana, the Pride of Owasso continued to excel and consistently led the state in students selected to All State with many continuing the same path I took to college on music scholarships.

Their success as band directors, especially in our hometown, should have been a source of at the very least comments from Bonnie about how their path was similar to the path I promised her, but Bonnie never said a word in regret.

In the end it was Megan's decision: she chose volleyball. Megan also joined a volleyball club in Tulsa, which meant year-round volleyball with lots of tournament trips. Bonnie and I embraced Megan's decision and were active volleyball parents, both with the high school team and the traveling club team.

Megan's volleyball skills were as a libero (the short one in the back with a different-colored jersey), and she continued to improve. As a result of her success, we started thinking about her playing college volleyball. We sent videos to some schools during her senior year and took her to tryouts.

We liked St. Mary's in Leavenworth, Kansas. Bonnie and I especially liked that it was a small school, but it also had a convent on campus with two hundred nuns. How much safer could we get? Never mind that the school was in Leavenworth—less than a mile from two major prisons.

Part of the application process was submitting the Free Application for Federal Student Aid (FAFSA) paperwork, which every family with college-aged kids knows about. The application requires tax returns, and, because I was self-employed, business financial statements.

Many years had passed since my first year in business when I did not file personal or corporate tax returns. While the company had grown, and I was paying a payroll service for my employees, my personal tax status had not changed. I was in a tight spot as I had no tax returns to submit with FAFSA. Instead, I told the school I would pay any difference between her scholarship and what was owed out of pocket, making my FAFSA problems disappear. Megan received a half scholarship, and I made up the $7,000 difference per semester.

That same year, a Houston customer who had European facilities and with whom I hit it off asked me to make a presentation at their facility in Leeds, England. Bonnie and I made our first European trip, flying into London and driving to Leeds. After the meeting, I asked where we should go sightseeing. They recommended York, which was only a short drive north. We arrived in the early afternoon. After a pub lunch, we visited York Castle. Standing on the ramparts, we noticed a large tower across town. We asked what it was; York Minster Cathedral.

We made our way across town to this imposing structure. It was late afternoon when we walked into the church. We had never seen a 13th century Gothic church before and were too awe-struck to say a word. The lighting in the room, as the shadows were growing outside, enhanced the spiritual experience.

For the first time, I felt the presence of God.

I was so moved that I just thanked God for allowing me to see this. I wondered how man could have built such a place. Bonnie and I left with chills running down our spine. We could not stop talking about the cathedral. We decided to return the following day for an official tour, which was informative but less moving than the previous afternoon. We will never forget being alone, the partial darkness heightening our senses, as we tried to take in what we experienced in York Minster.

Mom was as supportive of Megan's volleyball career as she was of her youngest grandchild's tee ball exploits. She would make it to every game or match, but, with Megan in college, driving to Megan's games four or more hours away was difficult. Still, that did not stop her. On one occasion, I had some business in northern Kansas near where Megan was to play, and I rented Mom a bed and breakfast in a nearby small Swedish community.

Rick drove Mom to meet me in town before the match. We found a tea house where the three of us sat around a small table, sipping tea and eating crumpets. Rick and I kept rolling our eyes or shaking our heads as Mom made a production out of everything served. The scene was not at all unlike the video I shot many years earlier of Mom, Bonnie, and Megan doing the exact same thing on our living room floor at their tea party—less the dress-up clothes and boas.

Once back home, Bonnie, Matt, and I made a weekend trip to Branson. We visited a cave where one of the attractions was rappelling. Matt, age nine, was excited, but Bonnie, not so much. I explained he would not get hurt and paid the money. As Matt got harnessed in, Bonnie looked down into the cave and in a stern voice repeated, "I don't want him to do this." As he started down the hole, Bonnie got even more upset. She could not watch and left the area.

The bond between Bonnie and our children is strong despite any arguments or tension in their relationships. The six years Bonnie spent adopting Megan cemented her bond with her daughter, and the two months at the Hampton Inn made Bonnie and Matt's relationship equally special. While I had no problem sending Matt down that hole or taking Megan white water rafting in Canada, Bonnie was much more protective. She had sacrificed more than I to bring our amazing children into our lives. However, at times Bonnie's intense desire to do the best for our children unfortunately resulted in relationship problems with both of them.

By 2007, Mom's health was declining, and she had to quit work. Her legs would not allow her to walk. She also experienced bladder issues that remained untreated. She would see one doctor after another and be dismissed without a thorough examination because of her size. Like everything else, Mom took this in stride. She gave to others and never tried to do anything for herself. She wouldn't insist on the medical care she deserved because she'd never make a fuss.

At this time, Megan entered a romantic relationship with an older woman she met in Leavenworth and dropped out of college. None of us knew that the woman was controlling and Megan cut off all contact with us. We were devastated. Wracked with worry, Bonnie and I sought a way to get her back into our lives. Later, they moved to Tulsa, and we were able to see Megan on brief controlled visits. Even though Megan was living in Tulsa, we were no closer to having her back in our lives than we were when she was in Kansas.

In the summer of 2008, Mom was admitted to the hospital with kidney failure, and her prognosis was not good. She was sent to the ICU with its strictly enforced policy of allowing no visitors under fourteen. This devastated ten-year-old Matt who was close to Mom, as were all her grandchildren. Matt complained daily, which had a major effect on his behavior at home and school. Bonnie spent a lot of time at his school advocating for his Individualized Education Program (IEP) to give Matt the personal attention he needed.

Mom's condition worsened. She was transferred to a different room for dialysis where she was in and out of consciousness. At one point, with several of us in the room, she sat up and talked with a clarity we had not heard since she became ill. For thirty minutes she told us stories about past lives—about being on a wagon train, a pirate ship, and other strange events we did not understand. Then, as quickly as it began, she lay down and returned to being unresponsive.

We took turns keeping vigil at her bed. I was there alone on the night of August 30th when her breathing became shallower. The nurses said she did not have long. I called Rick, Kim, and Leslee, but before anyone could make it, she passed away. Betty JoAnn Rauh was sixty-nine.

I was standing in disbelief telling her how much I loved her when Rick and Kim arrived. Rick went on a desperate search for blankets and covered her up as he grieved over her saying, "I just want to keep her warm."

Rick and Kim left when the nurses arrived to get Mom ready for transport, but I waited for her to be taken to Mowery Funeral Service in Owasso. After a couple of questions, the driver came in. I recognized him, and we realized we grew up together in Mingo where he was a couple of years behind me. He remembered Mom fondly and said how honored he was to take her. I told him how happy I was as well. Mom was in good hands as a friend from Mingo took her on this important journey.

I got home around 11:30. As I got into bed, Bonnie rolled over. 'Did you see that?"

"Yes."

For an instant, we'd both seen Mom in the doorway to our bedroom. She did not say a word, but we soon heard her talking in Matt's room where she stayed for a few minutes. We clearly heard her voice and felt her presence. In the morning, we asked Matt a few cryptic questions, but he had no knowledge of the event.

The next day, we visited with Steve Mowery about the arrangements. We chose a visitation at Mowery's and a service in their chapel. During visitation, I could not bring myself to go into the room. I just could not see her that way, so I sat in the lobby the entire time.

I wrote a eulogy that I knew I did not have the strength to deliver. I printed it and took it to Rick to see what he thought. After reading it, he kept his head down, rolled his eyes up at me, and said, "I don't know who the hell you are going to get to read this, but it sure isn't going to be me."

At the service, Rick went up to the podium and gave a beautiful, heartfelt eulogy—something I could never have done without blubbering. Here is the eulogy I wrote to my mom that was never delivered:

Generations ago, it was common practice for towns and cities to erect statues of people who fought battles or left an indelible mark on a community. These statues were designed to remind future generations of the courage and sacrifice needed to accomplish great things against tremendous odds. This is the story of just such a person.

Betty Jo Ann Rauh, or "Jo" as her friends knew her, was born in Poteau, Oklahoma, on Ground Hog's Day in 1939. To say her childhood was difficult would be a huge understatement.

In fact, there is enough material about her years before marriage to make a Lifetime Channel movie. The only bright spot she ever talked about was her singing. Her family and most likely anyone who ever worked with JoAnn knew it didn't take much to get her started singing. You might not know that she accompanied an uncle who was a traveling Pentecostal Minister as a child. JoAnn was quite the hit at a young age as she would sing gospel music from the pulpit at many a Tent Revival and other church services.

After graduating from Tulsa Central High School in 1956, she was married in 1957. She began raising her children while living in the bedroom community of Mingo, located at the north end of Tulsa International Airport. Mingo was your basic lower-middle-class neighborhood where the husbands either worked at American Airlines or Rockwell/Douglas, and the wives stayed home to raise the children. Sadly, the community is now gone, but those who lived there, especially throughout the 60's, found it a remarkable place to raise a family.

Much like her childhood, Mom's marriage was not easy, either. The saving grace was that her husband worked nights, so she accomplished a lot in the afternoons and evenings, making her quite popular in the community. Among her many talents were her cooking and sewing and her uncanny ability to become close friends with practically everyone in the neighborhood JoAnn's cooking was legendary, especially at school, where our classmates and their moms always fussed over something she baked for school. Anytime there was trouble in the neighborhood, JoAnn was among the first to respond to either lend a shoulder to cry on or to cook something for the family. Her sewing was also in high demand, as she sewed countless costumes and basketball uniforms for the school and mended clothes for neighbors.

In 1970, JoAnn's life changed forever when her husband took ill. She was forced literally overnight to face the reality that she was penniless, had not held a job since high school, and had three children to feed. Those first few months were extremely difficult as she struggled to provide even the most basic of needs for her children. She entered the workforce, cleaning houses and eventually cleaning three of what can only be described as roach motels. JoAnn even traded

ironing clothes with the local music teacher to pay for trumpet lessons. Life was hard, but she never lost her faith. She would keep the family together and improve her children's lives.

In 1973, JoAnn moved to Owasso, where she immersed herself in her kids' activities. Though we struggled financially, those were some of her happiest years as she immersed herself in everything in which her children were involved, especially the Pride of Owasso Band, where, once again, she was popular among parents and students alike, with many students calling her "Mom." Our house was a favorite hangout as our mom was "cool" to be around. She spent ten years as a Band Mom and took great pride as her sons went off to the University of Arkansas on band scholarships, which would not have been possible had she not traded ironing clothes with the local music teacher for trumpet lessons and encouraged her children's passion for music.

After her children were grown, her attention turned to work and grandchildren, not necessarily in that order. She worked at several different jobs, from a Tag Office to a Construction Company to the Car Rental industry, to name a few. Her energetic and sometimes frenetic work ethic made her a popular worker. Still, she never sought out career advancement for herself. Mom thrived on challenges at work, and the tighter the deadline, the better. It's no surprise that she was popular in every place she worked.

Only once did she try to climb the corporate ladder. Her work ethic caught management's attention, and she was on the fast track to the customer service manager position. She managed a large staff and was a rising star in the company. One day, she was asked to lay off 37 people. Soon after, she quit her job and never worked in management again. Laying off those people affected her for the rest of her life. In fact, while she was on her deathbed in the ICU at Hillcrest, she made a point of mentioning how troubled she still was over the lay-off that took place some fifteen years earlier.

Another curious incident occurred during her last 23 days in the hospital, which maybe only her co-workers would truly understand. One night, she was having a rough time and chewed out a couple of nurses. JoAnn felt so bad the next night, she had a pizza party for the nurses as her way of apologizing. It should also come as no surprise that Mom was quite popular among the nursing staff early in her stay at the hospital and before the pizza party. She made it a point to get to know each of her nurses.

But the job Mom was the best at was being a grandmother. She had a unique bond with each of her grandchildren and great-grandchildren. She had a way of making each feel special, and they could sit and talk to Grandma for hours. Grandma never missed an event, which included every concert, t-ball game, softball game, volleyball game, school program, awards assembly, parade, or any opportunity to show her pride in her grandchildren. No activity or event was too small for

Grandma to attend, and she always encouraged her grandkids to succeed in whatever made them the happiest.

She was truly the glue that built and held our family together and the source of our strength. Mom always put her family before herself and never asked what was in it for her. Her reward in life was the simple joy and pride in everything her children and grandchildren accomplished.

No, they don't erect statues of people anymore, but JoAnn Rauh's life was nonetheless heroic. From her rough childhood through her difficult marriage to her role as a mother and father raising her three kids alone, she fought many battles, exhibited extraordinary courage, and sacrificed everything for those she held dear. Like Will Rogers, she never met a stranger and befriended countless neighbors, co-workers, or anyone lucky enough to cross her path. She was an amazing person who never sought recognition for herself and is only now in heaven being rewarded for what SHE accomplished here on earth.

JoAnn Rauh's statue is, instead, the sum of what she left behind in all of us who knew her. Her acts of kindness, compassion, and love are her legacy, and her little corner of the world is a better place because of her impact on it. Who needs a statue that sits in one place and can only be looked upon when JoAnn Rauh's legacy can be measured in the hearts and spirits of the people she touched?

On the day of her funeral, the remnants of a hurricane from the Gulf of Mexico came through as if Mom were trying to keep people from making a fuss over her. The weather did not stop us from honoring her in the chapel and then again at the graveside service in the pouring rain.

Leslee and her family moved into Mom's house, which only made sense other than the fact it only had one bathroom. From Mom, Leslee had learned how to adapt and found a way to make the one-bathroom work.

Bonnie was close to my mom so, like all of us, took her loss hard. Bonnie's faith allowed her to say, "If there was ever anyone who earned her way into Heaven, it was your mother." We both knew that Mom was in a better place and would always be looking down on those she loved so much.

I found myself in a dark place as I grieved my mother's death. Part of me wanted to write this book about my mother's life. I spent a lot of time sitting out on our back porch just thinking about Mom. Several years earlier, Mom bought Bonnie and me a small solar light shaped like a globe for our backyard. Bonnie placed it under her mimosa tree. It stopped working a few years earlier when I hit it with a rock while mowing.

While alone on the back porch at night, I started talking to Mom when I noticed a light. It was that broken solar globe. I just stared at it. As I walked over to it the light went out. The next night, I anxiously waited for darkness, and when I went outside, nothing happened at first. Then, I could see a faint light in the globe that continued to get brighter. Not as bright as it was when it once worked, but brighter than it was the night before.

This went on for a couple of months before I said anything to Bonnie. I was afraid that the light, or what I thought was the light, would disappear if I said anything. Bonnie was so sweet in not trying to talk me out of sitting on the back porch after I told her. She saw the light, too, but chose not to make anything of it, keeping this something special for me.

During a spring storm, a large branch from the mimosa fell and crushed the globe. I took what was left and disassembled it, looking for the batteries. To my surprise, I discovered that I had removed the rechargeable batteries years earlier when it stopped working. That globe gave me peace as I worked through my grief.

Unfortunately, thoughts of turning out just like my dad still haunted me. My unfiled taxes caused me to become more and more paranoid as my heart skipped a beat any time a different car pulled up at work or home, thinking it was the IRS coming to get me. This went on for years as I did everything I could to repeat history and destroy my family just like my father did.

None of this impacted the way I treated my family or anyone else. I continued to be generous to my family and coworkers and went about my days living the Golden Rule as my mother taught me. My father was diagnosed with schizophrenia, which is defined as recurring episodes of psychosis or misperception of reality. My increased paranoia could have been interpreted as another symptom.

Chapter Seven

2009-2014

IN LATE 2008 the financial crisis started, and companies were not making expenditures on things like CAM software. Our bank balance was healthy enough, so I thought I could weather the storm. In 2009, the crisis worsened, and sales plummeted. As summer started, I could not see a way out. I received a letter from the IRS that scared me, so in my weakened mental state, I devised an insane plan where I would take some cash, run away, and start over somewhere else. I felt stronger than ever that this plan was my destiny.

I started withdrawing money from my accounts and buying disguises and hair dye to conceal my identity. My paranoia convinced me that the IRS would try to track me down. Bonnie had no idea what I was doing, but she knew about the financial crisis from the news and asked if we would be fine. I assured her while, at the same time, I was planning to leave her and the kids.

How could I even think of doing something like that? I was convinced that my destiny included destroying my family just like I thought my father did. I did not love Bonnie or the kids any less and never treated them like my dad treated us under similar circumstances. My financial crisis and urge to fulfill my destiny made me lose sight of reality.

In July, I realized I could not make the credit card payments and cover payroll. The cash was in a bag in my trunk along with new clothes and my disguise. I got in my car and headed south. I got as far as Paris, Texas when I realized I could not go through with it. I had left my cell phone in the office so I could not be traced, so I went to a pay phone and called Bonnie. I apologized and told her I was coming home. Bonnie just said, "Come home."

When I arrived, Bonnie was, of course, visibly upset, but she never raised her voice. She just asked, "Why did you do this?" I explained the taxes and credit card debt to her and told her I did not know what to do. "You need to call Rick."

Rick came over quickly. We sat around our kitchen table as I explained the mess I was in. Rick calmly told me I needed to find a good tax attorney and accountant and make it right with the IRS.

Rick was absolutely right, but what he asked me to do scared me. Bonnie and I sat together quietly that evening. I did not know what to say, and it seemed like Bonnie was unsure what to say to me. I had shaken our relationship to its core. However, there was no discussion about my sleeping in another room as Bonnie and I went to bed as usual.

During the night, I convinced myself I could not go through with the steps Rick outlined and decided to run again. The next morning, I told Bonnie I was going to the office. Instead, I went to the cemetery. As I lay on Mom's grave, I asked her to forgive me for what I was about to do. I would have never had the courage to leave while Mom was alive. What a coward I was for leaving then and asking Mom to somehow forgive me from her grave.

My new idiotic plan was to head west. As I got further and further from Owasso, I kept thinking I could not do this to Bonnie and the kids. I stopped for the night in Denver, where I made a fateful decision. I convinced myself the only way out was suicide.

The following day, after a little sleep, I got up and left the hotel, heading east without a plan as to how I would end my life. As I turned onto the ramp to the interstate, I saw a hitchhiker who looked just like Charles Manson. I could pick him up, and he would kill me. Then I thought it might be too painful, so I passed him by. As I got up to speed, I thought *what would pain matter*. I took the next exit and circled around to pick him up. On my second pass, I slowed as I approached him—but changed my mind again and sped away. Once again, I decided to make another attempt to pick him up. *Once he kills me, he'll have my contact information from my glove box and might hurt Bonnie and the kids.* I abandoned this plan.

I continued heading east, trying to come up with a new plan. As I approached the Colorado-Kansas state line, I remembered the Wonder View Tower. I could climb up there and jump off. I arrived in the parking lot just as a school bus unloaded a group of grade school kids. I could not jump off the tower in front of kids, so I returned to I-70 heading east.

My warped mind produced a foolproof plan. I got off in Russell, Kansas and went to the local hardware store where I bought two six-foot pieces of clear one-inch tubing. In the parking lot, I wrote my suicide letter to Bonnie. Then I drove to a secluded field near some oil tanks. I pulled over, stuck the tubes in my exhaust and rear windows, and got back in the driver's seat. All I had to do was push the button to start the car, and in minutes, it would all be over.

As I sat there staring ahead, I heard some strange birds that I could not see. Then a deep voice said:

"You are not your father."

I sat, dazed. For the first time in my life, I realized I was not like my father—a thought that had never entered my mind. I started piecing it together as I said out loud, "Wait a minute. I was never mean to Bonnie or the kids until now. I have always been kind to everyone. I am nothing like my father."

I put the tubing in the trunk and pointed my car towards Owasso. First, I called Bonnie and tried to explain the experience. She was devastated yet again and did not want to hear me all bubbly on the phone as I told her God spoke to me. She just said, "Come home." I called Rick and told him the same story and asked him to help me with the steps he recommended. He, too, did not understand why I was so upbeat after what I'd done.

As I continued the drive home, I looked at the clock and realized I had lost ninety minutes. My car, watch, and phone had changed from Mountain to Central time well before my stop in Russell, Kansas. I distinctly remember it was 3:17 p.m. when I got in the front seat after connecting the plastic tubes. It was now 4:45 p.m. I cannot explain the loss of time.

I arrived home around 8 p.m. to find Bonnie relieved to see me but still grieving over what I had done. Words cannot describe how much pain I caused her. She said, "All I could do was hug your clothes in the closet because I knew I would never see you again." Strangely, after my epiphany and encounter with God, I was still on a high note, but Bonnie was deeply hurt and did not know what to say or believe. She did not say much more. Reflecting on this, I am sure she probably was thinking I was indeed acting just like my dad, and my self-proclaimed conversion was part of my psychosis.

After I'd left her twice, Bonnie had no reason to believe me or anything I said. I feared I'd damaged our relationship beyond repair. I only hoped I could show her I was a changed man and how desperately I needed her in my life. I went to Rick and Kim's, Leslee's, and Bonnie's parents, telling them exactly what I had done in the clearest manner possible and apologized for the hurt I had caused them.

Bonnie and I talked about the struggles ahead. She shook her head while never questioning my resolve that I was a different person who was going to do whatever it took to solve this crisis and heal our relationship. Bonnie was more worried about how I was going to make a living for our family.

While we were talking, I wondered why she was not unloading on me. Bonnie remained calm as she patiently allowed me to tell her everything in detail. After, she said in a firm yet quiet voice, "You will never do this again and expect me to remain by your side." I promised I would never keep any secrets from her, and I would live the rest of my life devoted to her and the kids. My epiphany in that Kansas field changed my life forever.

The following day, I called the office of Paul Tom, the attorney Rick recommended, and made an appointment. I then had to deal with my business and talk to those working with me. The business would obviously close immediately. I asked Rick to take over as the CAM Reseller. He started negotiations with headquarters, which could not have been easy. He had to convince them I would be out of the picture as my standing with the parent software developer was destroyed. On the other hand, Rick knew I would need to make a living for my family, so he offered to let me work for him as a consultant, doing the same tasks I did before but with no control over his business finances.

Later that day, after telling Bonnie where I was going, I once again lay on my mother's grave, this time asking her to forgive me for what I had done. I am convinced she had a hand in the miracle that brought me home from Kansas.

Bonnie went with me to meet Paul Tom. He listened to my story and told me I was in a lot of trouble, but it could be fixed. He then got on the phone with a forensic accountant and made an appointment for me.

I went to my office and told my people everything as clearly as I'd told my extended family. I explained that I would close the office immediately. I would keep the office manager on for a month to help me compile my financial records for the accountant. The rest transitioned to working for Rick, who was able to negotiate a transfer of the Reseller Contract to his business and keep key staff onboard. His business model was to have everyone work from home to reduce expenses as he looked for a small office training room.

Paul Tom's plan included filing business and personal bankruptcy. The accountant would prepare and file my back tax returns, and we would just have to wait for what the bankruptcy judge and IRS decided. I was told it would get rough as my creditors would be coming after me, which they did. The legal and accounting process took all the cash I had in my trunk and much more.

The one bright spot was that Bonnie was not involved in any of my tax problems. She had every opportunity to leave me. Most women would have left a man who abandoned her and her kids not once but twice. Was she happy when the phone was ringing off the hook from creditors? Of course not. All we could do was change our phone number more than once and do our best to ride out the storm.

Bonnie continued to stand by me when I proposed we set up a new home business in her name. She agreed, and we started the new company with her as 100% owner. I was now going to be working full-time from home for Bonnie who gave up her craft and sewing room in the den so I could set up a home office. Working from home allowed us to spend more time together. There was still lots of scar tissue to repair, but our relationship slowly started to heal.

For several months, I left the plastic hoses in my trunk as a reminder of how close I came to throwing everything away. Bonnie never noticed them, but I saw them every time I packed for a road trip.

Rick continued to use my services as a consultant for sales and support. I also focused on recording training movies teaching the CAM Software we sold, which became something of a hit. Due to the worldwide success of my training tutorials, I was in demand to teach on-site classes. Companies would buy my tutorials and say, "Let's bring that guy in here for training." This meant I could raise enough money to pay all my mounting legal and accounting fees and continue to provide for my family.

Matt's behavior at school was becoming a serious matter as he remained bitter over his inability to be with his beloved grandma before she died. He was being bullied regularly and took out his frustrations at home. When in the third grade, Matt was diagnosed with Asperger's syndrome. We began taking him to regular therapy sessions. We even had a brain scan done at a Dallas clinic that showed the "ring of fire" around his inactive brain, which is shared by those on the autism spectrum.

We consulted his therapist about his recent behavior, but their only suggestion was to have him admitted to an in-house treatment center, which we did not want to do. Matt was getting worse, and we were concerned about our safety. We hid all the knives in our house and locked the door to our bedroom every night. He had an IEP (Individual Educational Plan) at school, but it was becoming clear to us that public schools had done all they were equipped to do for him.

Finally, Matt started destroying things in the house, so, at the advice of his therapist, we placed Matt in the recommended boot camp to protect us and to correct his dangerous behavior. The facility was in a secluded area ninety minutes from Owasso. We could visit once a week under strict observation and were required to attend counseling with him.

Meanwhile, Bonnie found a lump in her right breast. Her biopsy was positive for breast cancer, so she chose to have a lumpectomy. We broke the cancer news to Matt while at a counseling session in the facility. The counseling was helpful, and some breakthroughs allowed Matt to come home. I don't think Matt will ever forgive us for placing him at the boot camp. He was exposed to some boys who were there for crimes they committed, so it was a much harsher environment than we had been led to believe. Had we known how bad the place was, we would have never agreed to place him there.

As I thought about Bonnie's diagnosis, all I could think was that the stress I caused Bonnie was the reason she got cancer. Whether true or not, I will live the rest of my life asking God to forgive me or punish me for what I did to Bonnie.

Bonnie found a wonderful oncologist and started chemo, which was hard on her. I was more devoted to her than ever and tried every day to make up for the harm I had done. I never left her side during her treatments and did my best to treat her like a queen.

Bonnie always took great care of her hair and wore it in countless different ways over the years. During chemo, she lost her hair and, on Thanksgiving Day, asked me to shave her head. We went to a wig store and bought a couple of wigs to wear to church, which I now attend with her every Sunday.

Bonnie took breast cancer in stride like she had every other medical setback. She did not have the serious side effects from the chemo treatments others do. Her major complaint was the loss of her hair. When chemo was over, she went through radiation, which had its own side effects that in some cases were worse than chemo. One side effect was that the hormone therapy Bonnie had been on since her hysterectomy had to be stopped because of further cancer risks. This, of course, greatly reduced her libido, which was a fitting punishment I deserved.

Matt was starting eighth grade, and Megan was still living with her partner and not a part of our lives. As the school year started, we were called to the counselor's office almost daily. The public school reached its limit with Matt when the principal expelled him for using a poor choice of words about another student. We had to do something.

Bonnie and I found and visited a K-12 school in Tulsa for children with learning differences. We were excited about the school's focus on kids like Matt but concerned as to whether they would allow him to enroll at midterm. The principal agreed to make an exception. Immediately we withdrew Matt from Owasso Public

Schools and registered him in his new school. As time passed, we realized this new school was the perfect fit for Matt as it slowly changed his life.

In 2012, one of Megan's high school volleyball friends, Veronica, helped broker a way for Megan to visit us without supervision. Megan was experiencing back pain from her years of throwing herself face-first onto the volleyball court. Veronica convinced Megan's partner to allow Bonnie and Megan to go to acupuncture together.

We saw an opportunity to get Megan out of her living situation. When Veronica made sure Megan was alone, I went over, moved all her things out of the apartment, and took her home. Megan had to share a room with Bonnie's sewing machines and craft supplies, but she did not mind. She stayed with us for a few months until we found her an apartment in Owasso.

At the end of 2012, my bankruptcy was completed, and the phone calls and knocks on the door stopped. Bonnie and I returned to a normal life with Matt in a school, which helped him tremendously, as did having Megan back in our lives. We only later learned that Megan's relationship was much more dangerous than the woman's control over her. Megan suffered from physical and emotional abuse during this dark period of her life. The friction between Bonnie and Megan during Megan's high school years disappeared as they were able to make peace with each other.

Matt's new school told us about a summer camp in Texas for kids on the Spectrum. Matt did not want to go, but we insisted and drove him there for the one-week camp. He ended up having a great time, so, the next year, we signed him up for a two-week camp, which we did for a couple more years. After we took Matt to camp, Bonnie and I went on vacations including cruises to the Caribbean and Mexico and another trip to Hawaii. Bonnie and I were growing closer again as we enjoyed each other's company more than ever.

Meanwhile, I was much more in tune with my spiritual side after my encounter with God in Kansas, and I felt ashamed about all the years I hadn't gone to Mass with Bonnie and the kids. I hadn't approached Father Bradley, the popular priest at St. Henry's, because I felt embarrassed about all my baggage, much of which took place while he was Bonnie's pastor.

A new priest, Father Matt, was assigned to St. Henry's, which, in my warped logic, meant a clean slate. How silly I was to have wasted all that time not approaching Father Bradley! If I had only stopped for a moment and realized: he was a priest who, in confessions every week, heard much more serious problems than mine.

In the summer of 2013, I decided to become a Catholic. In September, the first meeting of the Rite of Christian Initiation of Adults (RCIA) took place. I was afraid I'd chicken out, so I didn't tell Bonnie where I was going. I just told her at 6:30, after dinner, that I was going to run an errand.

Nervously I walked into church. I knew how much harm I'd caused my family in the past and considered myself unworthy of being allowed to join any church. I recognized many of the people in the class who volunteered, which helped make me feel welcome and at ease. The initial class was wonderful as I hung on every word from Father Matt. I was so moved and excited after class that I could hardly wait to get home to tell Bonnie.

When I arrived home, Bonnie was sitting in the dark with a look on her face I'd seen before. "I thought you left again," she said through tears. It hit me how stupid I'd been not telling her where I was going. While she was eventually happy after I explained, it took a while for her to come back from the dark place I'd put her yet again by my actions. I promised to never keep a secret from her. The following Easter, I was baptized and became a Catholic.

Shortly after Easter, we learned Father Matt would lead a pilgrimage to Rome and the Holy Land. Bonnie and I talked about going but were concerned about her health. While her prognosis after breast cancer was good, the chemo, radiation, fibromyalgia, and her constant back, shoulder, and now hip pain were taking a toll on her mobility and endurance. She also required daily doses of MiraLAX for any semblance of regularity. I was blindly gung-ho about signing up, and Bonnie knew how excited I was. She put aside her own concerns about her health and agreed, I think, because of how much it meant to me. Bonnie and my mom are so alike, putting others before themselves.

Father Matt and a group of eighteen pilgrims, including Bonnie and me, left for Rome and Israel in November. Rome was difficult for Bonnie with lots of walking and stairs. However, she enjoyed every day and did her best while holding onto me like a crutch. One of many highlights was a private Mass under St. Peter's Basilica.

Israel offered even more to see, but if I chose only one highlight, it had to be the visit to the Cana Wedding Church. This church was built on the site where Jesus turned water into wine, which started his earthly ministry. We had the church to ourselves for this private Mass, during which all the married couples were asked to come up for a special blessing during Mass. It hit us: we were in the Cana Wedding Church, preparing to renew our wedding vows in this holy place surrounded by so much history.

All the husbands were shedding tears with me, the worst of the bunch. The girls were all dreamy-eyed, including Bonnie, as they remembered their wedding day and enjoyed this special Mass. Sadly, a few widows in our group sat in the pews, shedding their own tears as they watched and remembered their wedding day and the loss of their husband. When we returned home and gathered for the holidays, we could not wait to share our trip with family and friends.

At that time, we were also busy making plans for Megan's wedding. She had met a man named Jay, who moved into her apartment. Bonnie and I were not on board with this arrangement, but Megan's being back in our lives meant so much that we would have overlooked almost anything. After returning, Megan had become much more independent. We were proud of the strong woman she was becoming.

Bonnie and Megan dealt with the wedding dress and cake. I only wrote the checks since my input would not have mattered, anyway. Next was the venue and catering. Since we only had one daughter, I wanted to pull out all the stops and make her wedding special. God had been good to me since my mental breakdown, which meant I could afford a little luxury for our daughter.

We chose the White House Mansion in south Tulsa, which is exactly what the name sounds like: an old, three-story house with banquet space inside and out. For dinner, we chose *Catering by Orr*. (Ironically, owner Orr Nalp was the owner of the Fountains Restaurant at the time the waiter spilled the tray of iced tea down Bonnie's off-white dress at our Senior Prom.)

We especially enjoyed the "tasting" event with the goal of producing a menu. Bonnie, Megan, Jay, and I met at the catering office and were treated to samples of everything on their menu. We tasted multiple entrees with different preparations of chick, fish, steak, multiple side dishes, and copious amounts of dessert. Stuffed, we finally agreed on a menu and could not wait for the wedding.

Chapter Eight

2015 – 2021

O<small>N</small> F<small>EBRUARY</small> 10, 2015, our excitement about Megan's upcoming wedding took a back seat when I got a call from paramedics. Rick had had a seizure and was being taken to the hospital. I gave the paramedic Kim's number and raced to the office where Rick was already in the ambulance. Apparently, Rick was in his office while a class was being taught. Nearing the end of the day, Rick came out complaining he could smell smoke. Rick's office was across the street from a previously manned fire station, which was only partially used.

The paramedics explained that Rick tried to get into the building, but instead set off an alarm. He then tripped and fell in the parking lot. When the paramedics responded to the alarm, they discovered him frantically waving his arms. Rick's condition worsened in the hospital, and he was placed in a medically-induced coma and intubated. He remained in a coma for twenty-four hours while they ran tests to find out what happened.

The doctors wanted to remove the breathing tube and were having trouble waking him up. They said it was not normal, but asked if Kim and I would try. While nurses watched, we started gently, but as Rick resisted, we turned up both the intensity and volume. Within a few minutes, Kim and I were yelling in his ear and cheering every facial motion as we tried to wake him up. Rick finally responded. The nurse left the room to get the doctor to proceed with removing the tube. She returned to inform us that the doctor was busy with another patient.

Rick was becoming more and more alert. He tried to remove the tube himself. We explained the situation and started communicating with him as he wrote on a whiteboard asking questions in what appeared to be an odd game of charades. Finally, the doctor arrived, and Kim and I were asked to leave.

In the hall, one of the nurses told us she had never seen that before. We weren't sure what she meant. She explained that she was referring to how hard Kim and I tried to wake Rick up. It was clear to her and anyone who heard the yelling and screaming that Kim and I loved Rick very much.

Earlier, when Rick was in the coma and Kim was away, a doctor came in and asked about Rick's swollen ankle. I told him it was an old injury, that Rick had fallen and torn ligaments at a skating party in Mingo, and that the serious injury resulted in his having always had trouble with that ankle. The doctor assured me the injury was recent. Later X-rays confirmed that Rick broke his ankle when he fell at the fire station. I felt terrible for misleading the doctors into not looking at his ankle sooner.

Following an MRI, Bonnie and I were with Kim and Rick when the doctor told them he had an inoperable brain tumor. The doctor thought it was the slow-growing type that might respond to treatment. The first course of action was to wait for the swelling to subside, and then operate to fix his ankle. Rick was discharged on February 14th to attend a friend's wedding, but no one felt like celebrating Valentine's Day.

I visited Rick the following Sunday, but he was not there. I cannot explain why, but I somehow ended up at the cemetery where I found Rick and his son Sam at Mom's grave. Sam is Rick and Kim's only child, and they're close.

Sam was all grown up and had recently married Shelby, who was also from Owasso. Their wedding was unique: Rick and Sam spent several weekends clearing a field of trees and brush on Kim's dad's property in rural Arkansas for the outdoor ceremony.

I told Sam about how our mom protected Rick from his father and what a hard time we'd had growing up. I told Sam about how Rick and his grandmother got all the abuse and how strong his dad had been through those difficult times. The words just came out of my mouth as I told Sam these things about his dad. I doubt Rick would have ever shared as much detail, but he never tried to stop me. I wanted Sam to know how proud I had always been of Rick and how much his dad went through growing up.

The following week, Rick had ankle surgery and was ordered to keep his leg elevated. Rick was blessed with our mother's gift of gab and could converse with anyone. However, after the seizures, when any of us visited, we noticed Rick was engaging in even more conversation than usual. One time in mid-March when Matt and I visited Rick, he would have talked to Matt for hours as he hung on every word Matt said.

On March 21st, Rick and Kim planned a trip to take brownies to the paramedics to thank them for what they did back in February. While in the car, Rick had a panic attack. He told Kim he thought he was going to have a seizure and kept mentioning the redwoods and the ocean as he struggled to remain conscious. When they arrived at the fire station, he started feeling better. They had to wait for the paramedics to return, which gave Rick enough time to regain his composure. The paramedics arrived, and Rick and Kim had a pleasant visit from the car and went home.

Once home, Rick sat in his recliner for a while as the trip had taken more effort than he realized. In the hall on his way to the bathroom, he had a panic attack and collapsed. Kim called 911. The paramedics loaded him into the ambulance and worked on him en route to the local hospital.

Rick was taken to ER Room #1 where they continued to work on him. Kim called us, and Bonnie and I rushed over to find that Kim had just been told Rick passed away. We all spent time in ER Room #1 grieving and trying to understand how this could have happened. Kim called Sam and Shelby, and I called Uncle BJ in California and our co-workers as we broke the news as best we could. Rick was only fifty-five years old.

I was devastated. I lost my best friend. Bonnie's and my tears were only comforted by our belief that Rick and our mother were together again. My prayers for Rick also include the hope that he was able to make peace with Dad.

Kim now had to plan for a funeral. She used Mowery's Funeral Home like we did with Mom. We realized Mowrey's chapel would not be big enough for the expected turnout as Rick remained as popular as he was in college. Knowing how much Rick loved golf, we contacted a golf course with a conference center that Rick frequented. This idea seemed perfect, so we scheduled a visit.

Several maintenance issues with the building made it impossible for us to consider the site. As we drove away, we all agreed we were not meant to have the ceremony at the golf course.

Rick's wishes were to be cremated after a viewing at Mowery's, so we chose not to have a traditional funeral. Instead, we planned a celebration. Steve Mowery suggested the Owasso 7th Grade Center, which, back then, was our high school. The principal agreed, and we visited the school to make arrangements.

We held the ceremony in the gym, the perfect venue for a celebration. The school supplied a custodian who set up chairs on the basketball floor and on the stage for the speakers.

As predicted, the turnout would never have fit in a chapel or small church. Several people spoke, and I did my best to keep my composure as I offered a few words: stories about our childhood together and adventures our parents never knew anything about, something I knew I could not have done at Mom's funeral. I concluded my eulogy:

Rick had the rare gift of making a personal connection, something he got from his mom, which made him as beloved as she was. While it is devastating to lose Rick at such an early age, I am reminded that just as in life, in space Brown Dwarfs go unnoticed. At the same time, Super Novas burn so brightly, they light up an entire galaxy. Rick was a Super Nova. While his glow was short-lived, we will never forget the amazing light show Rick put on for us.

When Mom died, we had purchased plots at Graceland Cemetery with one for Rick and Kim on one side of Mom, and one for Bonnie and me on the other, along with two plots right behind for Leslee.

Rick's passing meant more than losing a part of me. There was the practical matter of work. After the reception at Kim's house, we found some alone time. Kim said, "I guess you'll want to take the company back over?" In a moment that can only be described as divine inspiration, a vision came into my head. "No, you're going to take over the company and run the business, and I'm going to help you."

I had no idea I was going to say this. My vision included all the logistics—which made perfect sense. Kim agreed, and, after she'd had some time to grieve, we easily transitioned into this new business model as Kim quickly learned new skills and became an exceptionally good business owner.

Bonnie and I had a rough time managing our emotions. Bonnie had known Rick since he was thirteen, so we were both grieving. However, we faced Megan's upcoming wedding less than thirty days away. We had to quickly shift our attention to the wedding while being mindful of the fact that everyone in our family was still grieving, and her Uncle Rick wouldn't be at her wedding.

A few months after the wedding, as part of my grieving process, I joined the pastoral ministry at the same hospital where Rick passed away. I used my credentials the following March 21st for private time in ER Room #1 as I reflected on a year without Rick. I repeated this meditation as a couple more years went by. To this day, I think about Rick every time I walk by the ER on my way upstairs to make my rounds.

Megan's wedding was a huge success. We talked about Rick a lot and how much fun he would have had. Kim was there supporting us, and we all continued to support her. We could all sense Rick and Mom's presence as if they were there to make sure we all had an unforgettable evening. The only minor incident was when the bartender came to me and said, "There's this kid over there that keeps asking for a drink." I looked over: Matt, age sixteen.

As the evening finished and Bonnie and I loaded up, the venue manager took me aside. "Your wedding was the best one I've ever seen." I figured she was being polite, but she explained, "There was so much love in the room without all the drama I see at virtually every other wedding." She was right. A large part was having Rick and Mom there. We were all having a great time just like all the times we had during family gatherings at Mom's, Rick's, or our house.

That summer, Bonnie's neck pain got worse. Her injection treatments were not helping. Our family doctor sent her to a specialist who told us the vertebrae in her neck had deteriorated to the point where there was a real possibility a minor fall or collision could leave her paralyzed. The surgeon suggested placing a titanium plate in the front of her neck and securing it with four 1.5-inch-long screws.

This scared both of us, but Bonnie was not afraid of another surgery. "What else can go wrong with me?" she said. "Why don't you trade me in for a new model?" Bonnie had made this same comment many times, but there would never be anyone else for me.

The surgery went well, but, again, Bonnie had trouble coming out of anesthesia. They needed to reopen her for a follow-up procedure. This time, she came out of anesthesia as expected, and we went home. The next day she started running a fever, and her neck became swollen and red. We returned to the doctor who diagnosed Bonnie with the MRSA infection.

The doctors chose an aggressive course of treatment that consisted of multiple rounds of antibiotics delivered by courier to our house where I injected them into her port following exact instructions. These injections went on for ten days and were stressful for both of us. I had to flush her port and attach the large bag (that had to be watched carefully for any malfunction) as it administered the drug over a specified time. Bonnie had to stay in bed until the entire course was completed. She recovered, and our life slowly became normal again.

2016 had the promise of being a much better year as we looked forward to Matt's high school graduation. He was taking welding at the local vo-tech, so we hoped he could find work that would allow him to live on his own. Bonnie and I sat through several school seminars about programs for kids like Matt who live in group homes, which we feared might be Matt's future. Matt was totally unorganized at home, and he resisted our attempts to introduce order or structure as we hoped to teach him some basic life skills. We also learned Megan was pregnant and due in late July. Bonnie and I were so excited to learn we would become grandparents.

After the neck surgery and MRSA incident, Bonnie started having more and more trouble getting up and down our stairs. I was not doing much better with my worn-out knees. All our bedrooms were upstairs, so the only solution was to move. Bonnie started looking for houses, as I showed about as much interest in the process as I had when she started Megan's adoption journey.

In May, Bonnie told me about a house she wanted me to look at. Knowing how difficult it would be to move after having lived in our home for twenty-six years, I reluctantly agreed. We drove about five miles east of town and entered an older housing addition. When we arrived, the house was one story—much smaller than our house— and quite different from anything I thought Bonnie would choose.

When we got out of the car and Bonnie started talking about the place, it became clear she had been here before and had already entered into negotiations on her own. The owner and his wife showed me the house, which looked much like it had when it was built in 1980. The kitchen was galley style with a small dining space on one end and the washer and dryer on the other by the door to the garage. There was only one living space, and the bathrooms were dated. The first two bedrooms had wallpaper and a border. The master bedroom had an unusual, mirrored built-in frame around the bed, which would have to go before Bonnie would ever sleep there.

At this point, I wondered what Bonnie was thinking. I hadn't seen anything to impress me— until we entered the backyard where we discovered dozens of mature banana trees surrounding the in-ground saltwater pool and a large pool house or what they called their cabana. This convinced me Bonnie was not losing it.

Behind the gated backyard was what looked like a second house. The owner took me out to The Shop behind the fenced backyard. The Shop included a large room with a small office and bathroom and an attached single-car garage. The Shop had central heating and air, which was a plus. "Matt can sleep in the office in The Shop," Bonnie said, as if she had already worked out the details much like her plans for our marriage. "He would only need to come to the house for a shower."

Now, I could see where Bonnie was coming from. She wanted me to have a quiet place to work, so she was willing to sacrifice the lack of amenities in the house in exchange for a party backyard for our extended family and The Shop, which would make me happy. Bonnie also wanted a separate place for Matt to live in to help him gain some independence. Clearly, Bonnie hit a home run.

Another advantage to this house was its acre of land that would give our dog more room to run. Bonnie loved dogs. Memorable dogs followed after Jasper died, including Dixie the Scottie, whom Bonnie decided to breed. What we did not know was that Dixie was unable to give birth without assistance—until a Sunday night drive to the vet culminated in a $900-dollar C-section. Then there was Teddy, a little white bichon frisé that Bonnie bought from a local breeder. Teddy only lived in a crate before Bonnie bought him. Once home, Teddy walked on carpet and grass as if he were walking on hot lava rocks. Teddy was Bonnie's dog and no one else's; he followed her everywhere. When Bonnie ran an errand, Teddy would sit by a window and whimper until he saw her car pull into the cul-de-sac.

After Teddy died, Bonnie wanted another dog, and I knew better than to object. She'd heard of a new mixed breed called a golden-doodle and contacted breeders. After several failed attempts, she contacted a breeder in Salina, Kansas. They went back and forth for a few weeks until they eventually agreed on a price. When she told me the price, I was more than a little shocked, but how could I say no after the rough couple of years she'd been through?

It was February, and Bonnie, Matt, and I headed to Salina to pick up the new family dog. In the back of my mind, I gave the odds of success at 50/50, given our track record in the past with other unmentioned dogs. Snow began falling as we passed Wichita. We met the breeder in a Salina parking lot. We knew the dog was one-year-old, so we were not expecting a puppy. We had no idea that Bonnie had spent all her time negotiating for a seventy-five-pound, one-year-old *puppy*. Oh, my, that dog was huge! I wondered if it would fit in our van.

While Bonnie and Matt were overjoyed at seeing the dog, I was doing the math in my head. *What is this dog going to cost me? How much more will I spend to feed it?* I never pointed out that the cul-de-sac house had a small yard. I listened as the breeder talked about the special food she made, how she took her showers with the dog, and other odd things that made me question her sanity.

I handed over the check that would have bought a used car. We loaded the dog in the van and headed on snowy streets back to Owasso. The atmosphere in the van was like Matt's first car ride from Antioch to Los Angeles and our first ride with Megan to Grandpa

Tilman's. Bonnie and Matt were as happy as I had seen them in a long time. I could not help but get caught up in the moment and forgot about the logistics as I was quickly taken by how amazing this dog was.

On the ride home, Bonnie and Matt discussed names. Bonnie always liked the character Fozzie Bear from the Muppets but decided it was too long, so they settled on Ozzie, which seemed to fit his good nature. We arrived late, and Ozzie made himself right at home. I tried to discuss where he would sleep, assuming it would be the garage or outside, but Bonnie and Matt shut me down, telling me if he could take showers with his owner, he could stay inside. I could not argue with their logic.

Ozzie made it all night without needing to go outside. The following day, Bonnie attached a sleigh bell to the back door, and by the end of the day, he was using it when he needed out. Matt's room was smaller and always messy, so there was no room for Ozzie there. Instead, he slept on the floor next to Bonnie's side of the bed. While he was always willing, I put my foot down about any thought of him sleeping in our bed. He would however, occasionally jump on the bed with us in the mornings at the smallest prompting.

During spring break, shortly after getting Ozzie, Matt and I were skiing when I got a frantic call from Bonnie. The breeder had called. Having come to realize how special Ozzie was, she regretted the sale and wanted the dog back. I told Bonnie to let her try. She called the breeder back and made it clear she would not give Ozzie back. The dog had bonded with Matt and was already helping him more than any therapy dog could. Bonnie did like she had so many times before: she just took care of it.

Back to the 1980 house tour. Bonnie so typically sacrificed for others. In this case, she was giving up her large kitchen and amazing master suite for a house that was too small for us to even share a closet or bathroom. Bonnie only thought of others as she sold me on her vision.

We found a realtor and put our house on the market. The realtor was concerned our upstairs bedrooms would be a problem, so she convinced us to start with a low price. We took the realtor's advice and had an offer after one open house.

We made an offer on the 1980 house, which was accepted. The real work began as we had to conduct multiple garage sales to downsize our possessions. I also decided to paint all the rooms in the house. Our inspector had spent about four hours poking and prodding all over and handed me a long list of things to repair, so I made all the repairs he suggested.

We agreed on an August 5th closing and planned to move in on August 6th. Our house buyers needed an August 1st closing, so we put our belongings in storage while we stayed in a hotel for a few days before moving.

We were so proud when Matt graduated from high school. We looked forward to his finding work as a welder and to his becoming independent. Before we closed on the home, Matt decided to make his own visit to the 1980 house. He drove up and knocked on the door, telling the owners his parents had bought the house, and he wanted to look around. It was so typical of Matt to do something impulsive like this without consulting anyone first.

Our old house was a buzz of activity as boxes were being packed and rooms were being painted. All the while, we waited in anticipation for Megan's due date. Her mid-July due date came and went, and, by the end of July, we had almost everything out of the house and were ready to move into the hotel.

On that last night in our home that we had shared for the last twenty-six years, Bonnie and I reflected on all the events in our lives that centered around this place. We talked about the day I showed her the house. "I thought I was dreaming when I saw this place for the first time," she said. How lucky we were to have found this place—and even luckier, that my actions didn't take it all away.

We had so many incredible memories of family gatherings as

well as all the milestones in our children's lives. While we were excited about the move, we were also sad about leaving this place that was so important to us.

With almost all the furniture packed and out of the house, we heard a cold, unfamiliar echo as we walked around downstairs talking about how much more we had to do. The only place in the house that felt like our home was our bedroom that still included our bed, which was the last piece of furniture remaining on this final night.

Bonnie and I agreed the one thing we would miss the most would be our master bathroom and especially our bathtub. From the day we moved in, our bathtub was the start of so many nights of passion. Bonnie and I, being creatures of habit, limited our sex to our bedroom other than the one time we used a rug in front of a fireplace. We both complained the next day about being sore and never experimented anywhere else.

Shortly after we were married, I would do my best to initiate sex, still holding onto the notion Bonnie somehow hid a wild side in her that was just waiting to be magically unleashed. While we did enjoy each other as my fantasy of more sex came true, I soon realized that the Bonnie I fell in love with was the same Bonnie I went to bed with. I would never need her to be anything other than the sweet, caring, and giving person she was everywhere, including our bed from the day we were married.

As the years went by and Bonnie's many health issues mounted, I learned to let Bonnie initiate any sex we had. One of our many habits was when Bonnie was in the mood, she would leave the living room, and as she got to the bottom of the stairs, she would say in her soft, sweet voice, "I'm taking a bath." If I was watching something on TV and not paying attention, she would add, "You're welcome to join me." At times Bonnie needed a bath without sex, but when she paused as she left the room and used that tone while looking ever so gently toward me, I knew this was my green light.

I would wait a few minutes for her to run the bath and get

ready before coming upstairs. We liked bubbles in our bath, and Bonnie's favorite scent was Bath and Body Works Moonlight Path. I never needed an aphrodisiac or stimulant; all I ever needed was to catch a waft of Moonlight Path. When upstairs, I would lock our bedroom door, then knock on the double bathroom door. Bonnie would always say: "I hope that's you."

Bonnie would usually light candles around the tub. Sometimes, she would already be in the tub waiting. Other times, I would get in first and watch as she cleaned her face at the sink. We would sit there facing each other as we talked about everything and anything. Our conversations in this intimate setting were similar to the countless times we would simply sit and talk about things other than the obvious.

When the water started to get cold, I would get out and go to bed, waiting in anticipation for Bonnie to join me. There was never any selfishness in what we shared. Our sex was not a physical act, but instead, an affirmation of our deep love for each other as our bodies were used as a way of expressing what we both felt in our hearts. Our love for each other never needed sex for satisfaction. I may have been wrong before we were married when I thought we would have lots of sex. What I instead learned is that what matters is quality and not quantity.

The next day, we turned the page on this house we loved so much and took apart our bed, removed the rest of our belongings, and checked into the hotel.

On August 3rd, Megan went into labor and was admitted to one of the Owasso hospitals. The labor took a while as Bonnie and I waited. In the early morning of August 4th, with Bonnie at her side, Megan gave natural birth to an eight-pound, thirteen-ounce baby girl named Ella while I waited patiently as far from the action as possible.

Later that day, with little sleep and running on adrenaline from Ella's birth, we closed on the 1980 house. At the closing, the owner asked me to come out to the house to go over some things. The gesture was kind, and we met the owner at our new home. He started by walking me through the main house, showing me several light switches with red tape on them, preventing them from being turned off. He explained these switches managed unrelated items such as outdoor lighting, the ceiling fan and critical plug-ins, which made no sense to me. None of the red tape was there when we saw the house before closing. It was clear that their home inspection was much less extensive than ours.

We went outside, where he explained the process of digging up the banana trees every fall, storing them in a large crate over the winter, and replanting them in the spring. He next took me on a ten-minute tour of the pool equipment and briefly explained how to winterize the pool, none of which made any sense to me either. We moved to The Shop, and he explained other unusual wiring and switches and showed me the fake toy cameras he used for security. He told me the heat and air system was on its last legs, and the toilet could only be used sparingly as it would easily clog and back up.

That night, I started to experience pain in my side. I am not prone to anxiety, so it was not buyer's remorse. The pain kept getting worse—so much so Bonnie suggested I go to the local ER. At the same time, a powerful lightning storm passed through Owasso as we headed to the same hospital where Megan and Ella were.

After some tests, I was diagnosed with a small kidney stone. I pleaded with Bonnie, the doctor, and the nurses not to say anything to Megan upstairs. My daughter was recovering from passing an eight-pound baby naturally, and I didn't want to embarrass her while I whined downstairs about a kidney stone no larger than a mustard seed. After I was discharged in the early morning, Bonnie and I returned to the hotel for a few hours of sleep before our family planned to meet at 8 a.m. to help us move.

We awoke to a phone call. Sam's mother-in-law's house in Owasso had been struck by lightning and burned to the ground.

Sam and Shelby were sleeping upstairs at the time, but everyone got out safely. Despite the tragedy, Sam and Shelby, who were running on less sleep than we were, arrived ready to help us move.

As the first caravan of furniture arrived at the house, the whole family saw the place for the first time. It was as if they had arrived at Disneyland as they ran around exploring everything. They quickly saw the potential of future family gatherings as I shared Bonnie's vision for both the outdoor space and The Shop—our party room for indoor gatherings.

Bonnie never made a fuss about her hard work in finding the place but beamed as her nieces and nephews ran around squealing at one discovery after another. As we settled in, I started seeing more of her plan. Bonnie knew I liked having a separate space to work, especially when I needed to record tutorials. All I had to do was walk from the patio door to The Shop for my quiet space.

My silly notion of being unable to work at home had long since disappeared. After my mental breakdown, I loved working at home. Now, with The Shop, I could experience going to work in the morning and walking home to have lunch and dinner with Bonnie where we would sit and just enjoy being close to each other. Bonnie would frequently come out to visit me, usually with some new way to reorganize The Shop for parties or to make it look less like a shop.

At lunch or at the end of the day, I would walk through the patio doors and see her sitting in her recliner or in the kitchen. For an instant, as we exchanged glances, I would get the same feeling inside I had so many times when I came home from college or from a long road trip to see her. Anytime our eyes would lock after being separated, it was as if we had no need for words, as our eyes could tell each other everything we needed to know.

We enjoyed simple pleasures like lunch or dinner together as we made each other laugh easily. Bonnie has a keen sense of humor, and I always like to joke around. It was laughter that helped us heal after

I left her. It was laughter that helped us get through breast cancer and every other setback we experienced together.

Bonnie and I especially enjoyed sitting on the back porch. Bonnie had transformed it into an oasis. She enjoyed growing flowers and watching birds, especially the hummingbirds who frequented her many feeders. Bonnie often told me about other plans to improve the house or yard. We both really enjoyed working together, making this place our own.

We often talked about what Mom would have thought of this place and how she would have been involved in every new idea or project Bonnie came up with. Some of Bonnie's ideas did not come from Pinterest; instead, at times, they seemed like something only my mother would have come up with.

During the summers while I was working, I'd hear noises from the pool and go out to watch Bonnie, Megan, and Ella having fun swimming. Ozzie also loved the 1980 house as he now had plenty of room to chase tennis balls, his favorite pastime. Ozzie grew to be over 120 pounds, which is unusually large for a goldendoodle. His hair was not as curly as other doodles but more like a retriever's with some curls—not unlike Bonnie's hair before cancer. Ozzie was such a gentle dog. From the time she walked, Ella would toddle over and lie on Ozzie. The two were best buddies.

Shortly after the move, Bonnie and I experienced home main-tenance issues. First, a large water leak between the two bathrooms required cutting into the wall and a little jackhammer work on the concrete floor. Next, the air conditioner in The Shop broke. Eventually, every major and minor system in the main house and Shop had to be replaced.

Aside from mechanical and plumbing problems was the issue of the main house's interior. All the rooms needed work. The first to go was an odd built-in cabinet and frame around the smaller master bed. Next, in what was to become Bonnie's sewing room, we had to remove the bright red border that went around the "Nebraska Room," so named for NU's football cry "Go Big Red."

The kitchen consisted of vintage 1980 original equipment and was too much of a job for us to even think about taking on ourselves. We quickly discovered that the neighbors were wonderful people, and we were among the youngest on the block. Our neighbors across the street had large trees in the front yard, which became the gathering place as we would sit outside and visit. One time we were talking about our kitchens. "If you ever drive by my house and see a fire in my kitchen," our neighbor said, "DO NOT call 911!" to which we all laughed as Bonnie and I shared the exact same sentiment.

Both bathroom walls had to be seen to be believed. In the main bathroom, the textured walls had sharp spikes that extended a quarter inch from the sheetrock. Accidentally brushing your arm against the wall would draw blood. A new roll of toilet paper would tear into shreds as it passed over the wall. The small master bathroom also had texture issues. Someone had created swirls of concentric circles and shapes that looked like something out of King Tut's tomb.

Bonnie and I installed some shiplap on the wall behind our bed in the master bedroom to repair the damage caused by removing the odd built-in mirrored cabinet. We decided to do the same in the main bathroom to cover up the potential insurance claim if someone required stitches after encountering the wall while using the bathroom.

While installing the shiplap in the bathroom, I fell off a step ladder in the shower. Bonnie did her best to catch me. We landed half in and half out of the tub. My ankle dislocated with my foot dangling sideways. Bonnie was also in pain, but she was more concerned about my ankle as she watched me pop it back in place, something I had seen Bonnie do before.

Bonnie's injury was much more serious and required "Tommy John" rotator cuff surgery. I finished covering both bathroom walls alone as Bonnie's arm was in a sling for a few weeks while she recovered from another surgery with its inevitable anesthesia side effects. The only other side effect was that I had to find a temporary barber. Bonnie had cut my hair since we were in high school, but she was now on the injured reserve list.

While the backyard was amazing on the surface, it, too, had issues. First, there was no fence around the pool. We were not going to take chances with Ella, so we installed a fence. Next, the backyard had lots of uneven flagstone slabs with fine gravel in between. With her mobility issues, Bonnie did not trust her footing on the flagstones. We chose to cover the area with concrete.

While the contractor was preparing the area, his tractor found our concealed septic tank by breaking the concrete lid as the tractor fell halfway inside. Workers prevented an even worse disaster by jumping on the back to keep it from falling in. Construction halted as I was in a panic organizing the installation of a new septic tank. Bonnie and I were forced to live in a hotel again while the new septic tank was installed to allow the concrete work to continue. This was followed by many more maintenance issues than I can list.

No matter how many things this house needed to be repaired or replaced, Bonnie took one issue after another in stride, and I never regretted her choice or vision for this place. We faced each of these challenges hand in hand, just as we had faced all the other challenges in our lives.

As Bonnie and I continued fixing what we could, Matt enjoyed his freedom living out in The Shop. Matt's attempt at welding did not work out, as his temperament was not suited for the harsh way people are treated in manufacturing. He was also a night owl who would come up to the house in the middle of the night for a shower or to raid the ice box even though we put a refrigerator and microwave in The Shop.

We tried our best to keep Matt from interrupting Bonnie's sleep. By this time, Bonnie was taking medication to overcome insomnia and was a light sleeper. We continued to argue with Matt more and more until he decided to move out to live with friends. Once again, we lost one of our children as Matt drifted from us and bounced around, living in places and with people we did not know. He eventually got a job at an Airsoft Gun Store, a hobby he enjoyed.

Alone in our house, Bonnie and I wondered where we had failed as parents. We had lost Megan for several years, and now we could not live with Matt. Bonnie said, "I wonder if we were not meant to be parents."

"God put Megan and Matt into our lives for a reason," I said. "It will work out."

"I sure wish I knew what we did to deserve this."

Bonnie missed talking to my mom who would have encouraged her as she had so many times in the past. I knew I deserved anything bad that happened to me, but not Bonnie who, like Mom, never did anything to deserve the many setbacks she faced.

While I was busy working out in The Shop, Bonnie enjoyed Megan, Ella, and Ozzie. Megan and Ella came over often, and Bonnie delighted in everything Ella discovered, just as she had in the many milestones she recorded on the calendar when Megan came into our lives. Megan and Bonnie were becoming closer every day.

Matt would attend our frequent family parties, which were becoming regular summer and holiday traditions. One year, Bonnie wanted to do something special for Christmas: she wanted to convert The Shop garage into Santa's workshop and hire a Santa to surprise Ella and all the nieces and nephews. We knew just the guy to hire, our close friend Doug from high school. He was our friend who Bonnie dated to satisfy her mother when she forced our separation. Doug was now a Mall Santa who also worked at corporate events. Doug was as excited as I was when I called.

The only problem was that while The Shop was our party room, it was also where I stored my tools. Bonnie made and hung drapes to hide my tools in the main shop. Then she wanted to cover up all my larger tools on both sides of the attached garage.

I went overboard, like when I created Bonnie's map to Fayetteville. I started with lots of PVC pipe and fittings, which I used to build a frame that extended from the floor to the 10-foot ceiling on three sides of the garage. I bought some Christmas-themed plastic sheets to cover the framework and added lights. Bonnie found an old wooden wingback chair for Santa's throne and painted it gold. She added a small Christmas tree, fake presents, and other decorations. It looked like a movie set. We kept this project a secret from everyone.

While the family was in The Shop after dinner, I slipped outside and brought Santa in quietly through the outside overhead door. When Santa was ready, he rang a large sleigh bell, and I opened the inside garage door to reveal Santa's Workshop to everyone's surprise. Kids, old and young, took turns sitting on Santa's lap. The evening concluded with our nieces and nephews in a line dance with Santa doing the Macarena.

That Christmas, we also surprised the family by creating custom calendars with family pictures that listed everyone's birthdays, including Erik (Leslee's son who died of SIDS), Mom, and Rick. The calendar was such a hit that we continue the tradition every year. Bonnie and I start asking for pictures in September, assemble the calendar, and hand them out at our Christmas gathering.

The following spring brought some good news. Matt, who had gotten away from the Airsoft Gun Store whose boss was demanding, rude and mean, had found a job delivering auto glass from Tulsa to Springfield, Missouri. Bonnie and I at one time worried he might have to live in a group home; instead, we celebrated his working a regular job and finding success in the adult world.

In late 2019, we planned to remodel the main house's interior. This project included gutting the kitchen and, throughout the house, changing the flooring that consisted of a hodge-podge of four different materials, which made no sense.

Bonnie was excited to shop for cabinets and flooring. Daily she showed me pictures of ideas she got online on her iPad. Sometimes, she walked to The Shop to show me something as if it was too important for her to wait until lunch or the end of the day.

By March 15, 2020, when the first Covid lockdowns started, the kitchen cabinets and appliances were removed, and we had moved our bedroom into The Shop. Our contractor agreed to continue working while we quarantined in The Shop for three months until the work was completed.

Bonnie made it sound to friends as if she were living in a shed or camping in a tent. I thought living in The Shop was fine. We had our king-size bed and nightstands, our couch and recliners, and a big screen and projector for our TV. In the evenings, after the worker left, we inspected the progress then showered before bed. The conditions weren't perfect, but we were not roughing it, either. We finally moved back into the house where Bonnie enjoyed her new kitchen, flooring, and the many upgrades we made.

Sadly, Megan and Jay separated and divorced later that same year. Like so many other divorces, no one was happy with the outcome. The agreement meant Ella would live with Megan for three days and then Jay for three days, which complicated planning for any events or trips. Bonnie and I were saddened by the negotiations and disagreed with the three-days-here and three-days-there agreement. "I can't lose Ella," Bonnie said when the negotiations became more of a custody battle than simple visitation rights. In the end, cooler heads prevailed for Ella's benefit.

After COVID, Matt was living in an apartment and shared the news that he got a job selling lawn care services for a nationwide company. He was excited about sales and even talked about having fun knocking on doors as he cold-called neighborhoods. After his training, he showed us his notebook, which was full of pages of notes about everything related to lawn care. Bonnie and I recalled when we spent hours trying to get Matt to write a one-page book report, and now he was making copious notes on his own. What a transformation.

Bonnie not only still dealt with her own health issues, but in 2020 became the primary healthcare provider for her parents. Richard, then 87, had been showing signs of dementia for years. In September, Virginia, 82, had a stroke which hastened her own dementia. Bonnie and I chose early on to do everything we could to keep her parents in their home as long as possible. At first, Bonnie cooked meals and dropped them off, but as their dementia progressed, they needed someone to serve every meal and dispense their medications.

Bonnie initially took on the role by herself. We eventually hired Leslee, who lived across the street, to share the four daily trips for breakfast, lunch, dinner, and their 8 p.m. medication, which included Richard's insulin shot. Leslee had been doing in-home healthcare for several years and was between patients. The fit was perfect, as the duties were taking a toll on Bonnie's health.

Megan was also a great help as she worked for a home health company before being laid off during the pandemic. Megan and Bonnie signed Bonnie's parents up for Nursing and Rehab visits. Mobility and memory were the primary issues. Both tenaciously fought using any device like a cane or a walker. Sadly, several years earlier Richard gave up his hobby of R/C Airplane building that had made him a legend in the Tulsa area. He also quit volunteering at the Air & Space Museum. Instead, he'd decided to retire to his recliner and watch TV all day, which resulted in his barely being able to make it down the hall to the bathroom since he walked stooped over at about the same angle as he sat in his chair.

As the situation worsened, we met with Bonnie's brothers, who had been uninvolved in delivering their parents' care, and explained our plan. One said, "We don't have any money," which angered me. Bonnie shook her head.

"We aren't asking you for a dime, nor will we ever. We're just telling you what we're going to do to make your parents as comfortable as possible."

Richard and Virginia had a few falls but nothing serious enough to change our arrangement. They could still make it to the bathroom independently and take showers, but we didn't know how long we could continue. Bonnie was becoming more stressed over her parents as their care consumed a great deal of her time. I was as supportive as I could be and always on call when one of them fell, needed help working the TV remote, or just to drive Bonnie there and back.

Our backyard became our place of solitude. We used the space Bonnie created to get a break from caring for her parents. While we hosted family parties on every major holiday, we mostly had the place to ourselves. I installed a sound system at the pool, and we enjoyed sitting in or around the pool listening to music. My playlist for the pool mainly included Hawaiian music.

I was in the pool by myself after mowing and a song with a catchy tune came on that I hadn't heard before. "Lava" is from the Disney Pixar Short about two volcanoes in love—or *lava*, as the lyrics go. While this is a kid's movie, something about the lyrics hit me hard.

The next evening when Bonnie and I were in the pool, I told her I'd found a song that was written for us. "Lava" played over the speakers. We stared at each other and cried. Bonnie said through tears, "It's the perfect song." These ending lyrics spoke to our hearts:

> "I have a dream I hope will come true,
> That you're here with me, and I'm here with you.
> I wish that the earth, sea, and the sky up above
> Will send me someone to lava."
> Oh, they were so happy to finally meet above the sea.
> All together now, their lava grew and grew.
> No longer are they all alone, with aloha as their new home
> And when you visit them, this is what they sing:
> "I have a dream I hope will come true,

That you'll grow old with me, and I'll grow old with you. We thank the earth, sea and the sky, we thank you, too. I lava you."

"I lava you."
"I lava you."

Chapter Nine

2022

IN THE EARLY summer of 2022, Bonnie's primary doctor contacted her to schedule a routine colonoscopy. The procedure took place in August. Afterward, the doctor told us the results were nothing out of the ordinary. On our way home, Bonnie complained about abdominal pain. She called the gastroenterologist, who assured her nothing related to her colonoscopy could have caused her pain.

The pain continued, but, like so many times before, Bonnie kept to her schedule. By now, we had hired Megan to work with Leslee to provide care to take the load off Bonnie, but Bonnie still did whatever her parents needed, filling in when Megan and Leslee were unavailable.

In September, I decided to attend the IMTS Machine Tool Show in Chicago. I asked Bonnie to go with me to get away for a few days. She was still fighting abdominal pain but agreed to go. We made several stops along the way, including Mass at the Cathedral Basilica of Saint Louis, which was especially important because back in 1999, Bonnie, her Grandma Tilman, and others from St. Henry's traveled to St. Louis to see Pope John Paul II who celebrated Mass at the cathedral.

Afterward, we visited the National Shrine of Our Lady of Snows outside St. Louis. Bonnie spent extra time in the Lourdes Grotto as we prayed for healing. I wanted the trip to be special, so I booked a room at The Gwen on the Magnificent Mile. That room was the fanciest in which we ever stayed—which says a lot as I always did my best to spoil Bonnie whenever we traveled. I hoped she would go shopping while I went to the trade show. She did her best and went to the adjacent mall but stayed only briefly.

We slowly made our way home, arriving on September 15, one day before Bonnie's birthday. To celebrate her birthday, I surprised her again with a trip to Pawhuska, the home of The Pioneer Woman Mercantile. I booked a room at the Frontier Hotel where we had stayed before, but this time I planned an entire weekend.

I asked Bonnie if she wanted me to cancel, but in typical Bonnie fashion, she said, "No, it'll be fun." I should have canceled, but I wanted her to have a special birthday. On Saturday, we visited The Lodge where the Food Network's Pioneer Woman series is taped. We had fond memories of traveling to The Lodge with Uncle BJ and Aunt Carla when they visited from California. (They returned the favor every time we visited them, including trips to Napa Valley, the Skunk Train, Fort Bragg, and Mendocino).

Bonnie and I enjoyed so many trips and adventures together. Even though she was fighting pain, she always managed to make the most of everything we did. Most of the trips we took were centered around my work; some we planned together, and I surprised her with others. Once, Bonnie surprised me with a weekend getaway to the romantic Jarrett Farms Resort that's only a thirty-minute drive. I came home from work to find a suitcase sitting by the door as she said, "Take this to the car and let's go." We stayed in one of their bungalows and enjoyed a quiet weekend we both remember fondly.

When we arrived home from Pawhuska, Matt told us he was offered a promotion to Regional Sales Manager in Midland, Texas. We encouraged him to take the job as it meant a sizable bump in pay, but we were not without our concerns. Matt kept going back and forth, but he finally accepted the position. He was to report for work on November 1.

On October 15, Bonnie's pain was so bad it reminded me of the kidney stones I had when Ella was born. We decided to go to the ER, thinking they would give her some strong pain medication and send us home. I waited in the lobby because they were packed with patients, and we exchanged text messages. She told me she saw the doctors, gave blood and urine samples, and went for an EKG. Bonnie asked if those were the same tests they did for my kidney stones. Next was a CT scan with dye as we awaited the results. Her next text read: "Please come on up…no kidney stone, but something is on my pancreas…"

We were advised to contact an oncologist and sent home. Bonnie tried to reach her breast cancer oncologist, but he had retired. His office suggested the Oklahoma Cancer Specialists and Research Institute (OCSRI), and Bonnie made an appointment. She asked to be put on the Prayer List at St. Henry's for guidance for doctors.

Bonnie and I had a quiet night as we sat and talked about what this meant. "Not again," Bonnie said. "I don't want to go through this all over again." I tried to reassure her. We had no idea what was wrong, but we both knew this was not good.

The initial visit to the cancer clinic was positive, and we were impressed with the facility. More scans and biopsies were the next steps in determining a diagnosis and course of treatment. Bonnie and I were both more than concerned, especially after we started researching pancreatic cancer on the Internet, which was not a good idea but unavoidable.

We broke the news to Megan. When we told Matt, he wanted to refuse the promotion and move to Midland. Bonnie insisted he take the job. We did not even know what she had, so there was no reason for anyone to change plans. We had a going away party for Matt in The Shop with no one knowing what we might be facing.

The following week, I rented a U-Haul and towed Matt's car while he followed in my car with his cat Kirby.

While in Midland, I sat in the U-Haul and listened by speaker-phone as Bonnie and Megan met with the specialist who was going to do the biopsy on her pancreas the following week. Scans revealed the growth was in a tricky spot to get a specimen, so the procedure would be to go through Bonnie's throat and pierce her stomach lining to reach the area for biopsy. We reminded him about the hardware in her neck, but he assured us it would not be a problem. I made it home before the procedure.

I'd held Bonnie's hand as she waited to be taken back for surgery countless times before, but this time was different. The breast biopsy did not scare me, but this one did—not so much because of the risk involved but because of what they might find.

Bonnie went through the procedure without any issues, and the doctor told us he was able to get a good sample. She had the biopsy on a Friday, which meant a long weekend as we waited to hear back from the oncologist.

The weather was unusually warm for November, which is not uncommon in Oklahoma. We sat out on the back porch and talked about many things. At one point, Bonnie asked me, "Are you happy?"

"I am always happy when I'm with you." She pressed me, saying, "No. I mean, are you *really* happy with how our life turned out?"

"We've been through so much together, but I wouldn't change a thing other than when I hurt you."

"There's so much more I want us to do together." I started talking about Ella to change the subject, not wanting to upset her.

The following week, the doctor asked Bonnie to come in for more blood work and for a meeting. He told us the biopsy came back positive for pancreatic cancer Stage IV. The cancer had already spread to her liver. We both took a deep breath as we looked at each other, stunned by the news.

The oncologist wanted Bonnie to get a liver biopsy before she started chemo on December 6. He was hopeful the cancer had not spread and needed the liver biopsy to determine which chemo regimen to put Bonnie on. The biopsy was scheduled for November 23, the day before Thanksgiving.

For the last several years, Bonnie has been preparing two Thanksgiving dinners: one for our family and one for the family gathering at her parents' house. I would smoke the turkeys, and Bonnie would make everything else. Her brothers and some of their kids would show up just in time to eat and do little else to help. This year, I told Bonnie she would definitely not be cooking dinner for them or us. Instead, we ordered a turkey dinner with all the trimmings from Cracker Barrel for Bonnie's parents' gathering.

The day before Thanksgiving was busy. Megan picked the food up for Bonnie's parents' dinner and put it in their refrigerator. I took Bonnie for a PET Scan at the cancer center. By some odd twist, I had a long-standing appointment with my orthopedic surgeon to discuss possible knee surgery. At the meeting, I explained Bonnie's crisis, and my doctor agreed to cancel another knee surgery at that time—the third surgery I'd cancelled. I then took Bonnie to the hospital for her liver biopsy. Matt was also flying home to spend Thanksgiving with us and would arrive later in the evening.

The hospital was oddly quiet, especially in the outpatient surgery ward, as few elective procedures were scheduled the day before Thanksgiving. When they wheeled Bonnie back into recovery after the procedure, she was complaining of tremendous pain. She was almost in tears. They asked her to rate her pain on a scale of 1 to 10, to which she screamed, "*TWENTY!*"

She pointed out that the pain was mainly across her chest and shoulders. They started giving her pain medication, explaining that, in rare cases, the diaphragm will convulse after being punctured during a liver biopsy. Bonnie, of course, was one of those who experienced this side effect on the extreme end of the scale.

We got home midafternoon. Bonnie was heavily medicated but

still in pain. Matt called to say his flight was delayed due to weather, and, upon arrival in Dallas, he would have to spend the night at DFW. Bonnie would not have any of this. "Go get Matt and bring him home," she said. "All I'm doing is going to bed." Reluctantly, I got in the car and drove the four and a half hours from Owasso to DFW. In the car, I was in constant contact with Bonnie while Megan stayed with her.

I arrived at DFW at 9 p.m., just as Matt's plane from Midland arrived. At 9:30, Bonnie started vomiting, so Matt and I raced home. When we arrived, Bonnie was worse. I tried to take her to the ER, but she wanted Matt and me to get some sleep. I woke up at 8:15 a.m. as Bonnie started vomiting again, and we went to the local ER. When they took me back to be with her, I realized she was in ER Room #1. Bonnie, like me, knew exactly where she was and what had happened in this room just seven and a half years earlier when Rick passed away.

They administered IV medication for the nausea and did a CT scan, thinking there might be internal bleeding—another rare side effect of a liver biopsy. The tests showed no bleeding, but her liver enzymes were elevated and rising. She also had inflammation around her pancreas. They decided to transfer her by ambulance to the medical center in Tulsa where she was NPO (nothing per oral—no food or liquid).

They asked a lot of questions with the goal being pain and nausea management, and they continued to pump fluids into her through her IV. I went down to the cafeteria and had my turkey dinner, which was surprisingly good. As I sat there eating and crying, I could only think about all the Thanksgiving dinners Bonnie and Mom worked so hard to prepare out of their love for family.

I contacted Bonnie's family and friends at St. Henry's. I told them the situation and that she was in no condition for visitors. The prayer group at St. Henry's and similar prayer groups at other churches and denominations associated with Bonnie's family and friends were also offering nonstop prayers for Bonnie.

During the night, Bonnie started vomiting again. They did an ultrasound and started new nausea medications. She hadn't had water or food in over thirty-six hours. They decided to perform a sort of gastric reboot by flushing out her liver, after which they would slowly introduce a liquid diet.

Bonnie loved to decorate the house and just about everything else for Christmas. This usually took place the weekend after Thanksgiving. With Bonnie in the hospital, we decided to surprise her by putting up the tree and all the trimmings. This may sound like a minor thing, but to Bonnie, nothing is minor about decorating for the holidays. She has boxes of decorations for Christmas, Easter, Halloween, and Thanksgiving, as well as fall, winter, spring, and summer.

Christmas required the most logistics. When we lived in the two-story house, I gathered all her decorations from the closets and attic, which necessitated leaving both of our cars in the driveway to make room in the garage for all the Christmas decoration boxes.

With our plan in place and Bonnie resting, I left the hospital and came home to help Megan, Matt, and Ella, who were already hard at work. We faced many challenges, such as what theme to use on the tree. Bonnie had multiple sets of ornaments she rotated from year to year. Once Megan and Ella, our creative managers, made their choice, they started decorating the tree as I tried to display her many wall decorations and candles.

The next challenge was which Nativity to put out. Bonnie has at least a half dozen Nativity sets with all the bells and whistles. This debate took some time, with Ella making the final decision. Megan threw in a wrinkle by wanting to put up a second Christmas tree. We agreed, and she ordered one at the Michael's store nearest the hospital for me to pick up on my way back to the hospital for the evening.

By Sunday, Bonnie showed a slight improvement as she had started a liquid diet. The doctors determined she was suffering from pancreatitis, which we did not fully understand. I went to my usual 5 p.m. Sunday Mass where there was an outpouring of love and concern for Bonnie. Many said they were praying for her. After Mass, I took Matt to the airport where he reluctantly flew back to Midland. He told me he wanted to quit and come home several times, but I reminded him that his mother would never approve.

On the following Tuesday, while Bonnie was still in the hospital, Rhonda, one of her closest friends from St. Henry's, planned a rosary at 7 p.m. That afternoon, the liver biopsy results came back negative, which was our first good news in some time. They also implanted her port in preparation for next week's first chemo treatment. With Bonnie doing slightly better, I decided to go to the rosary.

Typically, these kinds of rosaries are held in the small chapel, but they decided to move the venue to the main sanctuary because of the anticipated turnout. Rhonda had found a rosary text written for cancer patients that included beautiful passages instead of the daily mysteries. Rhonda led the rosary, which was very moving as the text between prayers was perfect for what Bonnie was going through.

After the rosary, I walked to the front and did my best to hold it together as I thanked them for their prayers and added the results of Bonnie's liver biopsy, to which there were loud Amens and Alleluias reminiscent of a Free Will Baptist revival. I explained that the doctors had told us this result only meant the sample they had taken was negative. To which I added, "What do doctors know? We all know a miracle when we see one." Everyone felt God was answering our prayers and that the negative biopsy was the first of many miracles to come.

Those in attendance hugged me to show their love for Bonnie and their excitement for even the smallest bit of good news. Bonnie taught many of their children and grandchildren in pre-school, and others had known Bonnie her entire life. From the back of the crowd, I noticed someone nudging her way through clearly on a determined mission to reach me as quickly as she could.

The scene was almost comical as barely five-feet-tall Chris, whose husband had recently retired as the church's deacon, elbowed her way to me. She grabbed my hand, placed something in it, and closed my hand in hers. She gave me a private prayer while everyone else was rejoicing in the biopsy news and not paying any attention to us. When she finished, she said, "Put this on Bonnie, and never let her take it off." I looked down to see a Green Scapular.

Being a recent Catholic convert, I knew a little about scapulars. My research discovered that a Green Scapular asks God for physical healing or spiritual conversion. I returned to the hospital and cried as I told Bonnie how many of her friends were there, to which she said calmly, "That's our church." I continued telling Bonnie about how amazing the rosary was and about my encounter with Chris. I then placed the Green Scapular around Bonnie's neck.

On Wednesday, Bonnie tolerated some oatmeal and got the green light to go home. The rest of the week and the following weekend, she made slow progress, eating and drinking little while still experiencing nausea and abdominal pain.

Monday, December 5 at 7:15 p.m. I sent a text message to some family and friends about the following day's first chemo session, which would be different from the chemo she went through twelve years earlier. The regiment included several IV bags with 5-FU (fluorouracil) being the primary medication. Each treatment would take four to six hours repeated every two weeks for six months.

The tricky part was one of the medications was to be taken home in a portable pump that dispensed the medicine over the next forty-eight hours. The side effects were severe. They explained that one side effect was that Bonnie would not be able to eat, drink, or even touch anything cold when wearing the pump. Just placing her hand in the refrigerator could cause frostbite-like neuropathy in her hands and feet. As if chemo were not bad enough, now we had to worry about frostbite.

Once home, I put some of my Irwin Quick-Grip clamps on the refrigerator handles sealing the door shut with oven mitts attached just in case Bonnie forgot about the frostbite warning. She still experienced slight nausea but ate some soup and took her pills.

Tuesday, December 6 at 6:30 p.m. Bonnie started vomiting up what little she had in her. By 9:30, she progressed to a cycle of vomiting every thirty minutes. By midnight, you could set your watch and know exactly when she would hug one of her large plastic mixing bowls. When finished, I would clean out what little bile she was able to expel and get ready for the next round. Bonnie would say, "Oh, Randy, here it comes again," as I would hold her hair back and squeeze her as tight as I could.

We frequently spoke with the night nurse at the cancer clinic who offered several remedies. Some required me to make the thirty-minute round-trip drive to the local all-night pharmacy. Several times, I raced to and from the pharmacy before Bonnie's next round, which continued like clockwork all night.

Wednesday, December 7 at 8 a.m. We were in the lobby of the chemo clinic with her mixing bowl in hand. They immediately took her back to a chemo unit, removed the 5-FU pump, and started an IV to replenish her fluids. We stayed for a couple of hours, and Bonnie got some sleep. We went home, where she slept most of the day, night, and following day.

To see Bonnie's strength was amazing as she hugged her mixing bowl all night announcing, "Here we go again." I was always proud of Bonnie's courage during her many medical challenges, but I was never prouder of her than I was during the previous twenty-four hours.

They decided Bonnie would come in daily for IV fluids. She could not tolerate anything by mouth. The nausea medication, especially the wrist gel, eased the actual vomiting. However, she constantly felt like she would start again, so she kept her mixing bowl within reach. Sleep was her only peace, but she complained about vivid dreams.

Sunday, December 11. We still had no answer as to why she was having so much nausea. The nausea got worse that night, and I took her to the ER where we were told it might take three or four days to get back into the medical center. They were able to stabilize her nausea and pain as they ran more blood tests and another CT scan. She soon responded to the new medication, and they sent us home with medication she could dissolve under her tongue.

Friday, December 16. After a rough night, we were back at the chemo clinic. The chemo lab at the cancer center was huge. They could administer chemo to over sixty-five patients at a time. Bonnie was sleeping with her headphones on when I heard a commotion. In the lobby, I could see Mr. and Mrs. Claus and elves approaching with an entourage singing Christmas carols. I also noticed they had a therapy dog. An advance person stopped at each cubicle, asking if the patient wanted Santa to visit or a picture with the dog. Immediately I said no to both. While Bonnie would have welcomed Santa, neither of us wanted to see the therapy dog.

Only a few months earlier, Ozzie had started losing weight, and his health began to decline. They tried several procedures to help him. By this time, I would have put a mortgage on the house to pay for any procedure Ozzie needed. He won over my heart long ago every time we walked into the house and saw his face after one of Bonnie's chemo or radiation treatments, or after visiting Matt in the in-house facility, or after Rick's funeral, or so many other times when he brightened our spirits.

In July, Ozzie could no longer stand or control his bowels or bladder. He made his final trip to Family Animal Medicine. I carried him into their private room where we watched him take his last breath as we wept. We all took Ozzie's loss hard. Bonnie and I had him cremated and placed his urn on a prominent shelf in our living room. Bonnie made a beautiful shadowbox with pictures, his collar, and one of his yellow tennis balls that he'd chase until his legs fell off. We truly lost a family member.

The wounds of Ozzie's loss were too deep for both of us. If asked to hold a dog for a picture, we would have both lost it. As I write or reread anything about Ozzie on these pages, I have to reach for Kleenex as I cry every time think about Ozzie.

With her headphones on, Bonnie was still asleep when the parade passed. Some ladies pushing a cart were handing out blankets to the patients. I recognized LeAnne Taylor, a breast cancer survivor and morning anchor on a local TV station. Several years ago, Bonnie and I walked in one of her breast cancer events at the baseball park downtown. I nodded to her as they passed while Bonnie slept. When the parade reached the other side of the room, LeAnne returned with a blanket and handed it to me, saying, "I just want her to have this."

I looked closer and saw it was a beautiful handmade quilt. I held it as I cried, thinking of Ozzie and Bonnie's love for sewing and the many things she had made for our children, for friends at church, and for all our nieces, nephews and grandnieces and nephews. She also embroidered work shirts for my old company and Kim's company.

Bonnie woke up, and I explained the parade and quilt. She held the quilt close and said, "They're who I want to have my fabric," referring to whoever made the quilt.

Up to this point, we only talked about how we were going to fight cancer and not about mortality. Holding back tears, I said, "That's a good idea."

During Bonnie's diagnosis and trips to the hospital, I kept family and friends updated. Most people would have used Facebook or Instagram accounts, but not me. I don't have any social media accounts. I do have a LinkedIn account, but I've have never posted anything on it. My problem or excuse is that my workload keeps me too busy for social media. The truth is that my lifelong lack of social skills or interest in sharing details about myself with strangers keeps me from social media. At home, Bonnie kept me informed about our family and friends through her Facebook account. This left me at a major disadvantage as to how to share important news about Bonnie's health with family and friends.

I knew I did not want to use Bonnie's Facebook account for such personal information, so I texted. Having sold software for thirty plus years and being the IT person who kept our software and computers running, one would think I would have created a website, blog, or email broadcast. Not me. I could have set up a group email or group text, but what if group members took offense regarding who was/was not included? This silly notion rattled around in my head, which made no sense when you think about it, but I have a history of overthinking things.

Bonnie's sweet nature made her a close friend to many—dare I say countless—family and friends, many of whom considered her their best friend. I was under enough pressure to share as much as possible without risking offending someone or leaving one of her best friends off my group text.

My poorly conceived plan included typing a single text to Megan or Leslee on my phone in real-time. I would then manually copy and paste the text message one at a time to about twenty other individual phones or groups, hoping they would pass my message on. Texting is not my preferred communication; I prefer email. I do not have Megan's text typing skills.

When Megan was in high school, AT&T called to discuss additional charges on my next bill. They explained how Megan had sent nearly 40,000 text messages the previous month, which they considered a possible record. How Megan became so proficient at texting on an early flip phone in the days before smartphones is unclear. Still, she almost managed to send one text every minute of every hour of every day when you consider the average month has 43,800 minutes.

My next problem was that I typed every text on my iPhone with my index finger. Hence, it took a while for me to compose the master text, which I then copied and pasted to send to the other phones. There was yet another problem. Due to the technical nature of my work, I tend to over-explain things, so my emails are longer than most; thus, my text messages reflect my same verbose attention to detail.

On the day Bonnie got the quilt at the chemo clinic, I sent this text using my unconventional manual daisy-chain texting method:

Dec. 16, 10:51 am

"We're at the chemo clinic. They've put her on fluids and are planning to start a new nausea medication. We'll be coming back on Monday for more fluids anda CT scan to check for blockages. She shouldn't be throwing up for this long after chemo. We might have to come in every day for more fluids since she can't take enough by mouth."

Bonnie and I came home, and she continued to struggle with nausea. She always kept that same mixing bowl beside her, saying, "This is getting old. I've got things I need to do." Several times, Bonnie expressed concern about shopping, particularly for stocking stuffers.

Every year, Bonnie always enjoyed filling the stockings. Her stockings, which she designed and created, were elaborate. Since her initial illness in October, Bonnie understandably had not done as much Christmas shopping as usual other than some online gifts. She had nothing to put in the stockings, which she mentioned often.

Saturday, December 17. Bonnie told me she wanted to go to Target for stocking stuffers. I tried to argue, but Bonnie's mind was made up, so all I could do was to figure out how to do it as safely as possible. When we arrived at the store, I grabbed a shopping cart in the parking lot for her to lean on. We made it as far as cosmetics when Bonnie said, "I've had enough. I'm pooped." and we slowly headed to the checkout.

While I was in the checkout line, Bonnie wandered to a kiosk nearby where something for a stocking caught her eye. Denise, the business manager for St. Henry's, came up behind me, surprised I was at the store after Bonnie's recent release that someone must have shared on Facebook said, How's Bonnie?"

I rolled my eyes and pointed toward Bonnie a few feet away. Denise did a double-take as I said, "It's her first Christmas shopping trip of the year, and I couldn't have stopped her if I wanted to."

Once home, Bonnie admitted her decision to go to Target may not have been the best. She was worn out. She rested that evening, still fighting nausea, and decided to go to bed early. One of our routines for a few years was she would go to bed alone while I sat up watching TV until I fell asleep. I would later try to come to bed without waking her. Sometimes it worked, sometimes it didn't. Bonnie was always frustrated that I could fall asleep in minutes while she struggled every night. She would have trouble going back to sleep if I made any noise.

Sunday, December 18. When I made it to bed, she was sound asleep. Around 7 a.m., I woke up, but Bonnie was still asleep. I eased out of bed to let her sleep and was surprised she did not wake up. I checked in on her about every twenty minutes, but she was still asleep. Around 8:30, I walked in and could tell she'd had an accident. I started trying to wake her up, and she slowly responded, but her speech was slurred, which scared me. This was not like her prior seizures, so I know that wasn't it. She wanted to get up but could not walk or talk clearly. I helped her to the bathroom, which is only about eight paces from her side of the bed.

I thought she may have had a stroke, so I called 911. The dispatcher asked about her symptoms. They questioned my stroke theory but said the paramedics were on their way. She still could not speak as I tried to get her out of her nightgown and clean her up. I could not do it by myself, so all I could do was wait for the ambulance.

The paramedics wheeled the gurney to the end of the hall. I gave them her symptoms and mentioned a possible stroke. One asked Bonnie to smile, which she did, confirming it was not a stroke. They mentioned concern about a cardiac event.

They got her in the ambulance, then asked about her medications. They said they could not get a blood pressure reading and were leaving for the medical center. I restocked her bag of clothes that I'd taken to a hospital too many times over the last few weeks and drove to the Tulsa ER. The waiting room was packed. Thirty minutes passed before I was taken back to be with her. Bonnie was now alert and able to talk. Several IVs were attached to her.

The hospitalist told us her BP was 40/20 when she arrived. Her low blood pressure caused her mobility and speech issues. They were concerned she had an infection and also about her kidneys. The next step was a full CAT scan to find the infection, but they needed to stabilize her blood pressure before they could move her. Two nurses came in to give her another IV and said it should help her BP.

Bonnie and I were fixated on her monitor as her BP barely changed. The nurses returned and shook their heads. Through the glass, I saw a huddle at the nurse's station. They returned with another IV saying, "This should work." Minutes later, they returned even more baffled when that IV made no difference.

By this time, seven IV bags were connected to Bonnie. She remained alert, but we were both concerned as we watched her monitor for any BP improvement. We also noticed severe spikes in her heart rate, fluctuating between 110 and 185 over two seconds and then racing back to 90. They explained as if it were no big deal that the IVs they were giving her to raise her blood pressure were the cause. They were focused on her blood pressure, which was not improving.

They brought another IV saying, "This one should work." I waited with my eyes fixed on the monitor as Bonnie slept. Within twenty minutes, her BP was 65/50, which was good enough for them to take her for the CAT scan. I took a break. Leaving her ER room, I almost bumped into a large cart by her door. The cart was clearly in the way, so I asked the nurse if I could move it. She said they had to keep the Crash Cart next to Bonnie's room. That was a gut punch as I was coming to grips with just how serious Bonnie's condition was.

Bonnie came back from the CAT scan, and the nurses prepared to move her to the ICU. Nurses and doctors, including those who had never been in Bonnie's room, came to watch Bonnie being wheeled to the elevator. They either knew Bonnie's case was unique, or they were offering prayers for her.

In the ICU, Bonnie was surrounded by nurses who asked me to leave as they settled her in. They hooked her up to even more monitors, and consolidated the IVs while commenting on how differently the ER staff and ICU staff attached IVs. While the ER staff was excellent and attentive, Bonnie received considerably more attention in the ICU. I sent another text:

Dec. 18, 7:49 pm

"Resting in the ICU. They did the CAT Scan, but it won't be until the morning before the Doctors review the tests. Her heart rate goes from 116-180 in seconds. They think it might be from the BP meds. Otherwise, she's sleeping when she's not being poked like she is now. They now have 7 bags going and need to add another one. Because of Breast Cancer they can only use her left arm so they're running out of places to poke her."

While Bonnie's blood pressure stabilized, her heart rate was all over the place. She slept a lot, but when she was awake, she talked as calmly as if we were home in her recliner. "Did you get something to eat?" she'd say, or "Why don't you go home and get some rest?"

"Wild horses couldn't drag me away."

The hospitalist explained why the ER staff paid so much attention to Bonnie. "The IVs they gave her are called *pressors*—the technical term is a vasopressor. A pressor is a form of life support. Patients usually only need one pressor to stabilize low blood pressure. Bonnie required three pressors, which is rare." No other details were shared.

We settled in for the night as Bonnie's medication allowed her to sleep, and I grabbed a cat nap on the couch. They offered a cot, but I did not want to fall asleep or be in the way if something happened in the middle of the night. The night nurse was helpful, and Bonnie felt comfortable enough to ask her some direct questions: "When can I go home?"

"You won't leave this room," the nurse said, "until we can remove all three pressors."

Bonnie and I were startled at this and just looked at each other. Realizing how serious this situation was, I called Megan in the middle of the night and asked her to come so she could be at her mother's side. I also called Matt who quickly left Midland.

The doctors arrived early the next morning. They started by telling Bonnie she was the first patient they had ever had a conversation with who was attached to three pressors. Patients with three pressors were usually comatose. They explained that Bonnie was suffering from sepsis shock because of her pancreatitis. She had multiple organ failures, including her kidneys, liver, and heart, which were only functioning now because of the pressors. They mentioned that some people from the dialysis unit would stop by to discuss options.

I sent this text to Leslee and a slightly modified text to the others:

Dec. 19 8:58 am

"I need to prepare you. Some major changes last night. We learned that the meds that Bonnie is on are what is keeping her alive. She has sepsis and multiple organ failure, including her kidneys, liver, and heart. Someone is coming in this morning to talk about dialysis to buy her some more time. We've got Matt heading this way.

She is alert and can talk now, but that may change. Please let anyone in the family who wants to see her to come to the 8th Floor Main Waiting Room. They only allow 2 people at a time."

Bonnie and I could not believe what we were hearing. The dialysis doctor soon came in and explained a procedure where they could put Bonnie on nonstop dialysis. They explained some patients respond, and others do not. I remembered that dialysis, one of the last things the hospital tried with my mom back in 2008, did not help.

They explained that the procedure included inserting a catheter in her neck. I was reluctant to put Bonnie through this. We both became confused. The earlier group of doctors told us Bonnie's organs had failed, and only IV pressors were keeping her alive; now the dialysis team was telling us about a hit-or-miss procedure.

Unsure what to think, I left the room to find the day nurse and ask her advice. She was reluctant when asked what she would do, but told me, "A patient down the hall tried this procedure, and it failed, but if we don't try, she might only have hours to live." I told Bonnie exactly what the nurse said. After a brief discussion, we decided to go through with the procedure.

Matt arrived from Midland and told his mom he wanted her to have her Christmas gift early. He gave her a large grey fleece blanket. Bonnie immediately asked Matt to cover her with it. When Matt put the blanket on her, she smiled for the first time in days.

The next to visit was the palliative doctor from Bonnie's cancer clinic. I had only recently discovered that palliative medicine is for patients with terminal illness. This doctor had a bedside manner in a good way that neither Bonnie nor I had ever seen. That's saying a lot, given Bonnie's history and the scores of doctors she encountered. He explained that his role was to help improve Bonnie's quality of life. While he did not make any promises, his was a special visit that gave us hope and one that neither of us would forget.

The two women hospitalists who were with Bonnie from the ER would insert the catheter which, due to Bonnie's condition, would take place in her ICU room. They told Megan and me we could stay, but being squeamish at the sight of blood, I chose to wait in the hall. I kissed Bonnie, and the doctor asked me to take her necklaces as I left. Bonnie wore a long chain with the miraculous medal of Mary for many years. I removed the medal and Green Scapular Chris from St. Henry's gave me at Bonnie's Rosary.

As I waited in the hall, I could see through the cracks in the blinds as one of the doctors stood on a step ladder wrenching the catheter into her neck, as if she were trying to fit a round peg into a square hole. She used all her leverage twisting and turning as she tried to insert the catheter.

This went on for a long time as I looked away from the window many times. Megan later told me her mom kept saying, "Oh, I'm so sorry you're having so much trouble," as if it were her fault. Yes, Bonnie was awake while they were trying to force the catheter tube down the side of her neck.

One doctor came out to tell me they could not insert the catheter, so it would have to be inserted through her groin, which is usually done under general anesthesia. She added, "This will be even more painful as all we can use is a local pain shot." Megan remained in the room as I waited outside in the hall until the procedure was finished.

When I walked in, Bonnie looked like she had been in a fight with a tiger. "How are you doing, sweetheart?"

Calmly she said, 'I do NOT want to do that again.' Megan rolled her eyes and shook her head, telling me all I needed to know about how difficult the procedure was.

By now, family and friends were assembling in the waiting room to take turns visiting Bonnie. Megan and I were walking toward the waiting room when an alarm went off. "*Code Blue!*" sounded over the speaker. We moved aside as a rush of personnel and equipment raced to the end of the hall and turned right toward Bonnie's room.

Megan and I quickly followed. The emergency was in the room next to Bonnie's. Seeing the hospital's response caused me to break down. I tried to walk away to cry in private. Megan was also moved but unsure why I was so upset. "Because this is what we may eventually see going into Mom's room and how we'll lose her."

After I gathered myself, we returned to Bonnie's room, which was blocked by all the staff standing in the hall. I began to tear up again, but this time not about Bonnie. Instead, I was moved by the sight of the doctors and nurses outside the room. They stood, silently watching those working inside, waiting to go in and take over if someone faltered. The scene was surreal. I was sad over the crisis for the patient's sake, but at the same time, my heart was filled with the love and compassion exhibited by these doctors and nurses in the hall. Bonnie was asleep and unaware of what was taking place—no surprise after all she'd been through with the catheter.

Visitors came to see Bonnie and comfort us. From the text messages, they knew she was in the battle of her life, and all commented on how alert she was during their visits. Bonnie's brothers arrived and had some private time with her.

After their visit, I walked them to the waiting room and reminded them that Bonnie was their parents' POA. "If she dies tonight, you'll be taking over."

They asked, "What's a POA?" I explained the duties. "Oh, we don't want to do that." Their answer didn't come as a surprise. I told them Megan was willing to take over POA duties if needed, to which they agreed.

Bonnie continued intermittently to sleep and greet every visitor who came by. She especially wanted to see Leslee's daughter Kaci, who, since Covid, had not attended family gatherings at The Shop. When she was younger, Kaci spent a lot of time together at our house with Megan, and Bonnie always had special affection for her. She arrived, and we gave them some private time.

As I stared at Bonnie while she slept, I noticed her breathing was now a two-step process. Her abdomen would rise when she exhaled, and her chest would rise when she inhaled. I asked the nurse if this was normal. "No, the sepsis fluid causes this, and it's not good." We noticed a large cart full of boxes in the hall, and I was told it was Bonnie's dialectic fluid.

For as long as I have known Bonnie, if she ever saw anything out of place, she did her best to fix it, so there was no reason for her to be any different at the hospital. She heard what sounded like water leaking in the toilet and told the nurse she thought the toilet was broken. "Oh, no, honey," the nurse replied. "That's you." She pointed to the clear plastic tube snaking its way from the dialysis machine, along the wall, and eventually draining into the toilet.

Tuesday, December 20. In the middle of the night, the nurse's pushing buttons on Bonnie's infusion pump woke me. She whispered that she was turning off one of the pressors. She might as well have splashed me with water as I jumped up asking her to explain. "We're just trying to see how she'll respond." While it was truly a miracle that they could remove one pressor, Bonnie still had two pressors attached.

Around 4 a.m., the nurse turned off a second pressor. My eyes were now glued to the monitor as I waited impatiently for every screen refresh to see her new BP and heart rate. The next sign Bonnie was improving was she needed a bedpan. The nurse explained this meant she was regaining kidney function. This good news had to be shared, so I sent the following text with pictures:

Dec. 20, 7:38 am

"This is what a miracle looks like. It is her Dialysis machine and her dolly full of dialysis fluids. After one night of treatment, they have turned OFF two pressors, which means her heart is back in business. One side effect is that she is on a bedpan regularly as her body is starting to do what it's supposed to. So, while we are glad for all the visitors yesterday, today might be a bit awkward with the bedpan. Next is to work on urine output then drinking and eating."

Next to visit were the doctors who had diagnosed her sepsis shock. One asked Bonnie, "What are your plans?"

Bonnie looked at Megan and me. "I want to see the birth of my granddaughter. My daughter and her fiancé Ray are expecting a baby in June."

The doctor responded immediately. "You won't be here for that."

Bonnie gave me a look I had never seen before: disbelief at hearing someone for the first time tell her she did not have long to live. Megan started to cry. All I could do was look back into Bonnie's beautiful eyes—those same eyes that stole my heart in a meadow in 1973. We continued staring at each other as we tried to accept the doctor's words.

When Megan and the doctor left, Bonnie said, "But I don't feel like I'm going to die. Randy, what are we going to do?"

"You're going to keep fighting like you always have."

"I'll get to see your mom before you do."

When Megan returned, I said, "I have something to tell you, Megan." To everyone's surprise, including mine, I told Megan how little I participated in her adoption, how her mother had done all the work. We never shared that at the time, I didn't want children because of my mental illness, and only because of her mother had she come into our lives. I apologized to Megan while Bonnie watched quietly. "This doesn't change how much I love you. I just want you to know how important your mother was in bringing you into our family." I felt I needed Megan to know the truth about her adoption in front of her mother. Given the doctor's grim news, I didn't want this to be a secret or something I shared much later.

Next came the dialysis doctors, joined by the palliative doctor. The kidney doctors shared their excitement, telling us they had never seen a patient respond so quickly to the dialysis treatment. After the previous doctor's devastating comment, we were not as excited as the kidney doctors at Bonnie's miraculous response. They turned off the last pressor and turned off the dialysis machine to test her kidneys as we anxiously waited.

The palliative doctor said, "If Bonnie remains stable and her kidneys start working on their own, there is a small window we can get her home on hospice care."

"I want to go home," Bonnie immediately responded. She didn't need to elaborate. I knew what she meant.

The hospitalist added, "There's a risk you may not survive the ambulance ride." She explained that Bonnie had a DNR (do not resuscitate) in place.

I cut her off. "I'm Bonnie's husband, and I cancel the DNR. I want the paramedics to do everything in their power to get Bonnie home to see her granddaughter." I couldn't forget the negative impact not seeing my mother while she was in the ICU had on Matt. I wanted Ella, who could not visit the ICU, to see her beloved grandma at least one more time.

How quickly our mood changed from the blow about Bonnie's mortality to our excitement about getting Bonnie home. We stopped thinking about any final outcome as we now focused on this latest miracle: Bonnie was coming home.

Tuesday, December 20, 10:30 a.m. Significant logistics were required to get Bonnie home. First was a visit by a third-party hospice person based in the hospital who explained the process adding, "You can consult with other hospice providers to compare services." We quickly dismissed wasting time shopping around and signed the papers to get the ball rolling.

Hospice scheduled delivery of the bed and other equipment for 3:30-4 p.m., the same time we scheduled hospital transport. Next, we made space at home. Bonnie and I decided to use the small back bedroom, our home office and Ella's playroom, where we'd installed a Murphy bed to make more room for Ella to play. We had a lot to do, but today's news that Bonnie was going home gave us hope.

I called Megan, who, along with Matt and her ex-husband Jay, with Ella's help, emptied the back bedroom, placing most items in Bonnie's sewing room and sunroom. I called the Murphy bed people who sent a team to move the bed, which they reattached to a wall in The Shop.

Bonnie remained stable as things were falling into place. Then I got a text from Megan who'd had lunch duty at Bonnie's parents. She sent a picture of a water cut-off notice on their front door. We'd neglect to pay their water bill—which was understandable. Bonnie, of course, was the most upset and blamed herself for not taking care of it. I stopped what I was doing, got on the phone with the City of Owasso, and navigated my way through their third-party delinquent payment provider. Paying the bill could only be done online, a painful process on my laptop given the hospital's 0.25 Mbps Internet speed.

Around 1p.m., I left Bonnie to go home so I could help with preparations and meet the hospice delivery people to sign more papers. When I arrived, I was amazed at the job Megan, Matt, Jay, and Ella had done to clear the bedroom and coordinate the Murphy bed transfer. They left one cabinet with Bonnie's photo albums and some of her potted plants.

The hospice truck arrived around 2:30. They quickly brought in and set up the bed, wheelchair, and other supplies. Around 3:30, the ICU nurse called to tell me they were waiting for the ambulance that was on a call. By 4:30, Bonnie was on her way home as we prayed for her safe arrival. The hospice nurse was already at our house waiting for the ambulance.

When the ambulance arrived, we could hardly wait for them to unload Bonnie. No one was more excited than Ella who held Bonnie's hand as they wheeled her into the house and down the hall. Trying to get six-year-old Ella out of the way was pointless as Bonnie was not going to let anything come between her and Ella.

The hospice nurse settled Bonnie in and taught us how to use her medication, oxygen, and aspirator if she began to choke. We only asked a couple of family members and Father Matt to come by. Bonnie was getting stronger and able to engage with visitors. As we settled in for the night, Megan and Ella wanted to sleep next to Bonnie, so I created a pallet for them on the floor to make it as comfortable as possible. Matt slept in The Shop, and I slept in our bed just across the hall.

Wednesday, December 21, 4 a.m. I was awakened by the sound of heavy breathing, reminiscent of the times Bonnie had seizures. Megan and Ella were already awake when I made it to her bed. We tried to wake Bonnie, but she did not respond. Her labored breathing reminded me of my mom's breathing the night she died. I ran out to The Shop and woke Matt. It started snowing as we raced back to Bonnie's side.

Bonnie's breathing became shallow, which worried us even more. Megan called the hospice nurse who said she may not have much time. The snow was piling up, so the nurse could not come out until later that morning. In Oklahoma, an inch of snow causes school and church closures.

We tried everything we could to get Bonnie to respond, including saying silly things to which she would have responded if only to correct us. At times, her breathing was so shallow we thought we were going to lose her—then she'd gasp and breathe heavily again.

This continued repeatedly for hours. Some moments her breathing was so shallow I said, "If it's time to go, babe, don't be afraid," as we all including Ella stayed by her side. The next day, I sent the following text update:

Dec. 21, 9:18 a.m.

"I think the end is near, but Bonnie is still fighting. She's been unresponsive since 4:00 am but continues to hang on. Megan, Matt, and Ella are here."

I sent Leslee a second text: "Prepare the family for bad news. I'll keep you updated."

Nothing we could do changed Bonnie's breathing or made her respond. With the roads nearly unpassable, I called close friends and family, asking if they wanted to talk to her on the phone. I explained the situation and that it may be the last time they would be able to speak to her.

I held my phone next to Bonnie's ear as, one by one, they talked to her in what may have been the most difficult phone call any of them ever made. I made over a dozen phone calls. Some used their speakerphone so everyone in the room could talk to Bonnie. Each call was harder and harder as each person was put on the spot to think of what their last words to Bonnie might be.

Around 2 p.m., Father Matt came by to offer the Viaticum (communion for someone near death) and Extreme Unction, more commonly known as the Last Rites. This ritual was strikingly different from the Anointing of the Sick. Father Matt's readings and prayers and placing a fraction of the Blessed Eucharist between Bonnie's lips was both somber and comforting. I walked Father Matt out and discussed possible dates for the rosary and funeral Mass, then sent the following text:

Dec. 21, 2:54 pm

"Bonnie is still fighting. Father Matt just left. He offered her the Viaticum.

She no longer physically responds to our voices, but that isn't going to stop us."

Even though Bonnie was not responding to anything we said or did, we kept talking to her, hoping she could hear us. I sat in the chair beside her, leaned over, and stroked her cheek. I looked down and noticed she was not wearing the long chain she always wore with a miraculous medal of Mary.

I thought of the rare times I'd seen her without her medal. I tried to remember where she got it and when she started wearing it. I remembered times when she had to get a new chain when one would wear out. Bonnie did not like a tight chain around her neck, especially after the plate had been inserted. She always needed to get a larger chain than usual to feel comfortable. I found her miraculous medal and carefully placed it around her neck.

I kept looking at her face. *Something else isn't right.* I couldn't put my finger on what was missing...

The next ten minutes played out like thirty as I jumped up and raced around the house. Megan and Matt were trying to calm me down, and Ella must have thought I was acting crazy as I ran all over the house, yelling, "Oh, God, please let me find it, oh, please!" I ran into the garage and looked through our cars, followed by a search of the kitchen cabinets and the bathrooms.

When I reached the bedroom, I went through all the drawers—then realized I needed to look in the hamper. I dug through the basket, throwing all the items in the hamper into the air. Then I felt it in a pair of pants. I fell on my knees, crying, then raced back to Bonnie's side. As Megan, Matt, and Ella stared in disbelief at how crazy I was acting, I carefully placed the Green Scapular around Bonnie's neck.

Minutes later, Megan and Ella changed places with me, saying over and over, *I love you, Mama* and *Love you, Grandma*—

Bonnie's lips moved. "Love you." Her voice was weak, but her words were clear, and we all jumped for joy.

Bonnie started tugging at the bandage on her groin from the catheter. I moved her hand several times asking her to leave it alone when she pulled her hand out of mine. "STOP!" She pulled the sheets back and pointed to a loose edge on the bandage with her eyes partially open. "See? This is sticking up." She then made "cat claws" at me with her hands and added sarcastically, "I was just trying to show you,"

I went through my painstakingly slow one-by-one text notifications and gave everyone the good news of Bonnie's first words. My phone started to blow up as people were asking if this was medically induced. I explained she had not taken any pain medication since the hospital.

One minute, I was talking to Father Matt about funeral arrangements, and now, we are laughing and dancing around the room euphorically. Quickly forgotten were the past twelve hours of agony as countless times we and those on the phone with Bonnie saw her near death.

Bonnie asked for some hot tea, which set in motion one of many times when we would run down the hall tripping over each other like Keystone Cops on steroids to do whatever she commanded. (If you're unfamiliar with the Keystone Cops, look them up. You'll get the idea.)

Limiting the spillage, we returned with the hot tea, which she did not touch. "I'm trying to wake up," she said. Quite an understatement. We told her about the snow, and she said, "Uh-huh." So, we opened the curtains to show her the four inches on the ground. She shook her head in amazement and went back to sleep, breathing normally.

Megan, Matt, Ella, and I continued to look at Bonnie as we tried to come to grips with the miracle we had just witnessed. We also looked at each other without saying a word, reflecting on what we had been through on that longest and most difficult day.

The hospice nurse came by and told us Bonnie's vitals were stable and that she might have been experiencing a "rally," which I remembered Mom did not long before she died.

None of us were going to leave Bonnie's side as we had no idea what might happen. While Bonnie slept peacefully, Megan and Ella used sign language and hand signals to talk to each other. Matt chimed in as they tried to remember the alphabet in sign language. I leaned over to Bonnie, who was sleeping and whispered, "Your kids are doing sign language." We all laughed. With her eyes still closed, Bonnie said, "It's for Santa and the deaf kids." She paused. "I've had a rough day. I want some pancakes, waffles, and bacon."

Now awake, she had her first sip of water. She kept asking to get dressed, so we helped her stand and put her robe on. I immediately—a relative term given how slow my text message method was—notified everyone that Bonnie was awake and invited anyone who wanted to brave the road conditions to visit her.

In Oklahoma, we rarely get snow without ice before, during, or afterward. This storm was no exception. A glaze of ice under four inches of snow made driving hazardous. I ran outside to shovel snow and scrape ice off the driveway.

Several risked the drive to see Bonnie as a kind of pilgrimage to witness the miracle for themselves. Even if it was a rally, Bonnie was now awake and coherent, so I wanted to make the most use of the time we had.

Rhonda and her husband Embry were among those who came. Rhonda organized the rosary for Bonnie. As Rhonda and Bonnie visited, Embry asked me to step into the hall. He said, "Do you want to get Bonnie's parents over here?"

I immediately broke down. Embry tried to console me as I said, "I forgot about them. Oh, yes, thank you."

Bonnie's parents' dementia made it hard for them to understand what was going on. During Bonnie's hospital stays and difficult times at home, I visited them, and they always asked where Bonnie was. I'd explain she was extremely sick, but I knew they didn't grasp how serious her condition was. No way could I take them to the ICU, so I had no plan for how Bonnie might see them.

Embry's suggestion was a gift from God. It was evening when we hopped into my Subaru and drove the five miles to Richard and Virginia's house. I told them to get their shoes and coats on so they could see Bonnie. Richard did not want to budge from his chair and movie while Virginia asked questions. Not wanting to waste time, I told them I would explain in the car.

Once in the car, I explained that Bonnie's condition was serious, and that this may be the last time they would see her. Virginia kept shaking her head saying it was not that bad, while Richard said little. I thanked them for raising such a sweet person, and told them how much Bonnie meant to me and how thankful I was to have Bonnie in my life. The drive took about fifteen minutes, and I did not stop talking the entire way.

I took them to the bedroom where I placed two chairs close to the bed. Virginia moved her chair back, and Richard pushed his chair as far away as he could. "Bonnie will be fine," Virginia said. "There's no reason for all this fuss." I added more details about Bonnie's condition and urged them to hug and kiss her. Richard made jokes like he always did. They didn't understand what I was telling them.

By this time, Bonnie was getting tired and dozing off as Virginia talked about whatever her boys were doing. Ella was in the room and said, "Love you, Grandma," which always perked Bonnie up and made her say *love you, too* back. As Virginia kept talking about random topics and Bonnie kept nodding off, I would say *do your thing, Ella*, and she would repeat *love you, Grandma*, which unfailingly got a response from Bonnie.

After ten minutes, Richard said, "Well, it's about time to get home."

"But this may be the last time you see Bonnie," I told him again.

He shrugged his shoulders and said, "That's too bad."

I tried to prolong the visit as long as I could, but even Virginia told me she was ready to go. Virginia touched Bonnie on the head, and Richard said goodbye as they both headed down the hall, leaving me looking at Bonnie and shaking my head. On the return trip, I again talked the whole way, sharing my feelings and love for Bonnie.

Back home, I saw an opportunity. Bonnie and I knew Megan and Ray were expecting a baby, but Ella did not. Megan planned on telling Ella on Christmas Day. Given the situation, we decided to tell her that night while we had time so Bonnie could share in the event. Megan, Ray, and I were in the room with Bonnie as Megan told her, "You are going to be a Big Sister," and showed her the sonogram photos. Bonnie and I held hands as we watched Ella's eyes light up as she screamed. Six-year-old Ella had been a very tough and brave girl during those dark hours when we thought we lost her grandma. She posed for a picture beside Bonnie, holding the ultrasound photos of Gemma, Bonnie's second granddaughter.

We got ready for bed wanting to stay as close to Bonnie as possible. I planned to sleep in a kitchen chair beside her while Matt slept in our bed. I was having trouble sleeping, so I went to my recliner. Megan and Ella were sleeping on a pallet on the floor. At 2:45 a.m., Megan rolled over and saw Bonnie's feet dangling off the side of the bed unique to her vantage point from the floor. She jumped up as Bonnie said, "I want to sit up." Megan ran in to wake me, and we did another Jack and Jill routine—tripping over each other down the hall. When we reached the door, Bonnie was already sitting up.

I ran into our bedroom and heard Matt talking, so I assumed he was on the phone. I turned on the light and yelled at him to get up, thinking he was wide awake. He stumbled about mumbling, "Where's my pants?" "Forget your pants. Come on!" We ran back and hugged Bonnie, crying with joy. Then I asked Matt, "Who were you talking to?" "No one." We decided later that what I heard was Matt practicing a sales pitch in his sleep.

We helped Bonnie back into bed, but I would not be out of position again, so I stayed in a chair next to her and catnapped. At 6 a.m., Bonnie rolled over, reached for her glasses like she did every morning, and wanted to know what time it was. She said she wanted to sit up again. Megan and I helped her to the edge of the bed. Then she said, "I need to go," which caused Megan and me to race around the room looking for the bedpan. "No," Bonnie said. "I'm going to the bathroom." Megan and I just stared at each other, mouths open, shrugging our shoulders and raising our eyebrows. Without a word, our body language said: what is she going to do next?

Megan and I said okay as Bonnie stood, and we helped her walk to her bathroom where she told us, "I'll tell you when I'm done." A few moments later, we heard a commotion and thought she'd fallen off the toilet, but it was only her rummaging in a drawer looking for a comb. Bonnie always liked her hair. She often grumbled about how her hair was not the same as before chemo for breast cancer. Nonetheless, she always paid attention to her hair with the help of her stylist, Dana, who cared for Bonnie's hair for years.

As we got Bonnie back in bed, Ray showed up with breakfast from Whataburger, a South and Southwest chain. While burgers are their specialty, they're open twenty-four hours a day and serve breakfast sandwiches and taquitos (an egg, potato and sausage burrito). We mentioned we had breakfast, and Bonnie said, "I want some applesauce," so we headed to the kitchen to bring her some. "No, I'm going to eat my applesauce at the table." Megan and I exchanged another *here we go again* look as I went into the kitchen to set up her applesauce.

Ella leaned over to Megan and said, "Grandma pottied." As Megan and I looked for an accident, Ella pointed to the tube from Bonnie's urine catheter, which was full of urine. Her kidneys were producing urine—another major milestone.

We got Bonnie in the wheelchair, and she immediately noticed we had put up the tree and decorated it. As soon as she got to the table, she said, "You need to reimburse Ray for breakfast."

I sent a text message that included: "Odds are she'll be sitting in her heated recliner next. Who knows what lies ahead all through Prayer and the Grace of God." Megan snapped several pictures of this momentous event as we enjoyed the best breakfast ever.

One picture jumped out at me as Megan showed me her phone. I sent that picture of what perfectly summed up our emotions via my next text message: Ella's back is to the camera while Bonnie is sitting in her wheelchair at the table. The shot shows a side view of Bonnie, with the entry wall by the front door in the background. On the wall are a couple of Bonnie's Christmas decorations. On the right is a vertical wreath she made. In the middle of the wall is a two by one-foot board with the red letter "J" and a round green wreath and the red letter "Y."

I sent the picture with the simple caption: LOOK CLOSELY AT THIS PICTURE.

We all laughed as the guesses started coming in. Some said, "She's sitting with Ella?" Others said, "I see a urine bag." But my Uncle BJ was the most observant: "Is that Whataburger I see on the table?" They do not have Whataburger in California, but he had plenty of them here. My sister Leslee made the same Whataburger guess; eventually, I had to give her the right answer.

Of course, that Bonnie was sitting under a sign saying "JOY" was the correct answer—and the best way in a single picture to describe how we all felt that morning. To this day, that Christmas decoration remains on that wall and will never be taken down.

The rest of the day, Bonnie napped and had a couple of visitors. I kept my text messages to a minimum. Megan and I decided to get Bonnie some CBD oil or gummies. Megan gave me an address where we'd meet. I had to run to the store for supplies and would meet her at the CBD store.

My errand was a trip to Reasor's grocery. The events of the day had me still on a non-CBD high as I walked through the aisles as if my feet were not touching the floor. I was wishing everyone I came close to Merry Christmas. As I left the checkout, I chickened out and stopped myself from shouting Tiny Tim's last line from Dickens' *A Christmas Carol*: "A Merry Christmas to us all; God bless us, everyone!"

I headed to the CBD store and became concerned. I'd seen a cannabis store named "Dank Factory" near the address Megan sent me. Ever since Oklahoma legalized medical marijuana, I wanted Bonnie to get a medical card, but asking Bonnie to use marijuana for her pain would have been like asking her to use crack cocaine.

I was relieved to arrive at American Shaman, a block south of Dank Factory. We got out of our cars, and Megan said, "Let me do the talking," which both reassured and worried me as it sounded like we were getting ready to do a drug deal.

The woman who helped us could not have been more understanding as she listened to Megan explain Bonnie's condition. She offered several suggestions using language I'd never heard before. We bought an assortment of oils and gummies. Afterward, I did not ask Megan how she knew so much about the topic; I wasn't sure I wanted to know.

That evening, we had a pleasant visit from a Lutheran minister on the Hospice Team, followed by the nurse. She said Bonnie's vitals were excellent, and her blood pressure was 117/76—exactly what it was when they turned off the dialysis machine. As an added bonus, her catheter hose was full, meaning her kidneys were working. Bonnie told the nurse she had no pain or nausea, topics on which Bonnie is an expert.

As I tried to sleep, many thoughts went through my mind: the JOY of the last thirty-six hours and all Bonnie and I had been through since we were kids, holding hands in the back seat after Spring River... I thought about our beautiful children and Ella. I wanted to put how I felt into words, so I wrote this text and sent it the following morning:

"Every family enjoys its own Christmas traditions. Bonnie's family, growing up, would have Christmas Eve dinner, followed by opening presents, and then wait

for Midnight Mass. My family opened presents on Christmas morning.

This year, the Rauh household is observing multiculturalism and adopting a modified Jewish Hanukkah tradition of multiple days of gifts. We have chosen a four-day celebration. What you do not know is that you have been observing this new tradition with us.

Let's recap: Our first gift was on Wednesday when Bonnie came home. On Thursday, we continued the festivities, with Bonnie first being given the great gift of the Viaticum by Father Matt, followed by her slow but steady progress from simple words to complete sentences. Friday, Bonnie got dressed, walked to the bathroom, and enjoyed breakfast and dinner at the table.

It's early Christmas Eve as I write this, and today's gift is Bonnie's having normal vital signs. A few minutes ago she informed me we need to wrap presents!

So, as this year's modified four-day celebration of JOY concludes, we look forward to tomorrow and the greatest gift of all: the birth of our Lord Jesus Christ.

Our new Rauh household tradition was only made possible through the prayers of hundreds, maybe thousands, and the grace of God.

Christmas Eve, 8:30 a.m. Megan and Ella were in Bonnie's bathroom, and I was in mine. I came out to see Bonnie sitting up in bed by herself again. She was ready for breakfast, which consisted of applesauce and a mini bear claw compliments of some dear friends from St. Henry's. She washed it down with her favorite, a hot mocha.

The nurse arrived and announced Bonnie's vitals were even better than the day before, and her BP was 138/76. With Megan and me as guardrails, Bonnie walked by herself to the bathroom where she brushed her teeth and then walked to bed. Sleeping in had done her good, so we let her sleep as much as possible.

I decided to shop for some items including air mattresses and bedding. My first stop was Ollie's Bargain Outlet, which had recently opened and marked my first time in the store. The entrance was through the south doors. Again, I greeted everyone I saw with Merry Christmas. I found a couple of pillows but little else. Checking out, I located the north doors exit. As I reached the exit, I turned and shouted, "MERRY CHRISTMAS, EVERYONE!"—which was more like George Bailey from *It's a Wonderful Life* than Dickens, but I managed to pull it off. As I tried to make my quick exit, the cashier said, "Sir, that door is broken." I then had to make my way back across all the registers with customers staring at me and exit through the south doors.

My next stop was Academy Sports for Air Mattresses. I picked up two air mattresses and proceeded through checkout, then performed ACT II of my George Bailey imitation as I exited the store without incident.

My last stop was Walmart for tissues to restock the house after I'd quickly depleted Bonnie's well-stocked supply. Because of its proximity to the exit, I chose checkout #6 where I gave an inspired ACT III at the top of my lungs due to the size of the building— "MERRY CHRISTMAS, EVERYONE"—then made a safe getaway.

At St. Henry's, like all other Catholic Churches, parishioners help at Mass by volunteering as ushers, lectors, or Eucharistic ministers. Myles, our deacon, makes up the schedule and sends it every month. I saw I was listed for all three Christmas Masses, which was unusual. Several friends offered to cover for me, but Bonnie was doing better, and I felt I was being called to serve.

The first Christmas Eve Mass at 5 p.m., the Children's Mass, was packed. I was assigned as an usher who also takes up the collection. I was nervous when I left home, knowing I would be gone for a couple of hours. I always leave my phone in the car or turn it off during Mass. After Mass, many were surprised to see me and wanted to know about Bonnie. When I walked outside and checked my phone, I had no texts. "She made it!" I screamed and hugged Roger, one of my Men's Club brothers, who helped me find my car as I could not see for the tears.

Once home, I did not have a minute to lose. While we had put up the tree and decorated the house, only a few presents had been wrapped. Wrapping presents was Bonnie's job. She always took time to wrap each present carefully and with the appropriate paper, ribbon, bow and name tag. On the other hand, the presents I wrapped looked more like someone wore work gloves while wrapping them.

Bonnie was in bed with Ella at her side while Megan, Ray, and Matt helped me wrap. The first challenge was to find the sacks and mostly Amazon boxes with gifts in them, which were in Bonnie's sewing room behind all the furniture from the back bedroom. We immediately got started, except we had one problem: the sacks and boxes included gifts for all of us. Our plan was that I would look in a bag or box, and if the gift was for Megan, for example, I'd ask her to close her eyes as I gave the gift to Matt or Ray to wrap. I repeated this procedure for each gift. We had a great time laughing when, in some cases, I forgot who a gift was for. We'd all make a guess or wrap it and put a random name tag on it.

We finished with only minutes to spare before I left to be a Eucharistic minister at the 10 p.m. Mass, which is our Midnight Mass. The Offertory hymn was "Hark! The Herald Angels Sing." As we sang, it was all I could do to keep from breaking out in laughter thinking of the last scene in *It's a Wonderful Life* where George Bailey sings the same song under the tree. Those who knew of my antics at Ollie's, Academy, and Wal-Mart also got a chuckle.

Christmas morning, Bonnie made her way to her recliner as we opened our gifts. Most were, as expected, for Ella. Matt commented that we did not get as many gifts this year—not in a mean-spirited way, but in a way Matt sometimes does before thinking his words through. I stopped him in his tracks a little more forcefully than I should have and reminded everyone of Bonnie's only shopping trip of the season to Target the day before she was admitted to the ICU. I said, "I will remind you when you open one of the Target gifts."

As gifts were being opened, especially when opening our stockings, I would say *Target* as a gift was opened. The atmosphere in the room became somber as we all watched the person open the gift and reflected on what Bonnie went through to buy that specific gift. We all knew how much Bonnie loved shopping for Christmas gifts. As each of the Target gifts was received, no matter how trivial, the recipient made a point of giving Bonnie a special hug and thank you.

As I stood in the vestibule before the last Mass at 10 a.m. on Christmas, it hit me. God guided Myles to put me on the schedule for each Mass. I was meant to be at all three Masses: to get and pass on hugs that well-wishers sent to Bonnie and to give hope and JOY to those who saw me and knew Bonnie must be doing better if I was at church.

When I returned home, we could all relax except Ray, who was busy assembling Ella's toys. In the afternoon, Leslee and her boyfriend Max came over. Leslee had been divorced for a few years. As I mentioned, Leslee was one of Bonnie's parents' caregivers, not just because she lived nearby, but because she had been doing the same kind of work as a private in-home aide for several years.

The wife of one client, whose mother Leslee took care of until she died, developed dementia, so Leslee cared for her until she died. A couple of years later, Leslee started a relationship with the client,

Max, with whom she attended high school. Sounds complicated, doesn't it?

Bonnie was back in her recliner as Leslee told us, "I got a Christmas present, too." Max had proposed. Bonnie was so excited, and we were so happy for them. Max made Leslee happier than I could remember her being. Max lives on a home-farm across the street from the local Macy's distribution center—an unusual location for cows, horses, pigs, goats, chickens, and other assorted farm animals.

That night, I was scanning through my phone and noticed some people I included in my text messages who had yet to respond, which seemed odd. These included Pat and Maria, who now lived near Durango, Colorado. Bonnie checked Maria's phone number on her phone; I was sending the messages to the correct number.

I asked Megan to contact Pat and Maria's children on Facebook to see if they could help me reach their parents, which was more complicated than it sounds. Justin, the oldest, lives in Vietnam; Lia lives in Tasmania; and Adele lives in New York City. Adele was the first to respond. She told Megan I was using their landline. *Landline?* Who still uses a landline? She gave us Maria's cell number. We all got a laugh out of it, but then it sank in that Pat and Maria knew nothing about Bonnie's illness. I realized my next phone call would be a difficult one.

I went into the garage to allow Bonnie to nap in her chair and not upset her with all I needed to say. Maria answered the phone. I started by telling her I had bad news as she put Pat on speakerphone. I explained I had sent dozens of text messages to her landline, which we all laughed over. I told them to sit down and have some tissues ready.

Starting with the colonoscopy, I walked them through everything that happened. When I got to something bad, I would say, "This next bit is going to be hard to hear, but I can walk twenty feet and hand the phone to Bonnie, so don't worry." I repeated this several times as we talked for about an hour. When I got them up to speed, I gave the phone to Bonnie. I imagine Pat and Maria must have felt like they were talking to a living miracle on the phone.

Maria finished the conversation by telling me she wanted to read all the text messages her landline prevented her from seeing. This started a lengthy process where I needed to take dozens of text messages and convert them into Word and PDF documents. Not wanting to leave Bonnie's side and afraid my typing might wake her, I moved my laptop onto the top of the dishwasher near a plugin where I straddled the cabinet, spending about an hour converting text messages into a file I could email.

The next morning, Bonnie woke up and wanted pancakes. It was like a five-alarm fire went off as we raced around the kitchen making breakfast. Bonnie and I usually ate little for breakfast: some yogurt with granola for me, and Bonnie would have a hard-boiled egg, oatmeal, or an occasional egg-in-the-basket where she would core a hole in a piece of bread and grill an over-easy egg.

I found some pancake mix and syrup in the pantry. Megan and I flew around the kitchen as she started making the pancakes while I started reading aloud the instructions on how to add water to the mix. Megan stopped me. "Dad, I can read." I went on making sausages and heating up the syrup. In my haste, I didn't take the lid off the syrup, which exploded in the microwave, causing the syrup to pour out the door and onto the floor. What a mess! We still managed to get breakfast on the table without burning the house down, and we had a wonderful time laughing and enjoying Bonnie as she ate her pancakes. Next to the JOY morning, it was one of the best mornings ever.

Later, the nurse visited and gave us more good news about Bonnie's vitals. By now, the reading aloud of Bonnie's vitals was like the climax to a game show: we waited in anticipation and cheered the results. Sometimes, I'd take a picture of the nurse's notes as confirmation of the good news. At one of the nurse's visits, she proclaimed that what Bonnie was experiencing was not a rally, but instead, she was improving every day.

That afternoon, close friends Patty and Dan came by with some soup. Patty is one of Bonnie's closest friends; they'd known each other since first grade. Bonnie was glad to see them and more excited about the soup. I gave her a larger portion than I should have, and she ate it all. Later, her nausea returned, but nowhere near as bad as it had been before.

Next to visit was a social worker who asked a lot of unusual questions about Bonnie's mental state and suicidal tendencies. The interview was required by law as part of hospice, but the conversation was uncomfortable and not one we wanted to repeat.

Wednesday, December 28. I sent out another text message, which now started with DAILY BRIEFING as if I were Bonnie's press agent:

> Bonnie has been upgraded to nursing three days a week instead of daily.
>
> This morning, she stood up by herself and was using the walker exclusively.
>
> She was having a little nausea but otherwise made daily improvement.
>
> Thank you for your continued prayers.
>
> PS We had just emptied her catheter bag because it was full.

Bonnie was now spending half her time in bed and half in her recliner, and she could come and go as she pleased with the aid of a walker. That morning, Maria called to tell me she was on her way to Owasso. We wanted to make her visit a surprise. Maria estimated she would arrive around 5 p.m. As five o'clock came and went, Bonnie wanted to go back to bed, so I made up a story that the social worker was coming back to ask more questions. Bonnie was not happy, but I knew it would keep her in her recliner.

At 6:07 p.m., Maria arrived, and Megan began filming with her phone. I walked Maria into the house announcing the arrival of the social worker. I wasn't lying because Maria actually is a social worker in Colorado. Bonnie looked up to see Maria and covered her mouth as she broke down, saying, "You came." They hugged for the longest time.

Maria stayed for a few days, which boosted Bonnie's spirits. While Maria was here, she helped us introduce Bonnie to the CBD oil and gummies Megan's previously unknown skillset had procured. Bonnie's nausea was becoming more of an annoyance than a problem. We started with CBD oil in her clear mixed-berry Ensure, which was the only liquid she could tolerate besides water. We next added a partial gummy. Bonnie protested as expected, but we convinced her it could not hurt.

Maria is one of the hardest working people I know and one of the most giving. The day before she planned to drive home, she asked where our cleaning supplies were. I was puzzled, but she told me she wanted to clean Bonnie's bathrooms. I tried to talk her out of it, knowing Bonnie always kept a tidy house. I gave in, assuming it would take her only a short time since both bathrooms were quite small and clean. Boy was I wrong!

Maria spent four-plus hours cleaning our two little bathrooms, which are smaller than most walk-in closets. I later talked to Pat on the phone and told him what she was doing. "When Maria puts her mind to something," I said, "there's no stopping her!"

Pat replied, "You have no idea."

Our next big decision was about an event we had planned before Bonnie got sick. We had scheduled my side of the family's Christmas gathering on New Year's Day instead of Christmas. The decision was whether or not to proceed. Like her cousin Maria, Bonnie saw no reason for us not to have the gathering as planned. She only said she could not go out in The Shop. We all agreed, and the party was on.

New Year's Eve. Bonnie asked me to shave her head. Even though she'd only had one chemo treatment, her hair was falling out in clumps, making her uncomfortable. Megan was in the room, and I asked Ella if she wanted to watch. At first, she hesitated, but as I started, she kept getting closer and closer until she was next to Bonnie. It did not take long to cut her hair because not much was left. While cutting, I asked Megan to get the trash can, but Ella said, "No, we need to give it to the birds." Puzzled, I asked her what she meant, and she said, "They can use it to make nests for their babies." Bonnie agreed, and Ella and I went to the backyard to find a good place to put Bonnie's hair. At that moment, I could sense in Ella a heart as pure as the one I always knew existed inside Bonnie.

As Bonnie, Megan, and Ella went to bed, I made a grocery store run to buy candy bars—lots of candy bars. Tomorrow was our Christmas party. The next morning, I set up tables and chairs in The Shop for our usual thirty people in preparation for our 1 p.m. gathering. When everyone arrived, they all took turns coming to the house, with Kaci spending most of her time there. Everyone took turns having private time with Bonnie as many of her friends and family had done over the last twelve days. Today, our family reflected on how much we had all been through and how blessed we were to have Bonnie with us.

After dinner, each family was eager to pose behind Bonnie's recliner for a family picture with her. She was draped in the blanket Matt gave her, and her bald head was covered with a stocking cap I got on my adventure to Academy. Everyone from the youngest to the oldest had the biggest smiles, but none shone more brightly than Bonnie's.

Back in The Shop, we played the Candy Bar Game—something Bonnie came up with a few years back. It started with my buying one of every candy bar I could find, focusing on the obscure, lesser-known brands. I then edited a PowerPoint I created with clues that are difficult at first and get progressively easier until someone guesses the candy bar and wins—what else? The candy bar!

The Shop is also an entertainment room with two projector screens and a third projector in a play area for kids. I would put up on the screen an obscure clue, e.g., *the absence of all magnitude or quantity*, followed by some guessing, followed by the next clue: *every game starts here*—followed by the next clue if needed: *1 – 1*. The answer? The Zero Bar.

I added a twist this year. I purchased several bags of mini-Almond Joys and placed the bars on all the tables. When we started the game, my first clue was: *what's Bonnie's favorite candy bar*. As guesses started coming in, I held up my palms. "Stop, everyone—it's right in front of you. Please pick up an Almond Joy." I raised my Almond Joy, "Here's to Bonnie!" Hands holding Almond Joy shot in the air as everyone shouted, "To Bonnie!"

Bonnie and I were so happy to have spent this time with our family on this special day. Bonnie's dream for this home she'd found was that it be a gathering place so our family could stay together, unlike so many other families in today's hurry-up society. Simple pleasures like a shared cookout, pool party, birthday party, and shared holidays are what hold a family together. Bonnie made this possible for our growing family.

We all slept well as Bonnie walked to the table for a pancake and half an egg the next morning. She was still having minor nausea issues, but the CBD products were, under protest, helping. She made it to the recliner and watched the Rose Parade like she did every year. When Megan was in the Owasso Band, they marched in the 2004 Rose Parade. Bonnie and I flew with her parents, and my mom and other family to Pasadena. We had a great time watching Megan and the Owasso Band in the parade.

As this year's parade ended, Matt returned to Midland. He'd

been home for almost two weeks and had to get back to work. It was so hard for him to leave. His departure was nothing like when I left Bonnie to return to school. This time, Matt had no idea if he would ever see his mother again. They had their private time on many occasions over the last two weeks as they talked and healed wounds between any mother and child that were no different from those most of us have.

By now, Bonnie was getting better daily as her vital signs remained strong. Her only complaint was occasional nausea, which was little more than annoying.

Tuesday, January 3. Bonnie complained of leg pain. With no clots or symptoms, the nurse suggested she take baby aspirin.

The next day, Bonnie's nausea worsened, and the lead nurse started her on a regular two-hour dose of alternating medicine for nausea. She said a lack of potassium might be causing the leg cramps, so Bonnie started drinking Pedialyte.

The next morning, Bonnie's catheter tube was bright red, so we called hospice. Hospice thought the baby aspirin was the cause, so Bonnie stopped taking them. As the nurse flushed the catheter, Bonnie saw the blood in the tube and said, "What's next?"

Bonnie continued to deal with nausea and leg pain. She would ask me to rub her legs, but I could tell she was getting frustrated with her lack of recovery. I noticed the first sign of depression.

Saturday, January 7. Bonnie had a good day. Her legs were still bothering her, but she ate and drank a little more. The pain in her leg continued to frustrate her. We, too, had lots of private time to talk about so many things. Death, however, was not one of our topics. Bonnie repeated, "I don't feel like I'm going to die," as I would shake my head and remind her of all the miracles we had witnessed, from her surviving the ER and three pressors to her making it home when they didn't think she'd survive the ambulance ride, to the twelve hours when we lost her then got her back after placing the Green Scapular around her neck. I told her God must have something else in His Plan for her.

While we did not talk directly about final plans, Bonnie commented, "There's only one song I want sung: Ave Maria. The rest are up to you." She also mentioned she wanted Monica, our cantor, to sing. Father Matt gave me a booklet Bonnie used to select from all the readings and prayers used at a funeral Mass. Bonnie and I sat together but did not discuss what this booklet really meant. Instead, Bonnie read the booklet carefully and slowly as she made her choices.

The next topic I hadn't planned on discussing; it just came to me. "If something happens to you, Bonnie, I want Megan to move into the house, and I'll move into The Shop. I won't live in this house without you."

I hadn't slept in our bed since the first night Bonnie came home. She didn't question my decision, but she pointed out some flaws with my plan that only Bonnie could have. "But The Shop doesn't have a shower. What are you going to do—come to the house to take showers? What about your laundry?" Bonnie had a plan for everything and was always the smarter of us. So often I'd throw out an idea—anything from work to home—and no sooner had I finished than Bonnie would come up with a solution. Bonnie liked solving problems. I think this is why she had so many close friends. She was so good at listening and offering suggestions without being judgmental or mean-spirited, just like my mom.

I asked Megan, Ray, and Ella to come in as I told them my plans in front of Bonnie. I wanted this conversation to happen with Bonnie present to witness it. While I talked, Megan and Ray hugged each other and cried while Bonnie never said a word. She simply sat and listened, giving silent approval. My plan was to pay all the bills while they lived in the house, so they could save money and eventually buy their own place. When they moved out, I would move back in.

After they left, Bonnie and I talked about many things, including Ozzie and how much we missed him. "If you go," I said, "you're taking Ozzie with you." She didn't hesitate. "That's fine with me." I told her how sorry I was for running away and for how much pain I'd put her through.

"I know. That was a long time ago." She paused. "You know I love you. Always have." I tried to tell her I caused her breast cancer, but she said, "No, my body has been fighting me since I was born." I promised I would take care of her parents. "I know you will." She shook her head. "I don't understand it. I don't feel like I'm going to die." I nodded. Bonnie had a restless night and barely slept because of leg pain.

Sunday, January 8. Bonnie was in even more leg pain which was now focused behind her knee on the same side as her pancreas. I gave her a dose of morphine that didn't help. I called the nurse who doubled the morphine, which did nothing. They sent the nurse who relayed that the doctor thought her leg pain was a nerve-related exit point for the internal pain she had been free of for so many days.

By mid-afternoon, the nurse had given her Dilaudid, lorazepam, scopolamine, and four times the usual dose of morphine. Clearly, the hospice team was doing everything they could to relieve Bonnie's pain. All the medications did was make her sleep, which was a blessing since she was no longer writhing in pain. The nurse told me to repeat the medications if she awoke in pain.

Megan and Ella came by to see her, but Bonnie remained asleep. In fact, she slept all afternoon. I went to Mass at 5 p.m. while Megan and Ella watched her sleep. Megan told Ella to try to not wake her up—so different from that first night when we thought we'd lost her, and Ella, Megan, Matt, and I tried so hard to bring her back from her shallow breathing. This time, Bonnie was sleeping peacefully, just like she was taking a nap: no shallow breathing, no reason for concern. As the hours went on, I became more concerned. Bonnie had been sleeping in the same position for over twelve hours.

Monday, January 9. I tried to wake Bonnie, but she would not budge. I called Matt and Megan to give them the news. Megan wanted to bring Ella over, but I did not want her to see her grandma like this again. I remember sitting in the hospital, helpless, when my mom was non-responsive before she passed. Megan dropped Ella off at Jay's and came over.

The nurse arrived and confirmed we were near the end. I emailed Rhonda to ask the Prayer Network for Dying Graces. I asked those who wanted to come over to remember how they last saw Bonnie while Megan and I remained at her side.

Father Matt arrived and anointed her. As he finished, he leaned over ever so gently, and putting his hand on her cheek said in a soft voice, "Pray for me." I did not expect that moving moment. As I walked him out, I asked what he meant when he asked her to pray for him. "We ask the saints to pray for us because they are in heaven. Bonnie surely lived her life and faced this battle with a dignity worthy of a Saint." He smiled. "Why shouldn't we ask Bonnie to pray for us if we know where she's headed?"

Father Matt's actions and words gave me an inner peace I hadn't felt since God spoke to me in that field in Kansas. I was ready to put my sufferings in the Hands of God and let Him guide me on this journey. I was no longer afraid.

I went back to Bonnie and just watched her sleep. After dinner, I sent Megan home, so Bonnie and I were alone like so many other times before. The secret to our success was we simply enjoyed each other's company. I am only whole when I am with her. I spent nearly five decades racing to be by her side. This moment was no different than countless others we shared in silence, just occupying the same space.

I started talking more and more, telling her how much she meant to me. I could tell she could hear me. I knew her face so well I could interpret the slightest twinge of her eyelids or lips. I repeated what I knew she was saying inside as I carried on this conversation between our souls for a couple of hours.

10 p.m. I turned on the local news on my phone and talked to Bonnie about the day's news events just like we always did in our recliners. After the news, since music was always a big part of our lives, I turned on Pandora. Music brought us together in the Owasso Band. I placed my phone on the pillow next to her and played movie soundtracks from romantic movies we enjoyed and over which we'd shared tears. I then played some Andrea Bocelli and wept as I held her in my arms when he sang "Time to Say Goodnight."

Next, I put on the soundtrack to the 1980's movie *Somewhere in Time* starring Christopher Reeve and Jane Seymour. This movie was special to us because we knew we had found our soulmates, and that we would travel across time to be with each other again. We would always shed a tear at the final scene when Christopher Reeve's character is reunited with Jane Seymour's in heaven.

12:30 a.m. Bonnie's breathing became shallower—no gasping or obvious pain, but her breathing simply slowed down. I reached under the sheets to hold her hand and noticed her fingers were turning gray. I knew I did not have much time, so I told her how happy she had made me and how proud I was of her. I promised her I would take care of Megan, Matt, and her parents.

12:52 a.m. My phone rang. Matt was calling from Midland. I hadn't talked with him since earlier that evening. I put him on speaker phone and placed the phone on Bonnie's chest as I held her wedding ring hand next to my heart. I told Matt everything that was happening.

Monday, January 10; 12:55 a.m. As Matt and I said, "Goodbye, Mom, we love you, and we'll miss you," Bonnie took her last breath.

A peace washed over me as I hung up the phone. I did not shed a tear as I placed her hands on her chest, positioned her legs, straightened out her sheet, and covered her up, leaving her face uncovered as if she were just sleeping.

I called hospice, then Mowery's Funeral Home. While I waited, I straightened the house as if I were expecting company. I organized all the hospice equipment and removed the air mattresses from either side of her bed.

Within an hour, the nurse arrived and filled out some forms after confirming Bonnie's passing. She told me she had to wait for Mowery's driver. We sat at the kitchen table, and I shared all that Bonnie had gone through.

The driver from Mowery's arrived. The nurse and driver went to the back bedroom, placed Bonnie's body on the gurney, and brought her down the hall next to her recliner. In a calm, gentle voice, the driver walked over to me and said, "Would you like some time with her?"

"WHY? She's not here!" I bellowed. "That body is why she's not with me."

Surprised, he wheeled her to the door, and I started to cry. For the last time Bonnie was leaving this home that she had created for me and our family.

The nurse destroyed the hospice medications and left. Angrily I went around the house gathering every last one of Bonnie's pill bottles and MiraLAX tubs and threw everything in a trash bag to dispose of them the next day at the police station. I never wanted to be reminded of all those pills and medications Bonnie took for nearly her entire adult life. I caught a couple of hours of sleep in my recliner, then sent another text:

FINAL UPDATE

"The love of my life has gone home.

Bonnie passed away at 12:55 a.m.

It was the most peaceful and beautiful experience of my life."

Chapter Ten

2023

DURING MY LAST phone conversations with Megan and Matt shortly before their mother died, I reminded them of my mother's visit to our house *after she died*. I told them not to be afraid if something unusual happened.

Before I go on, I need to explain that Matt, by nature of his Asperger's, is not prone to flights of fancy or mystical thoughts. He is the most skeptical person about any form of supernatural occurrence.

Around 8 a.m., Matt called. "Mom was here."

"What do you mean?"

"I felt her presence in the doorway of my bedroom, and I felt her touch my head."

I knew he was not saying this to make me feel better. That is not in his DNA. I thanked him for the call and went about all the things I had to do.

My first stop of the morning was to see Father Matt. He offered his condolences as we went into his office. We started thinking about dates, but I had yet to meet with Mowery's Funeral Service, so I could only talk about an outline of what we wanted, which was easy because of the book and form Bonnie had carefully filled out a few days earlier.

While Bonnie's form included readings and prayers, the music and who would be celebrating the Mass were undecided. I told Father Matt that Bonnie wanted Monica to sing, but we knew she was on maternity leave, having recently given birth to baby number seven.

Father Matt mentioned being the celebrant—

"I have different plans. I'd like to have four priests."

Father Matt was surprised. "Why four priests?"

"Because I don't know five."

Had I known 100 priests, I would have asked for 101. Part of me wanted the Catholic church to pull out all the stops to celebrate Bonnie after all she had given to St. Henry's, the Catholic church, and to me. I now loved the Catholic faith so much that part of me wanted a special celebration for Bonnie to shine the best light on the faith, especially for those non-Catholics who would attend her funeral Mass including my family.

I wanted Father Matt to be the primary celebrant. I also wanted Fr. Bradley although I hardly knew him because I rarely attended Mass when he was Bonnie's pastor at St. Henry's, but Bonnie was fond of him from when she worked in the preschool. I wanted Father Todd, Bonnie's cousin on Virginia's side of the family, and Father Bala, the associate pastor at St. Henry's.

Father Bala came to St. Henry's on loan from India not long before the pandemic. Bonnie and I treasure him as a good friend. When he first arrived, he asked me to help with some projects around his house. This led to Bonnie's altering and hanging his curtains, and other things we did for Father Bala cemented our friendship.

The meeting ended with some possible dates. Following Bonnie's wishes, the events included a rosary and funeral Mass with internment at Graceland Cemetery near Mom and Rick's graves followed by lunch in the church's Bamberg Hall.

The next stop was to tell Bonnie's parents. I'd already sent Bonnie's brothers the Final Update text, so I felt no need to call them. I slowly walked up the steps of Bonnie's parents' house, not unlike the way I did when Mom drove me over to meet them, which felt like yesterday. I stood in the living room of the house where Bonnie grew up and where we had spent so much time together and told them of Bonnie's passing as gently as I could. Richard said something like *that's too bad*, and Virginia shook her head in disbelief.

Next, I made an appointment with Mowery's. Megan went with me to start the process. I expected to see Steve, who cared for Mom and Rick, but he was on medical leave. We met with Steve's son Grant. I did not know Grant as well as his father, but I quickly learned I would enjoy working with him. The word "enjoy" sounds strange, but the peace that came over me the night before allowed me to put grief aside.

Grant mentioned the usual Catholic procedure, but I interrupted as I had with Father Matt. "I also want a visitation like Mowery's." He mentioned visitation usually took place at the rosary. Nonetheless, in addition I wanted a common Protestant style visitation so those who did not want to attend a Catholic ceremony would feel comfortable at a traditional visitation.

We talked about possible dates, but I was concerned about travel. Bonnie's relatives were from all over, and I wanted everyone who wanted to come to have plenty of notice, so I called Father Matt. We agreed on Wednesday, January 18 for the visitation and rosary, and Thursday, January 19 for the funeral Mass.

We then went with Grant to look at all the necessary hardware. I did what I had done so many times before. When Bonnie and I shopped for a big-ticket item like an appliance or car, I quickly decided and was ready to move on. Once, we remodeled the kitchen in the two-story house and went to pick out appliances. While the salesman tried to compare stove models, I looked at a stove and said, "We'll take that one," and did the same for the dishwasher, microwave, and refrigerator. Bonnie would protest—*wait! wait a minute!*—but it was too late.

I was not allowed to make the same mistake when we remodeled the 1980 house. Bonnie reminded me of the problems we had with the appliances I quickly chose. She made all the decisions on subsequent appliances. As I'd done with Megan's wedding, all I did was sign the checks.

As I went through Mowery's showroom, I was as calm as if I were shopping for furniture or appliances. Megan shook her head. "Why would shopping," I asked her as we finished in record time, "be any different here?" We walked past the urn collection, and I commented that Ozzie's urn was the same size as a person's. Who knew? Even Grant was shaking his head at this point. I'm guessing he wondered how I could be as calm and relaxed as if I were at the mall.

Back home, I met the hospice people who came to pick up the bed and other equipment. As I cleaned the bedroom, I thought about where I would sleep. I knew I would never sleep in our bed without Bonnie, so I moved a spare squeaky twin bed into the back bedroom. I positioned it so I would always have a view of the empty spot where the hospice bed had been as a constant reminder of where I last held Bonnie's hand and where she took her last breath. It would be some time before Megan moved into the house, and I moved into The Shop. The nights I spent in that room before I moved meant a lot to me.

The Men's Club held a regular meeting the day after Bonnie passed away. I showed up, to everyone's surprise. With the same inner peace, I smiled and engaged everyone more than usual, and asked the men if they would be Bonnie's pallbearers. That great group of guys was so important in teaching me how to serve my church. We enjoyed so many events together, and I could think of no one I would have trusted more with such an honor.

Matt called that evening around ten to tell me, "She's back."

He said they were having conversations. He heard his mom's voice, which may sound farfetched, but some of the quotes he shared with me could have only come from Bonnie's mouth.

For example, when Matt learned I'd asked Megan to move into the house, he was upset. He thought she would not keep it as tidy as Mom did. During this visit, he asked Mom if she thought Megan would tear up the house. She responded, "Not any more than you would," which is exactly what Bonnie would have said.

Of course, Matt would say he would have kept it spotless, but Bonnie and I know the truth. When Matt moved out of The Shop, Bonnie and I spent half a day cleaning his room with latex gloves and masks. At the end of the horrendous ordeal, Bonnie said, "We'll never get that day back."

In a story Matt relayed after his mom died, he was at home with Bonnie in one of his private times before she died. He wanted to see if he could figure out how his mom would contact him after she passed. He had heard others on the Internet talk about clouds, butterflies, or other natural phenomena that allow people who pass to contact the living. Matt asked his mom, "What is your favorite bird?"

Bonnie did not hesitate. "Wild or domestic?"

"Mom! I'm just trying to figure out how you'll contact me when you're gone."

"I don't know. I've never done this before." Bonnie's response was so smart and clever.

These conversations between Matt and his mother after she passed lasted three days, some of which he shared with me. Since then, Matt said he often thinks of what his mom would say and feels the answer. This has given Matt inner peace, which was unexpected, considering how close he was to his mother and how he reacted to the loss of his grandmother.

After leaving Mowery's, I went home and made several phone calls, telling family and friends our plans. On Wednesday Monica, our cantor from St. Henry's, called to discuss music. I thought she was on maternity leave. "I am," she said. "I would only come back for Bonnie." Her words meant so much to me.

Later, Megan got Ella back for her three days with her. I was worried about how Ella would feel coming into the house for the first time without Grandma. Megan and I talked about it, and I told Megan how scared I would have been at Ella's age.

To try to ease any concerns, we continued a tradition Bonnie started for Ella. When Ella was three years old, Bonnie bought a small red mailbox with a flag. She placed it on a bookcase in the back bedroom. Bonnie kept a stockpile of small toys and trinkets kids like. She would put an item in the mailbox when Ella was away. When Ella came over, Bonnie would say, "Ella, have you checked the mail?" Ella would run to the mailbox. Just as in real life, sometimes she had mail and sometimes she didn't.

I found Bonnie's stash of toys, and Megan put an item in the mailbox. When Ella arrived, she walked in as if nothing had happened. She got some toys and sat at the table, never mentioning Grandma. I asked if she'd checked the mail, and off she went running down the hall. She came back with a trinket, saying, "Grandma Bonnie must have left this for me." We did not know what to say other than how proud we were of our little six-year-old girl who had gone through so much over the last few weeks and was clearly stronger than any of us gave her credit for.

After Bonnie's passing, many friends and family visited to be with me. This meant a great deal to me. I still had the same inner peace from the moment Bonnie died, which was making me more of an extrovert than I had ever been. Rick was always the extrovert, but my inner peace allowed me to open up much more than I normally would have. Those who visited could tell I was different, not grieving as some might have expected. Some suspected I was holding my grief in, which was not healthy. They even discussed an intervention.

I texted the following explanation:

"I am not putting on a show or good face with visitors. My lack of outward grief is my way of healing after the countless times only my family saw my grief and breakdowns over every little thing these last few months.

One of the high moments while Bonnie was home was when she was sitting in her recliner with all of us gathered around. It was the first time we were all with her, laughing and enjoying ourselves in the living room where we had gathered so many times before.

Something Megan said reminded me of a Yogi Berra quote. I mentioned his name, and the kids had no idea who he was, so I looked up quotes and started reciting them. As I began to laugh harder at every Yogi quote, I had one of my worst breakdowns. After I gathered myself with everyone staring at me, I said, "We're having such a good time, and I know at some point we won't ever be able to do this all together again."

When Bonnie was here, I did my grieving. After she left, I can only describe having a peaceful, warm feeling I can't hide.

The Yogi line that broke me up? A reporter asked Yogi, "When the streaker ran across the outfield, could you tell if it was a man or woman?" Yogi replied, "I couldn't tell because it had a bag over its head."

On the Friday after Bonnie passed away, I traveled to Fayetteville with Kim and Sam to attend a celebration for Mr. Janzen who, while living in a memory care center in Owasso, passed away before Christmas. Jana was in my small text message group, and it was important for me to help support David and Jana at the loss of this great man who changed my life in much the same way Harlon Lamkin did.

One memory that stands out from the celebration was near the end when we sang "How Great Thou Art," arguably one of the most recognizable religious hymns of all time. Many famous artists have performed this, but it is unlikely you have ever heard it performed by over one hundred band directors and trained musicians in perfect four-part harmony. Anytime we sing that song at St. Henry's I think about that day and our tribute to Mr. Janzen.

That weekend, I needed to put together a slide show for the luncheon and visitation. I gathered all the photo albums I could find and asked Rhonda to help Megan and Ella pick out pictures. As they pulled out photos, I told stories about Bonnie and our early years.

I returned to the now-empty back bedroom for more photo albums and noticed something on the floor where the hospice bed was: there, clear as day, was a large clump of Bonnie's hair, which says little about my cleaning skills, as I had run the sweeper in the room. I returned to where the girls were looking at pictures and did my best not to break down as I told them what I found. Rhonda and Bonnie's nieces later got small locks of her hair, which meant a lot.

Not knowing Father Bradley well, I asked someone to contact him for me. He called and said Father Matt wanted him to deliver the homily at the funeral Mass, essentially a eulogy. We agreed to meet at the visitation to review some material. I told Father Bradley I wanted to send him the text message I sent Father Matt. After Mass the previous Sunday, I'd told Father Matt I wanted to tell him something I couldn't say in person without breaking down. I texted:

> "What I want to say is the one time I will certainly break down will be when I see four priests take their places behind the altar at the beginning of Mass. I cry just thinking about it.
>
> When we set the date, you asked me why four priests and the answer I gave is because I don't know five.
>
> The greatest gift Bonnie gave me was the Catholic Church that I love so much. Without her, I might be a Baptist or worse.

I had good intentions after we got married to join the church but allowed anger and bitterness to keep me home as Bonnie took our kids to Mass. Bonnie maintained an unshakable faith despite the countless times she asked in her sweet voice if I wanted to come with her to Mass as I made one excuse after another not to. The fact that she never quit trying or ever complained kept the smallest of sparks in me that took far too long to ignite.

While I can't top a funeral Mass or the Eucharist, the only way I can start to repay her for her faith and patience with me is to ask that the Catholic church provide her with a celebration that requires more effort than usual. If this means in my eyes that four priests coming to celebrate and thank Bonnie for bringing one lost soul such as me to God and the Catholic church, then this is my offering to her.

I can never repay Bonnie for being so loving to me in spite of my lack of support. All alone she was the only religious influence in our house. Bonnie loved me so much she could see past my anger and petty excuses."

Sorry for the Baptist joke. I could not resist. While I wanted to go all out for Bonnie, I made it clear to Father Matt that I only wanted one priest at my funeral. I have instructed Megan and Matt to hunt Father Matt down when my time comes.

Grant Mowery instructed me to go to the Graceland Cemetery office to pay the fee to open the grave. Graceland is the second cemetery in Owasso. The first cemetery, where Bonnie's grandparents and baby infant brother are buried, has been full for years. Mowery's used to own Graceland, but now it's owned by a local attorney who grew up in Mingo and was in the same grade with Rick.

Bonnie had a bone of contention with Graceland. Not long after we buried Mom there, Bonnie and I bought a bench and a tree. The tree did not survive the winter. When Bonnie checked on a replacement, she found the cemetery had been sold. The new owners would not honor the tree guarantee. Bonnie made a point of commenting about the missing tree every time we visited Mom's grave.

I sat down with the cemetery manager who was expecting me. She showed me the plot, and I noticed they had Bonnie on the wrong side. I pointed out this error, and she said placing the wife on the right and the husband on the left is customary. "We didn't sleep in our bed that way," I said, "and we're not going to lay any differently in the ground." She was surprised at my response and explained she would have to redo the paperwork, to which I replied, "That's fine with me. I have nothing to do."

My next task was to have posters made. I turned to Sherri, Steve Mowery's sister-in-law, who had grown up with Bonnie's extended family and was honored to help with her Fast Signs business. The same was true with Sheri at Art in Bloom, the Owasso florist who took such care in providing the flowers.

I now needed to write my own eulogy for Bonnie, which I planned to give after Father Bala led the rosary. I also had to educate my family, which included a variety of Protestants and Nones, about what to expect at a rosary and a Catholic funeral Mass. Typically, only Catholics attend a rosary, but I wanted my family to be there. I explained that, unlike Protestant funerals, the family and friends only speak after the rosary and not at a funeral Mass.

I created a "Catholic Mass for Dummies" document as set of lengthy, multi-part text messages to my family and non-Catholic friends to explain the beauty and ceremony of the rosary and Mass. I felt it was important for everyone to know a Catholic funeral Mass is special and how much a part Bonnie had in everything they would see.

Another concern I had was getting Bonnie's parents to the church. I decided to put Bonnie's brothers in charge. I figured they would only have one thing to do; how hard could that be? I called each of them and told them their parents would only be going to the funeral Mass. Their job was to pick them up and get them to church, take them to the lunch, and get them to the cemetery and back home. Their responses were identical: *I don't know… I don't know.* After about the fourth *I don't know*, I said in a harsh tone, "This is nonnegotiable. You are going to get your parents to your sister's funeral and back home. We are not going to debate it."

This exchange, of course, left me concerned. Even this simple request, the only one I'd made of either of them since I was fourteen, was possibly too much for them, so I put a backup plan in place. I told Leslee about our conversation, and she assured me she and Max would monitor from across the street with their blinds open to make sure the boys did what I asked or be ready to take over if they failed.

The day before the visitation, we went to Mowery's to take care of some last-minute items. When we finished, Grant said, "She's ready if you want to see her."

Immediately I said *sure* as if I were going with him to view a new boat. I then looked at Megan as I thought she might have a problem. Megan has always done her best to avoid any discussion of death. Whenever her mother or I would say *when we're gone*, she would interrupt. "Don't say that! I don't want to talk about that." Knowing she'd have major reservations about seeing her deceased mother, I looked at her, assuming she would not want to go—but she agreed. Megan was no longer the shy timid person she used to be. Instead, Megan had grown into a confident woman with many of the same qualities I admired in her mother.

Megan and I held hands as Grant took us to the same viewing room where Mom and Rick's visitation had taken place. We walked closer, and all I could say to Grant was, "You did the best you could. She had a rough time at the end." Megan and I stood there, not saying a word, as we were thinking the same thoughts. She did not look good at all.

I'd told Grant Bonnie didn't use much makeup, but clearly,

he'd taken my comment literally. That wasn't the only problem; something was missing. "Did she wear glasses?" Grant asked. The question hit both of us like a ton of bricks. "Of course!" Megan and I shouted. "That's what's wrong." Bonnie had worn glasses since third grade. For a time she wore contacts, and for a while following the old-fashioned Radial Keratotomy (RK) procedure done using a diamond knife, she didn't need corrective lenses, but she'd worn glasses for the last twenty years. I also asked Grant to apply more makeup.

As an added touch, Rhonda gave Bonnie some scarves when she lost her hair the last time. One of the scarves was silly featuring candy and junk food. I gave it to Grant to use on Bonnie. I thought it might bring a smile during the visitation.

With glasses in place and some modest makeup, Bonnie was ready for the visitation. Knowing how many people would come to visit after having only read about Bonnie's passing in the paper, I expected lots of questions. I created a two-page summary, "Bonnie's Last Battle," and printed a stack that I placed in the visitation room.

Sherri at Fast Signs had created a large poster from a selfie Bonnie took with Ozzie. Yes, Ozzie's urn was at the bottom of the casket next to Bonnie's feet where he walked, sat, and slept so often, just as I promised. Now they were together again.

My heart was full of joy as I greeted everyone. I walked with most of them to see her, pointing out the scarf and poster and telling them where Ozzie was. I thought it was a good way to lighten everyone's mood during this difficult time. If they saw me being open and welcoming, it might help put them at ease.

I broke down once as I saw Gloria and Rosemarie walk in. They were Bonnie's relatives on Virginia's side from Wisconsin. I cried as I said, "The Wisconsin group. I completely forgot about you," but they told me they had been kept in the loop on Facebook.

Father Bradley stopped by, and we used an adjacent room to discuss what he would say in his eulogy. He asked about the text I sent and if he could use any of it. I told him he could use anything we wanted. We talked for a few minutes, and then he left. The encounter was the first time I'd ever sat face to face with him. I found him to be warm and kind, as Bonnie always said. How foolish I'd been not to approach him after my mental breakdown.

During that day, I thought how silly I was not to go into the same room to see Mom at her visitation. How disrespectful and selfish I was to act that way. I could not help thinking of how far I'd come spiritually. I owed it all to God and Bonnie: God saved me from myself on my lowest of days, and Bonnie chose to stand by me and not to give up on me. We had said *for better or worse, for richer or poorer, in sickness and in health, to love and to cherish, till death do us part,* and in our forty-three year marriage, Bonnie and I literally experienced every one of those ups and downs.

With the visitation behind us, the rosary was that evening. I informed the family that Bonnie's casket would be open before the rosary. If they wanted to put something inside, they needed to do this before they sat down. Once they closed the casket before the rosary, it would never be opened again.

At the rosary, a section is typically reserved for the family. I asked that only the row where Bonnie and I sat during Mass be reserved. I sat at the end of the row as we took our seats. Just as Father Bala walked in, Matt came up and nudged me. He was spending the last moments he could at his mother's casket. After Father Bala finished, I walked up to the podium and started off with:

Everyone now knows the kind of fighter Bonnie was and how strong she has been since they found the tumors in October. Stories of her determination and strength to even those who knew her well may have come as a bit of a surprise.

The Bonnie we knew was kind, mild-mannered, soft-spoken, and just simply a sweet person. So, what clues in Bonnie's life led to how she fought her extraordinary battle, which, given her demeanor, may have seemed to be out of character for such a sweet person?

How did she summon the strength and courage to face one crisis after another?

We've all read the obituary, but that only tells part of Bonnie's story. Yes, she was born on September 16, 1958, but did you know she was only 3 pounds 7 ounces at birth?

Think about it: in 1958, the odds of survival for a small preemie had to be astronomical, but Bonnie was a fighter.

Show of hands. Did anyone ever hear Bonnie complain?

MEGAN, MATT PUT YOUR HANDS DOWN. Mom had every right to complain about your messy rooms, tattoos, and the COLOR AND LENGTH of your hair.

This scripted dig at Megan and Matt was well deserved. Megan colored her hair often and not in a subtle manner. I remember her being a brunette, but she wore multiple shades of bright and brighter red for some time. As for Matt, I never mentioned his hair goes halfway down his back. When Bonnie tried to get him to cut his hair, he always said, "But the girls love it." We would always reply, "What girls, and when are we going to meet any of them?"

I continued by recounting all the medical issues Bonnie faced, most of which even her close friends knew nothing about. After each of her setbacks, I would say, "But did Bonnie complain?" I also covered both adoptions and the hotel clerk in Thousand Oaks when Matt was born. I concluded my eulogy with:

Now, let's go back to Thousand Oaks when Matt was born. Did we mislead the hotel clerk into thinking Bonnie must have been an Olympic athlete? Or was he just the first person to suspect what we all now know about Bonnie?

Without complaint, she summoned the strength and courage needed throughan extraordinary grace from God to teach all of us how to face any challenge.

On a personal note, I want to thank those who have commented about my haircut. I recently changed barbers. My barber started cutting my hair in high school, and just one week before she died, she told me, "I can stand long enough to cut your hair." After a series of back-and-forth negotiations, she agreed to let someone else cut my hair.

Bonnie was also very smart and good at math. Multiple times when I was poised to make another impulsive decision, she would remind me, "Now about those haircuts." I always knew that at any time, she might produce an invoice, which always took the wind out of my sails.

I am so glad to have been able to share Bonnie's story with you.

May it encourage everyone that nothing is impossible with God. Thank you.

I then asked if anyone else wanted to speak. Several stood up and made moving comments about Bonnie, with some commenting on how much of an impact she had on their now-grown children from her time at Wee Angels Pre-School. Near the end, a small voice spoke up. It was Greyson, Leslee's five-year-old grandson. "I love my Aunt Bonnie," Greyson said, "and she was the best ever," which did not leave a dry eye in the room and certainly stole my thunder.

The next morning was cloudy, cold, and windy. The weather was not the best for the internment at Graceland. We had our family gather in the Old Parish Hall before Mass. The family present numbered seventy-five. Before we went in, I got everyone's attention, and, looking up at the ceiling, I moved back to the center of the room as if I was looking for a specific location. "Forty-three years ago, this is the spot where Bonnie and I were married," to which everyone responded.

Back then, this room was the entire church, which had been added onto many times since making this room a secondary meeting room. In the "Catholic for Dummies" primer, I explained how Communion worked: "Bonnie wants each and every one of you to join the Communion line with your arms crossed over your chest to get a special blessing from the priest. Bonnie wants each of you to receive this special blessing."

I pointed to some flyers I printed giving directions to our house. I sent another text saying I was opening the house and The Shop after the graveside, and encouraged everyone to come.

The turnout for Bonnie's funeral Mass was as large as expected. The family took up an entire section, and some had to wonder how Bonnie could be related to so many people. The Mass was as beautiful as I'd hoped, and, yes, I cried when the four priests knelt next to Bonnie's casket, which was placed in front of the altar before they ascended the steps to take their place behind the altar.

Monica was wonderful as she sang songs that usually make me cry during regular Mass. Malinda and Joyce were our lectors. When it came time for the homily, Father Bradley, in his soft, gentle voice, gave a beautiful commentary on the lives Bonnie' touched and her legacy. He did not use any of the anecdotes I shared with him except one line from the text I sent him: "The greatest gift Bonnie gave Randy was the Catholic church he loves so much"—and then repeated it for effect. Only he and Father Matt ever heard me make that statement. You could have heard a pin drop.

On the left side near Monica sat the St. Henry's Men's Club, all assembled in their red polo shirts. They were there to support me; no, to hold me up during this difficult day. The Men's Club had a much larger attendance that day than we ever have at any work function.

As Mass ended, the Men's Club took their positions and escorted

Bonnie's casket to the hearse. Outside, I said, "Make sure Art is not on the foot end of the casket. That's where Ozzie is," as a joke about Art, who is the oldest and smallest of the group. Art and Joyce, one of our lectors, also came with Bonnie and me on our pilgrimage. Art sadly passed away only months after Bonnie.

We then went to Bamberg Hall for lunch, where I worked the room like the maître d' at a five-star restaurant. I went table to table, talking to everyone with my newfound extraversion skill that I never knew I had.

Around 12:15, everyone was fed, and the driver for Mowery appeared. He was the same driver who picked up Mom from the hospital when she died. I hugged him, which must have seemed odd to everyone in the room. We talked about that night when he performed the same service for Mom.

We made our way to Graceland Cemetery, where the wind blew harder and the weather was even colder. I had decided to have a casket lowering, which is uncommon. Only Megan and I knew about this. I had never seen it done before except on TV. I had arranged with Sheri at Art in Bloom to have two dozen long-stemmed roses in position by the grave. Graceland has a small pavilion about thirty feet from Bonnie's grave. Father Matt gave a final blessing and prayer, and the Men's Club carried Bonnie to the casket lowering mechanism over her grave.

We all stood, shivering, as we watched the casket being slowly lowered into the burial vault. I asked Megan, Ella, Matt, and Bonnie's nieces and nephews to drop a rose on the casket before they lowered the vault lid. I also invited some friends to continue until all the roses were gone. They lowered the lid, and we were unsure what should happen next. I took Ella's hand, and we walked closer to the grave, picked up some loose dirt, and tossed it in. I do not remember what I said to Ella, but it was no different from the many times before when Bonnie, Ella, and I would go in the yard to show her something new to explore. This, too, was new for both of us.

Uncle BJ and I went to the church to pickup of the food, posters, pictures and flowers. We talked about what to do with the flowers, and I decided to take them to the memory care facility in Owasso where Mr. Janzen was living when he passed away. We unloaded the flowers at the front desk and asked the receptionist to give them to the residents and tell them, "These are from Mr. Janzen." As we made our way to Bonnie's car, I kept on walking and broke down for the first time of the day. I was weeping both for Bonnie and Mr. Janzen.

We then headed to Bonnie's house to join the gathering. On the printed invitation, I told everyone to come through the front door, look around at what Bonnie had created, and invited them to Bonnie's sewing room. They proceeded through the back patio doors to see the backyard, minus the beautiful flowers in January. They then made their way to The Shop, where I had Bonnie's slideshow on the projectors. We all sat around having a great time visiting.

The family headed home, and Matt stayed through the weekend. He asked if he could have Bonnie's mixing bowl, which, unfortunately, was her constant companion. He said he planned to blow it up into a million pieces. Megan, channeling Bonnie's common sense, said, "You can't do that. It would break up the set." All I could do was laugh as Megan sounded just like her mother.

On more than one night, Matt came up to the house and privately hugged Bonnie's recliner. None of us would sit in it as we were doing our best to get through each day. On Saturday, we visited a monument company in Claremore that Mowery's recommended. I was as open and engaging as I had been at Mowery's—at times, too much so for Megan as I made sure Ella was having a good time even as we picked out a headstone.

I did my typical *I'll take that one* approach to shopping, but we did give it some thought. I had one firm rule: our headstone would be shorter than Mom's. I did not want anything fancy, but I did want some Catholic items on the front. On the back I wanted:

MARRIED MAY 12, 1979

PARENTS OF MEGAN AND MATT

GRANDPARENTS OF ELLA, GEMMA

...AND OZZIE

We ate lunch at the Hammett House in Claremore, a favorite of Mom's. She loved to go there and especially liked their pies. We laughed and talked about when Bonnie was last there with us and remembered Grandma Rauh (JoAnn) and the times we shared there with her.

Sunday night, Matt headed back to Midland. In the seat next to him was the grey fleece blanket he gave Bonnie for Christmas at the hospital that she never took off. Matt said he would never wash it; it's one of his most prized possessions. Another of Matt's prized possessions is a batch of Bonnie's Club Cracker Bars. Bonnie made Matt a batch when we had the party before he moved to Midland in October. They remain in the freezer to this day.

What follows are only some of the Blessings God has showered upon me. I still cry every day, but I think all the blessings I received over the following months were God's way of healing the hole in my heart. As you will see, He turned my tears of grief into tears of joy.

The following Saturday, I asked Leslee and all Bonnie's nieces and grandnieces to come over to go through her jewelry. They were reluctant at my unusual request, but I told them Bonnie would want them to have her jewelry. I sat up a couple of card tables in the living room and displayed all of Bonnie's jewelry.

Aside from the miraculous medal, Bonnie wore jewelry like she wore makeup—little or none. That did not stop me from buying lots of jewelry for her over the years. She wore fancy jewelry at Easter or Christmas or on our many cruises, but most of it sat unused. Bonnie liked Rustic Cuff, and I bought copious amounts when I ran out of gift ideas.

The six girls, along with Leslee's oldest daughter Kristen (on FaceTime from home in Edmond, Oklahoma as if she were a bidder at Sotheby's), were hesitant at first but got into the spirit as I told them Bonnie was smiling down at them. I ordered pizza, and everyone had a great time as I told stories about Bonnie and her jewelry. We then went to Bonnie's closet, where they selected a few items to remind them of her.

Matt called me several times a day to talk about problems with his bosses and finding reliable employees. He was having a tough time alone in Midland and was in a bit of a rut. He wanted Mom's chair but didn't know how to get it to Midland.

At the car dealership where he worked, Ray had a trailer hitch put on Bonnie's CRV. I rented a small U-Haul trailer, and he helped me load the heavy beast. As we walked to the house, he said,

"I want to ask you a question."

"Sure, anything."

"I want to ask you for Megan's hand." Megan and Ray were in their thirties and both had been married before. He did not have to ask my permission for anything. I began to cry as I was touched by this respectful gesture.

My plan was to surprise Matt, who had no idea I was coming. I drove to his workplace and called him. I told him I needed the VIN number on his car because there was a question about the charges when he used AAA for a recent tow. Matt immediately sent me a picture of his AAA card. I shook my head, called him again, and said, "No, I need you to walk out to your car and take a picture of your VIN." As he walked to his car, I came up behind him saying, "Are you going to get me that VIN or not?"

He turned around and stared at me for about three seconds, wondering if I was real. We hugged and cried, which I had anticipated and is why I planned our meeting outside so as not to embarrass him. After getting that beast of a chair upstairs to his apartment, we went shopping for items he needed and made plans for the weekend.

Matt wanted to drive to Roswell, three hours from Midland. I laughed as I thought about our previous Roswell family experience. Many years earlier, I was to attend a conference in Phoenix. We made it a family vacation and drove out. Matt went on and on about wanting to go to Roswell. Bonnie knew Matt's fascination with science fiction and aliens meant we'd be there all day. She put her foot down. No Roswell.

After the conference, I took a different route home, and it just happened to take us through Roswell. As signs for Roswell appeared, Bonnie looked at me with squinty eyes. "If you stop in that town…" without mentioning its name—as if it mattered since Matt saw the same signs and was now on the edge of his seat.

I made a few slow passes through town, never stopping except for a traffic light as Matt, his face pressed against the window, begged me to stop. Bonnie kept saying, "No, we are not stopping."

Matt and I indeed went to Roswell the next day. We laughed along the way as if we knew some calamity would suddenly happen, like a flat tire or some other reason for us not to make it. In the end, nothing happened. We made it to Roswell safely. Bonnie was right all along, as usual. Matt wanted to explore everything, and I nearly had to drag him to the car to make the long drive back to Midland.

The next event in The Shop was the Super Bowl. I had hosted a Super Bowl party for the Men's Club for several years, and I agreed to host this year. At first, the wives didn't want to come, but I insisted Bonnie would not want them to miss out.

Bonnie was not a football fan, but she liked hosting such events, especially decorating The Shop. She ordered all kinds of football banners, tablecloths, and tableware. She even wrapped yellow napkins around ping pong balls. She put them in buckets on each table as referee flags everyone could throw at the two projector screens during the game. A third projector in the kids' area played Puppy Bowl at Bonnie's request and was always a big hit.

I decorated The Shop as Bonnie had. Of course, she would have thought up something new, as she always scoured Pinterest and other resources to find new ideas to make gatherings better. After halftime, I asked the wives to follow me to the house where we went into Bonnie's sewing room. "Now you see my problem. What am I going to do with this room?"

Like everyone who saw Bonnie's sewing room, they were overwhelmed by all the stuff she had. Larry's wife Denise, who is also into sewing in a big way, commented on how many kinds of craft supplies and fabrics Bonnie had. They all offered me luck but no solutions. I asked them to go through Bonnie's jewelry. They were also hesitant, but, after similar prompting, got into the spirit and took some pieces.

As each day went on, I remained faced with what to do with Bonnie's sewing room. In addition to one wall covered with small bats of fabric organized by color and texture, her closet was packed with all kinds of craft supplies. She also had her fancy sewing machines on an oversized table with all kinds of workspace, two sergers, and her computerized embroidery machine.

I remembered what Bonnie said at the chemo clinic when she got the quilt, but how was I going to find the quilters? I picked up the quilt as if it would provide me a clue—and on the back was a label: Trinity Baptist Quilters; Sand Springs—*duh*. That church is just on the other side of Tulsa. Their website mentioned the Quilting Club but didn't list an email or phone number. All it said was: Meets 8 to 11 a.m. Tuesdays.

I went to Lowe's, got three large plastic tubs, and started packing Bonnie's fabric per her wishes. I seriously underestimated Bonnie's organizational skills and needed three more tubs. Tuesday morning, I loaded the tubs in Bonnie's car and went to Trinity Baptist Church on a wing and a prayer.

I pulled into the parking lot and noticed some cars. I carried the quilt with me as I knocked on a side door. I asked the woman who answered if this was the Quilting Club; she nodded. I said I had some fabric to donate. She was obviously in a hurry, but she invited me inside. The room was busy with around ten women working at tables about the room. A couple of them approached me. I explained through tears how we got the quilt and Bonnie's wishes. I brought in the first large tub. One lady pointed. "Just put it over there."

"I have five more of these."

Everyone in the room stopped what they were doing. They hurried to the car looking like those crowds of people behind an army truck receiving water during a natural disaster. With excitement they grabbed the tubs. I tried to help but decided for my own safety to get out of their way.

Back inside, they went through the tubs, reorganizing the material, and commenting on the quality of the fabric and how colorful the patterns were. They showed me around and introduced me to their oldest member who was about to turn 100. They wanted to know about Bonnie. We talked for a while, then I said, "I should have mentioned this upfront, but I hope you don't have a problem getting these donations from a Catholic?" This was an obvious joke, but one of them said, "Sweetheart, we're all brothers and sisters in Christ," to which I gave a hearty amen as we all laughed.

As we concluded our visit, I mentioned in passing that I had to do something with her equipment. "Equipment?" one of them said. "Have you any idea how often our machines wear out?" I told them they should come out to Owasso and see if what Bonnie had would work for them.

The following week, a caravan of cars arrived at our house. They asked what I wanted for the machines, noting that Bonnie had expensive high-end equipment. "I know," I said. "I wrote the checks." I told them I didn't want money, but I wanted the equipment to go to people who would make good use of it.

I helped them load up as much as they could take, as the caravan was short on trucks and men. When they left, they again offered to pay something, but my mind was made up. They said they would give me a tax receipt, but I refused, saying, "I didn't do this for a tax write-off, either." A couple of men returned later for the rest. I was elated to have been able to follow through on Bonnie's wish.

Home alone, I tried to stay as busy as possible. Megan and Ray would be moving into the house in April, so I had plenty of time to pack, but I had much to do. Bonnie had suggested I add a shower to The Shop. I contacted Fabian, the contractor who did Bonnie's kitchen, and made plans for the addition to The Shop.

As I packed Bonnie's small bathroom, I paused. Moonlight Path. I cried as I opened the bottle and inhaled the scent, my mind replaying the many baths we took together in the two-story house. While we could not fit together into the bathtubs in this house, Bonnie would still go down the hall before bed saying, "I'm taking a bath," like so many times in the other house. I'd wait until she filled her tub before taking my shower.

As the scent of Moonlight Path seeped between the two bathrooms' thin common wall, it was as if we were back in our big bathtub enjoying each other before bed. When I got out of the shower and joined Bonnie back in bed, the smell of Moonlight Path on her and in the air was all we needed to set the mood…

Many people questioned my decision to move out of the house. The best way I could explain it was that Bonnie placed every item in every room and on every wall. I could not sit in this house and see Bonnie in everything around me. My primary role in decorating was to ask Bonnie, "Where do you want the nail?"

She decorated this house out of love. I could not imagine myself looking at each item and remembering where we were when we bought it or how much fun we had hanging shelves or pictures.

I slowly took all our things off the walls and put them in storage. I told Megan to decorate the house however she wanted. When Megan and Ray eventually move out, I will not be replacing Bonnie's things on the walls but replacing Megan's, which will be much easier.

Another thing that occupied my time was my search for the

letters Bonnie wrote me during those three years we were apart while I was at college. You have seen some of these letters, but before I moved into The Shop, I did not have any of them in my possession. I estimated she wrote 300-400 letters during my three years of college before marriage. After we were married, I gave her the box of letters and lost track of them over the years.

I was in the Shop attic looking desperately through boxes for the letters when I came across a box of video tapes. I had forgotten that Bonnie and I made home movies two times in our lives: when Megan was little and when Matt was little. I cried with joy as I plugged in the old cameras and saw Mom, Rick, and Bonnie talking and laughing.

I found more old pictures we had not gone through when we put together Bonnie's slideshow. Many were of our high school and college years. I scanned them and had some printed on glass and decorated the walls around my work area in The Shop with these special prints.

On the wall by The Shop's from door, I mounted the big poster of Bonnie and Ozzie. Sherri at Fast Signs created two more identical-sized posters of Rick and Mom, which I placed on either side of Bonnie. Rick's picture shows him holding a plate of ribs at an Arkansas Band Alumni tailgate party. Mom's shows her with that goofy smile she gave after saying something funny.

Still searching for those letters, I dug through some other picture boxes and found a box of Mom's that was too small for the letters and would probably only have pictures of us kids or something. Inside was a manila envelope marked "Randy." Inside was a stack of letters—Bonnie's letters. I have no idea how Mom got them, but it didn't matter.

The thirty-seven letters covered about four months of my second year in Arkansas. I carefully opened each envelope and read each letter feeling her beside me. Bonnie used stationary ranging from Snoopy to flower designs, and Mom once gave her some scented stationery. I will treasure those thirty-seven letters forever.

Much earlier, I described that Bonnie and I signed each other's 1973 yearbooks with her closing with "Love, Bonnie," which gave me the courage to approach her. What you do not know is that while I was searching for Bonnie's letters, I found our old yearbooks and stumbled upon what Bonnie wrote. I screamed, as only then did I remember how much what she wrote meant to me at that time and the impact it had on me. I took a picture of her simple yearbook entry:

> Randy,
> I've really enjoyed knowing you this year. I hope that
> we're friends again next year.
> God Bless.
> Love,
> Bonnie Helm

I saved the picture on my computer as "The Moment," printed it, and placed it, along with a couple dozen other photos, on the walls next to where I work in The Shop. Few couples can pinpoint their "Moment" like I can.

As March arrived, Megan and I were busy packing to prepare for our respective moves. I was taking pictures and mementos down, and Megan and Ray were packing their separate houses when it hit me. I had not met any of Ray's family. I knew most of them lived within forty miles of Owasso, but I hadn't met any of them. If there was going to be a wedding, I would offer to host a get-together at The Shop.

I didn't want to scare Ray's family off by the sheer size of my family, so I only invited a select contingent that included Leslee, Max, and Kim. Usually I'd smoke some meat, but I chose takeout from Oklahoma Joe's BBQ. The twenty of us had a great time getting to know each other. Toward the end, Megan said something to Ray, who left and returned holding a piece of paper. Everyone started laughing. I was puzzled until Megan asked me to sign their marriage certificate.

Turns out I was hosting a wedding and didn't know a thing about it. Megan, not prone to surprises like her Dad, said she told me they would get a license. Ray's brother Sam, who is licensed to perform marriages, already did his part. He needed Ray's mom and me to sign as witnesses. I told Megan I must not have paid attention when she explained their plan. Everyone had a good laugh at my confusion as Ray's mother and I satisfied our legal obligation. Afterward, I told everyone Megan's second wedding cost me $500, saving me about $20,000 over her first wedding. The evening was special.

Megan and Ray planned to move into the house on April 1st. The Murphy bed was already in The Shop from when it was moved the day Bonnie came home from the hospital. I was still sleeping on the twin bed, however, next to the spot where Bonnie died. My new shower was done, but I had trouble leaving that room where we experienced so much and were last together.

In early March, I taught a three-day class about seven hours away. This was the first overnight trip since Bonnie's passing. The trip, class, and nights in the hotel were similar to all the times I did this before until I started to pack my bags on the morning before the last day's class. I started doing what I always did: rushing to get packed with an extra bounce in my step, getting that same euphoric feeling—then I realized I did not have Bonnie to go home to. I had no reason to get excited or to experience that familiar rush of hormones every time I traveled home. Yes, I still had Megan, Matt, and Ella to come home to, but it was not the same. I sobbed in the hotel feeling completely alone.

When the time came for me to move into The Shop, I sat in the then empty room, looking at the place where the love of my life drew her last breath. I knew this day marked a new chapter in my life, but letting go of that room was hard.

To pass the time, I digitally transferred the home movies I'd found to my computer. During spring break, Megan, Ella, and I made a trip to Midland to visit Matt with a stop by Peppa Pig World in Dallas as Ella's main draw. While in Matt's apartment, I told the kids I wanted us to watch a movie. I set up the projector I always have in my laptop bag and showed them one of the home movies of their Grandma Rauh and their mother. My surprise hit them hard when they saw them and heard their voices.

I also scanned all thirty-seven letters from Bonnie and those I received from Mom during college—which was my second surprise. I first gave them a letter Mom wrote me in which she was trying to understand why I was not getting along with her—not to make them feel bad, but to make them realize issues they had with their mother were no different from those most children have with their mother. They cried as I told them that the problems were no different from those I experienced with my mother, which came as something of a shock.

Our next family gathering was Easter. Even though some in my family do not attend church, we always have an Easter celebration to remind us of when Mom would host Easter dinner. I surprised my family by showing them an edited collection of the once-hidden home movies. In preparation, I placed tissue boxes on every table. (I had plenty after my Christmas Eve Wal-Mart trip.)

To set it up for effect, instead of having the projectors running and featuring something as usual, they were turned off. As we finished dinner, I said, "Oh, let me put something on TV." In the home movie, I inserted a black and white clip of the opening credits of Gilligan's Island where they're singing the theme song. When the lighting strikes, I inserted a clip of a movie reel melting. They hear me say onscreen *I wonder what the girls are…* as I take the camera into the living room of the two-story house. It's 1990, and we find Bonnie, Mom, and Megan, sitting on the floor having a tea party. The movie featured other clips, including all of us opening Christmas presents when Matt was two.

The room was filled with laughter and crying as everyone was overcome with the emotion of seeing Grandma Rauh and hearing her talk fifteen years after her death, as well as seeing Uncle Rick and a young Bonnie on the couch helping the little ones open presents. Sharing that movie may have been as special as the time Bonnie orchestrated the Santa visit.

During this period, Matt was having a difficult time with his managers, one of whom I was convinced had undiagnosed bipolar disorder. He bounced all over the place, changing his mind as fast as the West Texas wind—and then blamed Matt for his misman-agement. By the end of April, they offered Matt his old job back in Tulsa, and he moved home.

Matt and I both knew we could not coexist in the Shop. Matt is a night owl, and I need to work, so his only option was the Pool Cabana, which is not insulated and has no running water. The com-promise was that Matt would use The Shop bathroom and shower, and I'd place portable air conditioners in the Cabana—which worked out and gave him his own space. I'm so proud of how far Matt has come and how much he has grown up. Does he drive me nuts sometimes with his blinders approach to life? Yes, but I would not trade the time I'm enjoying with him for anything.

Much earlier, when I talked about Bonnie's and my going to Spring River, I mentioned the date that I didn't remember until I recently reread Bonnie's letters and found a postscript on one talk-ing about our wedding plans and that May 28 was Our Day. I had forgotten the actual day of the trip until I'd found her letters. We never visited the site after our 1973 trip.

I scoured Google Earth and other mapping software, looking for something I could recognize on Spring River. I never knew the name of the place. All I knew was it was on Spring River. I found an abandoned park that looked like a possibility. I recognized the sandbar we all played on and spotted a meadow in the direction we had walked together.

On Sunday, May 28, 2023, courtesy of the Google Earth coordinates, I made the 70-mile drive to the abandoned park. I found the road closed and weeds growing through the pavement as if it had been closed for a long time. I parked Bonnie's CRV, climbed over the Road Closed sign, and walked up the old road a quarter of a mile. I sensed I had been there before. As I reached the end of the road, I saw the river, and to the left, the sandbar. Behind me were two concrete park benches obscured by tall weeds nearly covering them. I remembered we ate our lunch on those benches. This was the place.

I looked to the left and saw the sun shining through the clouds, revealing a clearing. I made my way through waist-high weeds, not thinking about the ticks as I kept walking—

There it was: the meadow where Bonnie and I lay side by side on the grass on our first walk together.

Sunday, May 28, 2023, marked fifty years since we'd been there in that exact spot where our journey together began. I'll always remember that special moment, as a flood of memories came to me. All I could do other than cry was thank God for allowing me to be there both on this special day and, more importantly, on that day fifty years earlier.

By the first of June, pregnant Megan was getting huge. She got upset every time I reminded her in my less-than-diplomatic way: "Are those pants large enough?" or "Be careful walking. You can't see the ground." You need to know Megan is only 5'4" with a petite build, so any comment from me about her size, no matter the context, was never taken well.

Megan was due to give birth to Gemma on June 7, but she'd been late with Ella, so we weren't concerned when date came and went. We were concerned, however, about her plans for this birth. She'd told Bonnie and me that she'd be using a birthing center with midwives and would be having a water birth. Bonnie was vocal about her concerns. I figured that if Megan gave birth naturally to

Ella, who weighed 8 pounds, 13 ounces, she could probably have Gemma anywhere easily. What did I know?

In addition to living in the house, I neglected to mention that I hired Megan as my assistant. On June 12, Megan visited The Shop as she did daily. Megan complained about a bit of pain but never called it contractions. On June 13, she was with me around 3 p.m. when she winced and said she needed to go back to the house. She later called to tell me she was going to the birthing center and would call me when I needed to come. Around 5:30 p.m., she called and said I'd better come on in. I told her I was eating dinner and would be there shortly. I figured I had all kinds of time.

I arrived at 6:30. Ray opened the locked doors and led me into what appeared to be a classroom with a rack of exercise balls and chairs set up in front of a projector. He told me Megan was down the hall. I sat down for what I expected would be a long wait. Twice, I heard not a scream but a faint noise coming from the birthing room. At 7:10 p.m., I heard a cry and knew it was over. The midwives, Ray and Megan's close friend Natalie, and Ella were in the room with Megan. After all Ella had been through at Bonnie's side, being present for her sister's birth was not unexpected.

One of the midwives came out to tell me Megan did well, but that the birth was unusual. To me, everything about this place and method of birth was unusual, but what she was talking about was that Gemma was born *en caul*, which, of course, I interpreted as they had a doctor "on call."

She explained that Megan's water did not break; Gemma was born in the tub with her amniotic sac surrounding her. This happens every 1 in 80,000 births and is a sight to behold. They call it a "veiled" or "mermaid" birth. Some say the sac forms a crown around the head that is held in place by angels. Per legend, babies born in en caul have special insight into the future, and their parents are especially blessed.

Trying to take all this in, I waited until it was my turn to go back and meet my new granddaughter. After what seemed like hours but was actually only thirty minutes, I was brought back to what looked like a suite from a four-star hotel. The lighting was dim as Megan and Ella surrounded little Gemma in a beautiful white-draped four-post canopy bed with tiny white lights hanging around the top. In the corner of the room was the round white bathtub where all the excitement had taken place only minutes earlier.

I stayed for a while taking in the moment and feeling Bonnie's presence all around us. I could not help but think all of this was only made possible because of Bonnie's six years of hard work, culminating in Megan's becoming part of our lives. This eventually led to Ella, who has enriched my life more than I can say, and now Gemma, who will help me focus on the future.

Had I stood beside Bonnie during the first adoption process instead of entertaining my silly notion that I would eventually destroy my family, we would have together been able to speed up the process. We would have had a different baby and a different future. No, Bonnie's painful search alone, which resulted in Megan, was part of God's Plan, as everything else has been that's written on these pages.

I am beginning to realize His Plan for me includes moving Megan and Matt in with me, no matter how awkward or inconvenient it may seem. When Megan brings Gemma out to The Shop to visit me every day I'm in town, my grief is put away as I marvel at this incredible gift He gave Bonnie and me. Whenever I hold Gemma, I feel Bonnie sitting next to me, leaning over my shoulder as she did in the back seat, first with Megan as we drove to Grandpa Tilman's and later with Megan as we left the hospital in California with Matt.

A few weeks later, I was fortunate to teach a class in Wisconsin, visit some of Bonnie's relatives, and make several other detours. I decided to take a longer than usual detour as I took the ferry to Mackinac Island, a place Bonnie and I always talked about visiting and where *Somewhere in Time* was filmed. I walked around town and had lunch in the Grand Hotel where many scenes were shot. As I walked around this quiet island where horse-drawn carriages and bicycles are the only form of transportation, I thought about Bonnie and how we listened to the music from the movie during her last moments. The day was special.

Back home, Bonnie's parents' health took a turn. By the end of September, we had to place them in a nursing facility. Their dementia made it impossible for them to stay in the house without constant care. We tried to bring in an outside home health provider to help with showers, but both parents refused. Virgina started wandering off from the home, and multiple incidents occurred where Richard was taken to the ER and finally placed in hospice care.

A hospice nurse told us about a small nursing facility in a small town about forty-five minutes from Owasso. Since she was their POA, Megan researched the place and discovered this was the only facility within their budget that would take a couple in the same room.

We visited and were taken with how small and clean the place was. After much discussion and some hesitation, we agreed it was the best we could do. I doubted our decision, wondering what Bonnie would do. Would she have found a way to keep them in their home longer? Guilt was weighing on me as I'd promised Bonnie I would take care of her parents, and now—on my watch—I was placing them in a nursing facility.

They both wanted to go home but were easily redirected. We visit as often as we can. I will always question my decision to have them placed in a facility and will not know if I did the right thing until I hear from Bonnie when I see her again.

Not long ago, Megan came out to The Shop and told me she found something. Inside a large baggie was a yellow roll of paper that could only have been one thing. She found the map I made for Bonnie before her first trip to Fayetteville. Officially, it measures 96" long and consists of thirteen pieces of paper still firmly held together with black electrician's tape—and smaller than the ten feet I estimated when I wrote about the event before Megan's discovery. The map now sits in my nightstand beside my Murphy bed in The Shop alongside Bonnie's thirty-seven letters—both of which are among my most prized possessions.

Recently, when Ella was in The Shop, she pointed to the pegboard behind my computers. "What are those cards?" Not knowing what she meant, I looked a little closer and noticed an item I had forgotten about that had been sitting in plain sight: a Christmas gift Bonnie gave me several years ago after my mental breakdown and her breast cancer.

Bonnie took a deck of standard playing cards, punched two holes along one side of each card, and used key rings to make a book. The front says "52 Reasons I Love You." On the inside of each card, she glued a note:

You Keep Me Warm

You Make My Heart Melt (Still)

We Finish Each Other's Sentences

You Don't Complain About Honey Dos

You Run the Sweeper

You Put Up with My Pain

You Loved Me Even When I Was Bald

You Are My Soulmate

You Open the Car Door for Me

You Are So Like Your Mom

You Trust Me to Cut Your Hair

I Can't Be Me Without You

I Know God Sent You to Me

The last two have special meaning for me. During this journey, I've learned a lot about grief. I've read several books on the subject, the best of which is *Grief, A Beginner's Guide* by Jerusha Hull McCormack (Paraclete Press). I recommend it to others who have lost a spouse.

Bonnie's playing card love note, "I Can't Be Me Without You," is especially true as I struggle with the hole in my heart, the one I ask God every day to fill. In McCormack's book, she recounts a letter from someone still grieving the loss of her husband from thirty-one years before:

> When it was clear that he was dying, she said to her son: "Your dad and I have lived together so many years I feel we have become one person. When he dies, one part of me is dead, too. Life will never again be enjoyable for me."
>
> Then her son said something surprising: "Since you and Dad have become one person, Dad will continue to live through you. Whenever you enjoy something wonderful like this blue sky [they had walked outside the hospital wards on a lovely April morning] or anything beautiful, you must remember my dad in you and with you. You are enjoying wonderful things together."
>
> So, she writes that whenever she was sad, she would remember what her son had said, and that gave her the courage to overcome her deep grief.

After finding this book, when alone I constantly talk to Bonnie and include her in everything I do. I'm sure people I drive past think I am singing to the radio. Instead, I am carrying on a conversation with Bonnie, sharing all my thoughts, hopes, and dreams.

I have one other large poster of Bonnie and Ozzie. I placed that poster behind my Murphy bed above my pillow. I reach up and touch that poster every morning as I say, "Good morning, sweet-heart," and I say, "I love you," every time I fold my bed up against the wall in the morning.

While driving on long business trips, I play lots of music Bonnie and I enjoyed. When a special song or movie soundtrack comes on, I hold my right hand out over the passenger seat to hold her hand like I did so many times before. I still keep a handkerchief in my pocket, a practice I never did before Bonnie's final illness. I usually have to replace it with a clean one after every road trip.

Part of my grieving process includes following through on my Christmas Eve text where I proclaimed a new Rauh four-day Christmas celebration. I ordered some small gifts from the Catholic Company, and on December 21, Ella opened an Advent Candle. We lit the first candle, explaining we would use the Advent Candle to mark our four-day celebration. I sent a picture of everyone sitting around the candle with a note recalling what happened a year ago to a small group of family and friends. The text read:

> "This may look like an Advent Candle, but this candle marks Day One of our
>
> First Annual 4-Days of Christmas celebration. Today's highlight: In nothing short of a medical miracle and by the grace of God, Bonnie came home from the hospital one year ago today."

We lit the second candle the next day, and Ella opened a box with a Christmas ornament with this inscription around the outside: MERRY CHRISTMAS – FROM HEAVEN. The message in the middle read:

> "I love you all dearly,
> Now don't shed a tear,

I'm spending my Christmas
With Jesus this year."

I sent a picture of the ornament with this text message:

"Day 2 of our celebration recalls the longest day of all. At 4 a.m., we thought the end was near. Later that morning, I held the phone to Bonnie's ear as close friends and family said their goodbyes. In the afternoon, Father Matt gave her the Viaticum. Shortly after, I discovered the missing Green Scapular, and by the grace of God, she started to respond.

What followed was a stream of people who braved the ice and snow to see another miracle from God for themselves. This day without a doubt included the lowest of lows and the highest of highs.

This was the day that brought Bonnie back to us."

On December 23, we lit the third candle, and Ella opened another round candle with a red cardinal on it that said:

"You need not shed another tear. Your sorrows can go free. And when you see a bright red bird, please say a prayer for me.

In Loving Memory
Bonnie Rauh
1958 - 2023"

I sent a picture of Ella holding Gemma next to the candles along with this text:

"Day 3 started with Bonnie making it to the bathroom for the first time.

Later, we had Whataburger for breakfast and played guessing games with a sign on the wall. Little did we know we would have 16 more days of JOY ahead of us.

We lit the last candle on Christmas Eve, and Ella opened a box with a memorial garden angel inside:

Bonnie Rauh

1958-2023

In Loving Memory

Unseen and unheard,

but always near,

so loved so missed,

and so very dear.

I sent this final picture with this text message to friends and family:

"Day 4 started off without any of the usual drama. We all slept in until 8:30 and had a simple breakfast at the table. The rest of the day was uneventful unless you count my making a fool of myself by shouting holiday greetings at three local merchants, disrupting their tranquil Christmas Eve ambiance.

I have learned grief is complicated, and everyone grieves differently. My grief journey includes plenty of low spots, but there have also been countless blessings God has showered me with, I think to help me with my grief so I can serve Him. You all are part of those blessings God has given me. Thank you for your love, prayers, and support for me and my family. As we all continue to heal, we should remember Bonnie was placed in each and every one of our lives for a reason. May we continue to remember her and, when needed, offer this simple prayer: "Bonnie, Pray for Us."

This last gift was placed next to our tombstone. I hope to continue this four-day celebration every year and make it something Ella and Gemma will someday celebrate with their families.

Sam's wife Shelby, a medical doctor, told me she presented Bonnie's case to the head of emergency medicine who offered his thoughts. He said Bonnie should never have made it out of the ER on December 18. He said no one remains conscious with three pressors, and no one comes back from multiple organ failure after one day of dialysis. Studies show that patients with three pressors have a 92.5% mortality rate.

Doctors predicted Bonnie would not leave the hospital or make it home in the ambulance. Instead, she enjoyed twenty days at home, eighteen of which were without pain medication. She was alert and coherent for the same eighteen days. One by one, family and friends shared their deepest thoughts with Bonnie as they were given a chance to tell her things so few have an opportunity to do before someone dies.

Bonnie and Mom. The lives of these two extraordinary women are similar in so many ways. God had a plan for Bonnie and one for Mom that led them through tremendous heartache, pain, and difficulties few have experienced. They were both blessed with an equal measure of passion for life, service to others, a kind shoulder to lean on, and a love for everyone they met.

I never asked Bonnie why she wrote "Love, Bonnie" in my yearbook. I suspect she wrote the same thing in everyone's yearbook because of the kind heart she had. I was only part of her mission on earth as she shared God's love with everyone. Bonnie now teaches all of us how to muster the strength to carry our own Crosses, no matter how heavy they become, with the same dignity she showed us.

The same can be said for my mother, JoAnn. She suffered devastating hardships that she overcame only through the grace of God, which made her the rock on which her family was built. God's plan for her included her tireless service to others, even as she ignored her health issues to always put others before herself. She never asked for anything and did not deserve how others treated her. Still, God's plan included those struggles as part of the Cross she carried with the same grace Bonnie showed.

These pages are my long overdue unwritten love letter to each of them. As time marches on I find myself more in love with Bonnie as I reflect daily on the nearly fifty years we had together. When we are finally reunited, the first thing I plan to ask Bonnie is, "Can I have this dance?"

Thank you, Mom and Bonnie, for everything you did for me and continue to do each day through your prayers. May your story inspire others as much as it inspires me as I try to honor your memory.

https://www.aletterunwritten.com/

www.ingramcontent.com/pod-product-compliance
Lightning Source LLC
Chambersburg PA
CBHW021714120626
46545CB00004B/1554